Homo Americanus

Other Books of Interest from St. Augustine's Press

Homo Americanus
The Rise of Totalitarian Democracy in America
Zbigniew Janowski

St. Augustine's Press

South Bend, Indiana

Library of Congress Control Number: 2021932277

∞ The paper used in this publication meets the minimum requirements of the American National Standard for Information Sciences – Permanence of Paper for Printed Materials, ANSI Z39.48-1984.

St. Augustine's Press
www.staugustine.net

TABLE OF CONTENTS

To my friend, Jonathan C. D. Clark, from whom I learned about
the significance of hierarchy in history,
and in memory of Leszek Kołakowski, the author of *Main Currents of
Marxism*, who taught me about the danger of ideological mind pollution

The Homosos is *Homo Sovieticu*s, or Soviet man, regarded as a
type of living being and not as a citizen of the USSR. Not every
citizen of the USSR is a Homosos. Not every Homosos is a citizen of the USSR... Such a man is generated by the conditions
inseparable from the existence of a Communist (or Socialist)
society. He is the carrier of that society's principles of life. He
preserves its intracollective relations by the very way of life he
leads... The Homosos is the product of human adaptation to
certain social conditions. That is why he can never be understood outside his normal environment any more than a fish can
be understood from its movements when it has been thrown
onto the sand or into the frying pan... If one looks at the Homosos from the viewpoint of some abstract morality, he seems
to be a completely immoral being. The Homosos isn't a moral
being, that's true, but it isn't true to say that he is positively immoral. In the first instance he is an ideological being. And on
that basis he can be either moral or immoral, according to circumstances.

Alexander Zinoviev, *Homo Sovieticus*

PREFACE

Only few Americans seem to understand that we, here in the United States, are living in a totalitarian reality, or one that is quickly approaching it. Any visitor from a country formerly behind the totalitarian Iron Curtain quickly notices that the lack of freedom in today's America is, in many respects, greater than what he had experienced under socialism. The other thing that our visitor notices is that thirty years after Eastern European countries shook off the yoke of Communism, the former socialist countries are in some respects freer than the U.S. (This is certainly true regarding freedom of speech; university teaching has not been dominated by PC ideology, and curricula have not undergone ideological transformation.) His third observation is that freedom in the post-Communist democracies is shrinking, and the post-Communist reality starts to resemble life under Communism.

This time, however, it is not to be explained by the limited experience in self-government, occasioned by almost half a century of Communist rule, or the existence of the remnants of the old ideological thinking, but by democracy's rapid expansion. As democracy left its intended and original *electoral* confines, it moved to regulate virtually all aspects of man's existence. In this respect, it acts very much like Communism; the difference being that Communism had a built-in ideological drive and vision which stemmed from its philosophy of History, while democracy appears to invent its own ideological objectives *ad hoc*. They do not follow any objective trajectory, while that of Marxism was designed by the laws of historical development, over which man was believed to have no control. They are grounded, rather, in the psychology of group behavior, and its goals are conjured up by social activists and political demagogues. In so far as human psychology underlies democratic politics, its goals, as Plato and Thucydides observed, are bound to be short-sighted, erratic, and, therefore, more difficult to counteract.

The weak constraints on democracy are what allow its totalitarian

1

appetite to become monstrous. It is believed that democratic procedures are not supposed to be limited to the elections of officials, but ought to be applied to *all* aspects of human interactions. In doing so, democracy devours ever-greater areas of our lives, including intimacy, which had previously been reserved for individual negotiations, via natural, time-honored social mores and *hierarchical structures*. This is not surprising, nor should it be. Already, in 1835, in his *Democracy in America*, II, 56, Alexis de Tocqueville painted a fatalistic picture of the future of the democratic nations:

> I think, then, that the species of oppression by which democratic nations are menaced is unlike anything which ever before existed in the world: Our contemporaries will find no prototype of it in their memories. I seek in vain for an expression which will accurately convey the whole of the idea I have formed of it; the old words despotism and tyranny are inappropriate: The thing itself is new…

The word Tocqueville so desperately needed to describe what the future holds for us is *totalitarianism*. Everything in his analysis of democracy—his remarks about the majority, its intolerance, its oppressive character, its thirst for control of the individual, its hostility toward individual greatness and classical virtues, its mediocre taste, and its disregard for Truth and Tradition—points in one direction: Tocqueville was anticipating democracy becoming totalitarian. What is totalitarianism if not a total control of man's mind and soul, and the intolerance of diversity?

Only someone shortsighted, or someone who values equality more than freedom, would deny that today's *citizens* enjoy little or no freedom, particularly freedom of speech, and even less the ability to express openly or publicly the opinions which are not in conformity with what the majority considers acceptable at a given moment. It may sound paradoxical to contemporary ears, but a fight against totalitarianism must also mean a fight against the expansion of democracy. This is likely to sound shocking to many people today, especially to the believers in "the people." However, if we go back in time, we will quickly realize that such a view was shared by every major thinker: Plato, Aristotle, Thucydides, Polybius, Jefferson, Franklin, Constant, Tocqueville, Mill, Arnold, Nietzsche, Ortega y Gasset, and, above all, democracy's first critic, Edmund Burke. Each of them, in his own way, had sent a warning to the future generations, and each pointed out what he saw to be a troubling aspect of democracy.

Why, then, do we, the people who see Tocqueville's predictions coming true, idealize a system which the thinkers of old found so problematic and defective? There are several reasons. Partly because, for the greater part of the 20th century, democracy's focus was the fight against communism and fascism. Secondly, for a long time, that is, so long as the enemy existed, democracy appeared benign, and, consequently, democracy's shortcomings went unnoticed. The attitude toward democracy was essentially what we find in Winston Churchill's famous saying: "Indeed, it has been said that democracy is the worst form of government, except for all the others that have been tried from time to time." In other words, we have better things to do than look for democracy's shortcomings. It also followed, at least seemingly, that because democracies defeated fascism and Nazism, and re-sisted Soviet totalitarianism, democracy must be better, and certainly it can-not be totalitarian!

Daily life in 21st century democracies, however, presents a different pic-ture of democracy. Its new face can and should make us doubt its benign character, and in some respects, the totalitarian tendencies are so obvious, that one finds it impossible to defend America and democracy against the charges of those who defend the new authoritarian despots. Anastasia Lin, a Canadian actress and human rights advocate, who came to Canada from China when she was thirteen, sees things in a similar way. In her "The Cul-tural Revolution Comes to North America" (*WSJ*, April 8, 2019), she writes:

> The emerging call-out culture in the U.S., Canada and elsewhere in the West bears more than a few similarities to China's Cultural Revolution, in which writers, artists, doctors, scholars and other professionals were publicly denounced and forced by mobs to engage in ritual self-criticism.[1] The goal is not to persuade or

1 For a first-hand, terrifying account of such practices, see the conversation bet-ween George Urban and Bao Ruo-Wang ("Thought-Reform in a Chinese Pri-son") in *Stalin and Stalinism. Its Impact on Russia and the World*, ed. by George Urban (London: Maurice Temple Smith, 1982). The book is a collection of

debate; it is to humiliate the target and intimidate everyone else. The ultimate objective is to destroy independent thought... China did not become a tyranny overnight. Too many people in my father's generation chose not to stand up for their neighbors, friends and even family members when they were under attack. They learned to obey instead of challenge, to pick sides rather than think for themselves. They assented to obvious lies because they didn't want the mob to turn on them next.

Our uncritical attitude toward democracy should make us doubt our ability to assess reality properly, when empirical evidence showing democracy's oppressiveness is before our own eyes.[2] However, the very lack of a critical attitude could be an indication that we have been trapped in a "democratic ideological bubble," which operates the same way in which communism possessed the minds of people living under its spell, and as long as its spell operates, there is little chance to free oneself from its influence.[3] In contrast to the old thinkers, especially Tocqueville and J. S. Mill, we seem to be blind to democracy's shortcomings. The least criticism of democracy is met with either disbelief or outrage, and few persons could question the idea expressed in Churchill's saying without doubting their own sanity. To have doubts about democracy is to commit heresy. The reason, in my opinion, is that democracy and equality—in America—are taken to be synonyms, and thus to question the former is to cast doubt on the latter.

Equality is our New Faith. This is what links liberal-democracy and communism. Even the most commonsensical and empirically grounded criticism of equality is unacceptable. The best evidence of it is the accusations

interviews that were previously published in *Encounter*. Thought manipulation, intimidation, threats, and mass killings were a common practice in each Communist country. An excellent account, full of first-hand stories and examples of Hungarian Communism, is *The Revolt of the Mind. A Case History of Intellectual Resistance Behind the Iron Curtain* by Tomas Aczel and Tibor Merey (New York: Fredrick A. Praeger, Publishers, 1959).

2   See Ryszard Legutko, *The Demon in Democracy: Totalitarian Temptations in Free Societies* (Yew York: Encounter Books, 2016).

3   For the analysis of the ideological operations, see Alain Besançon, *The Rise of the Gulag. Intellectual Origins of Leninism* (New York: Continuum, 1981).

of sexism, misogyny, ageism, homophobia, racism, xenophobia, and the apologies on the part of those who, as if in a moment of temporary insanity, allowed themselves to make a "heretical" statement. In acting this way, we behave the opposite of Orwell's Winston, whose great discovery was that commonsense is the greatest heresy of all. However, we need to be mindful that as long as criticism of equality is anathema, we can only expect further deterioration of the quality of public and political life, and the institutions which influence it. The rejection of the old hierarchical criteria of judgment, and of evaluating individual excellence, for example, in education, is probably the most glaring evidence of the destructive influence of democracy on the life of the mind, the consequence of which is a vulgarization of the public square and cultural life.[4]

All of this raises the question: Can democracies survive? The Greek experience, the collapse of democracies in 20th century in Europe, in Africa in the second half of the 20th century, and the instability of democracies in South America, do not seem to give much hope. However, in contrast to the 20th century, our enemy today is not a Fascist, Communist, or authoritarian alternative, but the moral and intellectual malaise which democracy itself creates and, as Nietzsche insisted, is bound to create. It is not an external enemy, but, as Plato described it in his *Republic*, Bk. VIII, a disease of the disintegrating soul. Democracy in 21st century is no longer a system that requires responsibility, intellectual alertness, and moral discipline from its participants. It is a realm which promises to fulfill everyone's infantile and unrealistic whims.

Looking at how democracy operates today, John Stuart Mill—probably the greatest champion of free speech and universal suffrage—would be outraged. Particularly painful for him would be the status of free speech, which now means the freedom to express only the views which pretend to express the views of the majority. According to Mill, freedom of speech is needed and exists only in societies with conflicting views. Securing it is important for advancing man's historical progress and society's well-being. That is why the opponents' opinions are sacred to those for whom such views seem contradictory or even offensive. The collision of diverse opinions—provided

---

4   There is nothing new in my observation. One can find it in many places in J. S. Mill's writings, especially in chapter 3 of *On Liberty*.

that it is regulated by the principle of *rational* discourse, which sifts rational opinions from nonsense—forms the basis of civil and civilized society, and those engaged in public debate should not be afraid of their opponent's views or of losing the battle. Defeat is always temporary and gives the defeated party breathing space to prepare a stronger argument to reignite the battle. Only those who cannot formulate an argument feel offended and convict the opponent of insensitivity, discrimination, and of being too judgmental. Such an attitude is childish and reflects an infantile social mentality.

Society ruled by intellectually adolescent adults is bound to lose not only its freedom, but against any civilization that understands that there is a difference between children and adults, and that adults always win.

Hopefully, the few observations and thoughts that a reader finds in the following chapters will serve for deeper reflection on how to stop the progress of democracy's malaise and how to regain our own sanity to help us return to civility.

***

This book revolves around four topics: the state of America and democracy today, liberalism, equality, and totalitarianism. The last topic may appear strange in an American context. Yet many insightful and reasonable persons, including those who may be less critical in assessing our reality than I am, are likely to agree that there is something wrong with American democracy today, or that it is undergoing a dangerous mutation which makes America resemble former ideological regimes. Of course, news outlets, such as the *New York Times, Washington Post, USA-Today, National Public Radio, CNN,* and *MSNBC,* would all disagree. For they are convinced that the problem is not democracy, liberalism, or equality but *too little* democracy, liberalism, and equality. They spare no effort to harness their propagandistic machines to convince the American people that our problems and the problems in the rest of the world result from too little of each of the above. As long as the problems persist, so, too, will they venture tirelessly to expand equality even further by making the state, as Mathew Arnold warned us, more powerful than the American Founding Fathers intended.

The absurdity of the idea that we suffer from too little equality was ingeniously ridiculed by the American writer, Kurt Vonnegut, in his short story *Harrison Bergeron*. In it, Vonnegut depicts the future of American society, in which, thanks to several additional amendments to the Constitution, all Americans *finally* became mentally, physically and socially equal. The only function of the state was to ensure equality, and those who dared to see things differently were killed. What makes Vonnegut's story, authored in 1961, so grotesque is precisely what makes American social life tragic in 2021.

One can easily question the claim that the root of our societal problems is too little democracy and equality: The enormous expansion of equality, in the last three decades or so, created many new problems, solved almost none of the old problems, and limited individual freedom to the point that nothing but comparison with life under communism can do justice to what life in America is like today.

By all comparative ideological standards, the new American is as ideologically minded as the former Homo Sovieticus was, if not more. It is not an exaggeration to say that the difference between Homo Americanus and Homo Sovieticus is the former's near-total lack of awareness of living in an artificial reality. The lack of cynicism on Homo Americanus' part, was the saving grace of Homo Sovieticus. Cynicism allowed man under communism to distinguish between the dictates of the totalitarian state—which he followed to save his life and that of his family—without losing his mind. Homo Americanus is a real believer. He is a product of an egalitarian ideology. So are his views and emotions, which naturally create a bond, and these form the base of his relationships with other people, often finding expression in social institutions. Yet the new Homo Americanus does not seem to see it, nor is he frustrated by the fact that his emotional and instinctual needs are not fulfilled. He does not feel a dissonance between what he wants and what the egalitarian ideology requires him to want, which is the reason why he is complacent in accepting rules, regulations, and laws that the former Homo Sovieticus rebelled against and despised.

This explains why the idea of being dissident is unknown to the new Homo Americanus. He may be familiar with the term from history books, but he cannot imagine being one because he does not know what he is supposed to rebel against and why. He is intellectually passive, complacent in his behavior because he cannot distinguish between natural and ideological realities. He accepts his predicament without a word of protest. His daily consumption of ideological slogans has the same effect on his perception of the world, as do the doses of *soma* on the citizens of Huxley's *Brave New World*. Like them, he is appalled by nature and natural relationships. In such an artificially constructed reality, human instincts and emotions, including human sexuality, are subject to regulations, as they are at present in the U.S.[5] For this ideological reality to continue, this must be so because it has no other foundation but abstract thought.

The possibility of citizens' emotional awaking could have disastrous existential effects on the life of an ideological state. It could, as it befell the protagonist in Yevgeny Zamyatin's *WE*, Winston and Julia in Orwell's *1984*, and Helmholz and Marx in Huxley's *Brave New World*, make them doubt the legitimacy of a system which makes them act according to an ideological script. In all three novels, the collective WE that stole their individuality, their souls, made them rebel against it. In Zamyatin and Orwell, the discovery of the sexual relationship unsupervised by the state was liberating emotionally, but it was at the same time an act of rebellion which had to

5 I discuss this problem in greater detail below, in the chapter "Sexual Liberalism." After writing this, I came across an article "Sex Choreography evolves to shield vulnerable actors" (*NYT*, January 20, 2020), in which we read that "intimacy coordination has become highly sought." How unnatural the natural will become on the screen remains to be seen, but everything seems to indicate that we are moving further and further in the direction of a reality that will present a very distorted image of human nature, propelled by ideological dictates. The picture accompanying the *NYT* article shows the intimacy coordinator directing a White man with open mouth to kneel between the crotch of a standing Black man. In their *The Revolt of the Mind*, Aczel and Meray relate a conversation over the script of a book about a Communist love story. Ravai, a Communist cultural activist, not being satisfied with the original scenario of the character Julia Nagy, a Communist student, falling in love with progressive bourgeois professor, which was unsatisfied to the girl, decided to give advice on how to rewrite the script: "Let us understand each other [said Revai]. I am not saying that a Communist can and should fall in love only with a Communist. She can fall in love with a non-Communist, but with a real Communist the two feelings of love and devotion to the Party cannot run parallel. One can love only a person who shares one's thoughts and ideals and who, if not today, then tomorrow, can become one's partner not only in love but also in the struggle for the new world."

be punished through reconstruction of the mind. To prevent rebellion, the schools and colleges in the U.S. took over sexual education. In imposing strict and ideological sexual norms—totally unknown in the former Communist countries—America admitted its docility. The aim of such policies is to preclude the possibility of shaping human relationships outside of the ideological framework, and only those which are sanctioned by egalitarian ideology can be said to be legitimate.

***

I would like to express gratitude to several friends who were kind enough to read different chapters, or the whole manuscript, and who offered suggestions and criticisms. In the first place, I would like to thank Katia Mitova and Ryszard Legutko. Both of them lived under socialism, in Bulgaria and Poland respectively. Their comments made me believe that my criticism of today's America is not off the mark. In the next place, my gratitude goes to Nicholas Capaldi, Jonathan Clark, and Wayne Cristaudo, and, last but not least, two of my former students: Jacob Duggan and Christopher Kramer. They were the first ones to read the earliest versions of each chapter. Both are young Americans; they have neither the Communist experience nor the memory of the older America. Yet their reaction to what they read confirmed my feeling that the views I expressed are essentially correct.

Throughout the book I use the word "man," and the personal pronoun "he" (and the possessive "his"). Each time I use them, I use them in the generic sense (meaning man and woman), as they used to be used. My usage is not intended to "exclude" or "offend" anyone, but, rather, to be as linguistically as precise as possible and stylistically elegant. Therefore, the reader will not come across "man and woman" (or "human beings"), "he or she" or "his or her"—all of which appear superfluous and stylistically cumbersome.

CHAPTER 1 | COMMUNIST LIBERALS

Morality in Europe at present is herding-animal morality; and therefore, as we understand the matter, only one kind of morality, beside which, before which, and after which many other moralities; and above all higher moralities, are or should be possible… The lofty independent spirituality, the will to stand alone, and even cogent reason, are felt to be dangers; everything that elevates the individual above the herd, and is a source of fear to the neighbor, is henceforth called evil… Supposing that the abused, the oppressed, the suffering, the unemancipated, the weary, and those uncertain of themselves should moralize, what will be the common element in their moral estimate?

Friedrich Nietzsche, *The Natural History of Morals* (202, 201), *Beyond Good and Evil* (260)

When I visited Lviv, Ukraine, in 1980, then part of the Soviet Union, the members of our Polish tour group roamed around the city, trying to find what was left of Polish culture. Lviv was one of the major Polish intellectual and cultural centers for centuries, only to be included by the Soviets in their Socialist empire. The most natural destination was churches. We knew about the miserable state of religiosity in the Soviet Union and the persecution of the Church. With over 90% of the population declaring itself to be Catholic, Poland was a religious anomaly in the Socialist Bloc. Even those who never attended Sunday mass declared themselves to be Catholic just to show their opposition to the New Faith.

Visiting Lviv was like a pilgrimage to a Mecca of national memory, which now lay outside the mother-country, and which only before the war was part of Poland. However poor and neglected Lviv looked, the old architecture soothed our national spirit and memory of Poland's greatness; the real, symbolic and imaginary, all of which made us who we are: a people who through the entire period of Communist rule bravely stood up to the ideological commands of the Socialist Big Brother.

With the exception of one famous Boim Chapel (built in 1609 and finished in 1615), most churches were "closed." One was a massive storage facility (one could see piles of furniture and chair legs sticking out through the broken stained-glass windows). Another one, open to the public, was a museum—museum of atheism! The interior was painted white, most likely to cover the religious frescos, with a long white drapery, hanging from the ceiling like a drying bed-sheet, just above where the altar once stood. On it, there was an image of Lenin's bust; in the nave, where in a regular church one finds the scenes of Jesus' way to Golgotha, there was some information about socialism, progress, stages of historical development, and other jargon of the New Faith. To us, living under the same Socialist ideology, the idea of a church being turned into a museum of atheism was shockingly strange and morally uncomfortable.

But the shock did not last for long; we knew well what it was about. The Soviet Communists wanted to make a point: Since history is progressive, the old buildings, including churches, should not be turned into mere utility buildings—like a bank I saw a year after in an old church in Zurich, and elsewhere in the "bloody consumerist West," as the Communists called—but must serve as an illustration of how history unfolds itself: Forces of history clash, and the more progressive forces must win because the New Faith is in the historical right.

However wretched and perverse the guardians of the New Faith were, one must appreciate them for taking history very seriously. They knew all too well that if the Marxist theory of historical development was incorrect, socialism could not be the historical winner, and the whole Socialist edifice (i.e. half of the globe) was bound to collapse.

The image of Lenin on the alter was an illustration of the rightness of the Socialist creed: Jesus Christ and Christianity were the historical losers and Vladimir Lenin and socialism were the winners. And as if history wanted to make a point, not far from the chapel we saw a newly wedded couple getting out of a car to lay a bouquet of flowers in front of Vladimir Ilych Lenin's monument. The scene was surreal.

Our Polish attachment to history saved our national soul; the New Faith robbed the Soviets of theirs, leaving them morally empty and politically weak.

To every former denizen of the Socialist paradise, the behavior of today's Americans is painfully reminiscent of the old Homo Sovieticus, and even more of the Chinese man of the period of the Cultural Revolution. Books were burnt (for the second time in China since 3rd century A.D.), just as they are disposed of now in American colleges; monuments were torn down, just like they are in the U.S.; awards with names of cultural icons decried as symbols of oppressive ideologies, were renamed, just as they are in the U.S., and, last but not least, the correct chronological notation—B.C. and A.D. were replaced by Common Era (C.E.) and Before the Common Era (B.C.E.)—was strictly observed by Communist editors and censors of books and journals, just as it is today by American teachers and editors who scrupulously remove B.C. or A.D. from student papers and publications. The goal of the new politically correct notation is to infiltrate the American public and students' subconscious minds, telling them that history was always secular, and that religion and past ideological formations, are a relic of the "obscurantist and intolerant" past, just as the Communists taught. Oppressive patriarchal ideology corresponds to bourgeois ideology under socialism; the capitalist system, which oppresses the "toiling masses," finds its equivalent in the American CEOs not sharing their profits with hard working Americans. Socialist realism in art, presenting ordinary workers immersed in their labor, finds its equivalent in American mural paintings presenting oppressed minorities. They do not have any artistic value, but it does not matter because it is not art but message that is important, and the message is oppression.

All this should sound awfully familiar to someone who knows history, but it is not familiar to the American people. A few incredibly well-educated scholars see it, but their voices are often too timid to be heard; they are too scared to stand up, or they have given up, just like those under socialism who knew that the Roller of Historical Inevitability would crush them.

A few examples. In October 2017, Christ Church in Alexandria, VA, of which George Washington was a founding member and vestryman in 1773, pulled down memorial plaques honoring him and General Robert E. Lee. In a letter to the congregation, the church leaders stated that: "The plaques in our sanctuary make some in our presence feel unsafe or unwelcome. Some visitors and guests who worship with us choose not to return because they receive an unintended message from the prominent presence of the plaques." In August 2017, the Los Angeles City Council voted 14-1 to designate the second Monday in October (Columbus Day) as "Indigenous Peoples Day." According to the critics of Columbus Day, we need to "dismantle a state-sponsored celebration of the genocide of indigenous peoples." Some of the opponents of Columbus Day made their intentions clear by attaching a placard on the monument: "Christian Terrorism begins in 1492." In June 2018, the board of American Library Association voted 12-0 to rename the Laura Ingalls Wilder Award as the "Children's Literary Legacy Award." Wilder is a well-known American literary figure and author of children's books, including *Little House on the Prairie*, about European settlement in the Midwest. In a statement to rename the award, the board wrote: "Wilder's legacy, as represented by her body of work, includes expressions of stereotypical attitudes inconsistent with ALSC's core values of inclusiveness, integrity and respect, and responsiveness."

The list of examples like these is endless. However, what is astonishing in each of the three above cases is the justification of the verdicts made about history by the official decision makers. First, contrary to what the leaders of the church in Virginia claim, history is not about making us feel comfortable. If it were, we should remove the Jefferson Memorial and Washington Monument in D.C., which are seen every day by thousands of passers-by. One can also wonder about the church leaders' Christian spirit of forgiveness. If George Washington were alive today, would they tell him that he is "unwelcome" in his own parish because his presence makes other parishioners uncomfortable? Following Jesus, one wants to shout out: "Let he who is without sin cast the first stone," or throw at them two of Jesus' other favorite words: You vipers, you hypocrites! You talk about Columbus being a "Christian terrorist" or "Father of Genocide," but are afraid to pass judgment on the horrific acts of human sacrifices committed by the Aztecs, Mayans, or Incas?

Such attitude does not bring us any closer to understanding history, human motivations, or human psychology. Renaming the Wilder Award because her work abounds in expressions of attitude "inconsistent with ALSC's core values" is a reiteration of what the Communists in the Soviet Empire and China were killing their enemies for. It was a common practice in the Soviet Union and its satellite countries to rename awards and names of streets, or to turn the churches into "museums of atheism" for exactly the same reason that ALSC gave: the legacy of the past was "inconsistent with the core values" of the present-day socialist society. If the communists believed in anything, it was the necessity of fighting against the "undesirable attitudes." This is not different from what we observe in the attitude of the American progressive ideology today.

After the collapse of communism in Eastern Europe and the Soviet Union, the former "socially progressive values" were found morally abominable, the monuments of "new" heroes were torn down to be replaced by monuments of the "old villains," and history had reversed its course. The old awards and medals returned, the streets regained their original historical names, and the "museums of atheism" became houses of religious worship again.

The events that followed the burial of the Communist past ought to be a dire warning for the present-day progressive social reformers. They can end up in the graveyard for the disgraced proponents of Progress, buried there while still alive by the specter of their victims.

It has already happened to Hillary Clinton. On September 14, 2018, the Texas Board of Education voted to remove her name from the list of famous historical figures. History can be a real bitch.

CHAPTER 2 | THE AGE OF GREAT DEMOCRATIC APOLOGIES

Persons of genius, it is true, are, and are always likely to be, a small minority; but in order to have them, it is necessary to preserve the soil in which they grow.

John Stuart Mill, *On Liberty*

For my part, I am persuaded that in all governments, whatever their nature may be, servility will cower to force, and adulation will follow power. The only means of preventing men from degrading themselves is to invest no one with that unlimited authority which is the sure method of debasing them.

Alexis de Tocqueville, *Democracy in America*

The Homosos' biggest loss is his separation from the collective [...]. The soul of the Homosos lies in his participation in collective life [...]. Ideology unifies the individual consciousness and unites millions of little 'I's into one huge 'We.'[...] The most powerful weapon against rebels in our society is exclusion from the collective. When rebels are thrown out of normal collectives, they are unable to create stable and coherent collectives in their place, not so much because of the authorities' vetoes and repressions as because of the rebels' isolation from the conditions of normal collective life... My first friend treated me as an enemy not because he was worried about the Soviet system but because I had transgressed the accepted norm and behaved in a non-Soviet manner.

Alexander Zinoviev, *Homo Sovieticus*

1.

The 1930s in the Soviet Union came to be known as the period of the Stalinist show-trials, confessions, apologies, and purges. The second decade of the 21st century is likely to be known as the decade of *democratic* apologies and ostracism. In America, apologies have reached the level of a national epidemic. At the time of writing, the most recent came from Alabama Governor Kay Ivey and Andrew Cuomo but the list of former distinguished persons includes Ralph Northam (Governor of Virginia), Larry Summers (former U.S. Treasury Secretary and President of Harvard), Megyn Kelly (popular American TV anchor with a sixty-nine million dollar contract, and who sparred with Mr. Trump during presidential primaries), the actors Richard Dreyfuss and Dustin Hoffman, and, the English Nobel Laureate Tim Hunt. This time, however, apologies are not ordered by the First Secretary of the Communist Party or the Executive Committee of the Polit-Bureau, rather they are forced upon us by the social pressure of "the people." The fear of the mob is great enough to make even the most distinguished individuals bow before their tyranny.

Nietzsche predicted it all. Like Cassandra, he prophesied the masses' moralizing mode when he asked: "What will be the common element in their moral estimate?" Nietzschean "herd morality" is now the social norm. The former beloved of the masses are now prostrating themselves before the masses. As Nietzsche would have it: Never before were the apologies so cheap and the crimes so light!

The relationship between the individual and the masses is nothing new. It was of interest to psychologists and sociologists alike. Freud, Jung, Fromm, Ortega y Gasset and David Riesman are best known for their contributions to our understanding of group behavior. They described how the masses act and the psychology behind group behavior. However, they left out the most pertinent *political* question that should be of concern to us all: What are the conditions under which a popular government, which allows the masses to exercise political power, might break down?

Traveling in America in the early 1830s, the French aristocrat Alexis de Tocqueville noted that a democratic society is more tyrannical than any absolute ruler could ever be:

The most absolute monarchs in Europe cannot prevent certain opinions [...]. It is not so in America [...] no monarch is so absolute as to combine all the powers of society in his own hands and to conquer all opposition, as the majority is able to do [...]. The majority possess a power that is physical and moral at the same time, which acts upon the will as much as upon the actions and represses not only all contest, but all controversy. I know of no country in which there is so little independence of mind and real freedom of discussion as in America.

And, in conclusion, Tocqueville adds:

If ever the free institutions of America are destroyed, that event may be attributed to the omnipotence of the majority, which may at some future time urge the minorities to desperation and oblige them to have recourse to physical force. Anarchy will then be the result, but it will have been brought about by despotism.

Tocqueville's observation overlaps with what we find already in Plato. In his *Republic*, Bk. VIII, Plato describes the process of the dissolution of authority in a democratic society, which, as a result, plunges democracy into anarchy, only to be followed by tyranny.

One should read Tocqueville as saying that despotism—monarchical or democratic—is despotism, and when it reaches its peak, when the suppressed minority will have no other means of defense, it will cause rebellion and will bring down democratic institutions. Following Lord Acton's famous dictum, "Power corrupts, absolute power corrupts absolutely," one might say: As the power of the masses increases, so does their intolerance of contrary opinions, and what was traditionally true of absolute monarchy is true of democracy in its final days.

Looking at the present through the prism of the French aristocrat's assessment of how democracy operates, today's apologies should not surprise us. They are signs of the individual's *increasing* servility to the absolute sovereign—the masses. And what the masses demand apologies for is a *lack of unconditional commitment to equality*. Any remark—however sound or factual—that questions equality meets with condemnation, rage and hysteria. As Orwell put it, "The heresy of all heresies is commonsense."

The apologies did not spare the offenders from losing their jobs, and yet the new offenders continue to apologize. If so, what needs to be explained is why anyone would be willing to subject themselves to public humiliation. To look for a *rational* explanation of so many individuals' personal motives would most likely be a waste of time. The answer must be sought in human psychology, and in the relationship of the individual to the masses.

The 21st century democratic "purges" are a strange hybrid of Ancient democracy and 20th century totalitarianism. In 507 B.C., when the Athenians invented democracy, they introduced the method known as ostracism, which consisted in banning the guilty for a ten-year term. The procedure was based on two questions: *Do you want to find someone guilty? And whom do you wish to accuse?* If the accuser amassed 6000 votes, the accused would be sent into exile. The purpose of ostracism was purely political: It prevented any one individual from accumulating too much power. Ostracism was a handy mechanism that disposed of political opponents. Unlike the Stalinist methods, our method stops short of killing or torturing anyone; unlike the Athenian method, it cannot force anyone into exile. The crimes are many: sexism, misogyny, racism, homophobia, xenophobia, Islamophobia, or ageism. If the public finds the accused guilty, it will cost him his job, social standing, and membership in any prestigious institutions. All of this is done to discourage others from committing the same crime.

It would be a mistake to think that the apologies are made for opportunistic reasons. The new apologizers know that the people who had apologized before them lost their jobs, and that they will lose theirs, too. Yet the new offenders apologize. Why?

2.

Democratic confession works like a simple psychological procedure and comes down to *admitting that I committed a crime and am feeling guilty about it.* The confession gives the apologizer a soothing feeling of being reintegrated into society. The apology, similar to a religious ritual, washes the sins away by contrition. It is done in a Protestant rather than a Catholic way, and the wave of apologies is limited almost exclusively to nominally Protestant countries. The sinner, like in Calvin's Geneva, prostrates himself before "the community of the faithful," rather than in the privacy of the Catholic confessional facing the priest, who is bound by the secrecy of confession, listening to the sinner, and aligning of the penance. Penance is public, as are our sins. After the confession, in your heart of hearts, you know that you are no longer a social pariah, and the ritual allows you to distance yourself from your former views. You are a new man. The transformation may move you to express genuine surprise at your former self. As if transformed by a coup de grace, the people you offended no longer appear as before—the fearful enemies—but as a community of brothers and sisters. You might even wonder: How could I have had such offensive views before?

Of all those who confessed in recent years, Megyn Kelly's confession captures the process of this transformation best. After she "offended" the public with her remarks about "Blackface," within hours she came to understand the evil of her ways. In her apology, she said:

> I have never been a PC kind of person [...] [but] it is not OK for [blackface] to be part of any costume, Halloween or otherwise. [...] This past year has been so painful for many people of color [...]. The country feels so divided and I have no wish to add to that pain and offense. *I believe this is a time for more understanding, more love, more sensitivity and honor, and I want to be part of that. Thank you for listening and for helping me listen too.*[1]

Kelly's confession could serve as material for a new novel about totalitarianism were it not for the fact that this novel was already written by a Russian writer Yevgeny Zamyatin, who experienced Stalinist persecution personally. In his *WE* (which served as material for Huxley's and Orwell's books), Zamyatin captured the psychology of self-annihilation in a manner almost identical to what we heard from Kelly. The novel ends with the "reintegration" and "happiness" of the protagonist, whose name is D-503. No one in *WE* has a name. Everyone is a number: I am We; other numbers are We, and no one can escape We. Here is the final scene:

1   Emphasis mine.

There we were tied to the tables and subjected to the Great Operation. On the following day, I, D-503, went to the Benefactor and told him everything I knew about the enemies of happiness. How could it have seemed so difficult before? Incredible. The only explanation I can think of is my former sickness (the soul).

Individuality means having a soul, a soul with individual desires and thoughts. We follow D-503's peregrinations in Zamyatin's novel, and as his soul awakens, he thinks of it as a sickness. The Great Operation ends the suffering of the *sick number*, just like the sensation of love, understanding, and sensitivity cured the American anchorwoman.[2]

Kelly is one among hundreds who thought that she did something wrong. In 2005, the former Treasury Secretary, then President of Harvard, Larry Summers, said the following:

> I must apologize for recent comments of mine that seem to suggest women lack the innate ability that men have to excel in math and the sciences. To be sure, my intention was to spark controversy and debate. But I certainly did not set out to offend anyone, and I regret that my remarks have upset so many people—

---

2   It appears that the process of ideological transformation has no end. Recently, on Feb. 26, 2021, two years after she was fired, Megyn Kelly, appeared on Bill Maher's TV show. What occasioned her appearance was Kelly's withdrawal of her children from school for imposing PC ideology on them. The 8–9-year-old students were supposed to take part in the so-called trans-education program. The children were asked to signal the extent to which they were "confused" about their gender. During the conversation, Kelly mentioned another case of the spread of the new iideology. One of the Manhattan schools came up with a chart for anti-racist re-education of the whites. The chart presents 8 categories into which all whites belong: white supremacy, white voyeurism, white privilege, white benefit, white confession, white critical, white traitor and white abolitionist. Given the perverse nature of the two cases, no reasonable person should deny that American schools' sole purpose now is to shape the minds of the American children at the earliest age possible. This in itself in not surprising; what is is Kelly's awakening that ideology that cured her during her apology is now threatening her children. As Kelly put it, "there is no way to get away from this..."

particularly members of the fair sex, whose delicate sensibilities should not be subjected to this type of emotional distress.

And in another statement, he said:

I welcome this opportunity to again express regret for my remarks about women, which have caused so much turmoil and bad feeling. I want to assure my female colleagues that I do not question their abilities, nor do I challenge their aptitude for achievement in math, the sciences, engineering, or any other field of endeavor. It is my sincere hope that they can now put this unfortunate incident behind them and won't worry their pretty little heads about it anymore.

Sir Tim Hunt, the English scientist who, along with Lee Hartwell and Paul Nurse, was awarded the Nobel Prize for discovering "key regulators of the cell cycle," caused a fury by making a humorous comment at a conference: "Let me tell you about my trouble with girls. Three things happen when they are in the lab. You fall in love with them, they fall in love with you, and when you criticize them, they cry." Again, within hours, a storm erupted over his comment, and Hunt issued an apology: "I'm very sorry that what I thought were light hearted ironic remarks were taken so seriously, and I'm very sorry if people took offence. I certainly did not mean to demean women, but rather be honest about my own shortcomings."

Hundreds of apologies revolve around the same crimes, and they come down to "not knowing" something one should know, or not realizing that something "I did not know" can be as offensive as the things I know to be offensive. This is a bizarre form of dialectical thinking because it makes one an offender on account of ignorance; ignorance of the sensitivity of people I do not know. So, instead of blaming them for being "oversensitive," or for not knowing what a joke is, the accused are deemed guilty of not being sensitive enough to fathom that there are others who are especially sensitive, or that the accused are much less sensitive relative to the offended. Not being sensitive enough is, as Tim Hunt put it, a "shortcoming" which one must admit during an apology.

To redeem the situation, and prevent people from saying "offensive" things, we embarked on the great project of *institutional training in the workforce*. Various institutions in America send people to regular "sensitivity trainings." Pharmacists, doctors, the police, non-profit organization employees, and hundreds of others must participate in it. The goal of the trainings is to "raise the employees' level of consciousness."

The parallels with the former socialist countries are inevitable. There, too, the professional trainers—called ideological officers—with degrees in Marxist-Leninist philosophy would organize meetings for the employees, explaining to them the nature of labor, relationships in a socialist work-place, socialist economics, and the nature of oppression and exploitation in the "corrupt consumerist West." In the 70s and 80s, not too many people would take it seriously. Some would skip the trainings, others would openly disregard it, but, most importantly, almost no one would believe what was taught. It was a formality that people were willing to put up with to keep from being harassed. This is not so in America today. The ideology impresses itself on people's minds with a force unimaginable to the former denizens of the countries of real socialism, and most of them, like the present author, wonder how one can take it seriously. We ask ourselves: Can it really be true?

But the parallels between socialism and democracy have their limits. Under socialism, it was the Communist Party that posed a threat to your life. Under democracy, it is the people. The process of extermination under democracy was described with a terrifying vivacity by Tocqueville in his *Democracy in America*:

> Such is not the course adopted by tyranny in democratic republics; there the body is left free, and the soul is enslaved. The master no longer says: "You shall think as I do or you shall die"; but he says: "You are free to think differently from me and to retain your life, your property, and all that you possess; but you are henceforth a stranger among your people. You may retain your civil rights, but they will be useless to you, for you will never be chosen by your fellow citizens if you solicit their votes; and they will affect to scorn you if you ask for their esteem. You will remain among men, but you will be deprived of the rights of mankind. Your fellow creatures will shun you like an impure being; and even those who believe in your innocence will abandon you, lest they should be shunned in their turn."

Sir Tim Hunt's story exemplifies this fragment. The Royal Society's President said that Sir Tim Hunt *deserved* to lose his position. Hunt's friend and Nobel Prize co-recipient, Sir Paul Nurse distanced himself from his friend, and told the *Telegraph* that Hunt's "chauvinist" comments had "damaged science." Finally, Sir Hunt was forced to resign from The Royal Society. The person who came to his defense was his *former* wife!

What should we think of Sir Tim Hunt's case? The first thing that comes to mind is that in a democratic society, even science must lose its independent status, and that scientists, from whom we should expect commitment to objectivity and Truth, will abandon their colleagues and Truth. *Platon amicus sed magis amica verita est* (Plato is a friend, but the greater friend is Truth), said Aristotle to mark his departure from his beloved teacher. The old formula that led Europe's intellectual commitment for twenty-four centuries has been abandoned today. Your genius and the pursuit of Truth matter not. The opposite is the case. In a statement, the Royal Society announced:

> The Royal Society believes that in order to achieve everything that it can, science needs to make the best use of the research capabilities of the entire population. Too many talented individuals do not fulfill their scientific potential because of issues such as gender and *the Society is committed to helping to put this right*. Sir Tim Hunt was speaking as an individual and his reported comments in no way reflect the views of the Royal Society.

Since when is the objective of science and its institutions to be ideologically involved? Whose side is The Royal Society on? On the side of Galileo or that of the Inquisition? No doubt, Galileo and Copernicus' views were "offensive" to everyone around except those whose concern was science, not religious fairy-tales. The position of the Royal Society is a serious departure from everything we know about how such institutions operated in the 17th century. If we admire Copernicus and Galileo, it is because their commitment was "to put science right," not to make the public feel good about the centrality of their mental universe.

Today's Royal Society, however, is not alone in believing that science is subservient to the public's ideological goals. In a recent conversation on American *National Public Radio*, a female scientist, after explaining that the level of testosterone—which is higher in males than in females—also accounts for the leadership qualities, in humans and animals, prompted the host to ask a question about women in politics. In responding to the question, the scientist remarked that one has to be aware of how the public may react to such findings. Really? The Catholic Inquisition maybe a bygone of history, but ever since 19ᵗʰ century, the Inquisition has been replaced by the democratic public. In the times of Darwin and Spenser, the Inquisition wanted to stifle the influence of science to protect the religious view of the world; today, the democratic mob does the same to protect the egalitarian world-view against scientific evidence that men and women are different.

3.

The danger of the new dialectical thinking is that we no longer operate in the realm of facts, physical reality, established social norms, shared moral and intellectual assumptions, or even a common understanding of the normal and abnormal, sane and insane, but we must operate in the realm of someone else's mental universe, which we are forced to "respect." My crime is no longer of a traditional nature. It cannot be measured by criteria of truth and falsehood, empirical evidence, good or bad arguments, harm in the form of bruises and broken bones, or even violation of the rules of politesse or civility, which in the past would disqualify me from being a member of a "polite society." *It is all mental.* As a consequence, the distinction between the public and private realm disappears, and is replaced with a subjective mental realm. Indeed, it gives way to a multiplicity of distinct mental realms.

My perception of the world and, therefore, my existence is a psychological onslaught of someone's perception of the same world, and my crime lies in that I do not recognize that someone else feels differently. Neither Summers nor Hunt *knew* that women can feel differently; Kelly did not know that Black people can feel differently than Whites, straight people do not know that gay people feel differently, Christians do not know how Muslims feel, and Muslims do not know how atheists feel about being converted to Islam, or any religion for that matter. Finally, women do not know how men talk or joke. In short, no one knows how anyone feels. *Everything comes down to feelings, and feelings create social reality and establish historical facts.*

Confession is the realization that there are an infinite number of universes, in fact, as many universes as there are individuals who feel differently, and all of those universes are equally legitimate. In all of them, facts are *everything that is felt to be true*. Facts are feelings and feelings are facts: The objective universe dissolves and disappears. I cannot claim that my universe is better, more valuable, truer than that of anyone else, and I have no right to impose my views and language on anyone else. My saying that the Italian Dante is the greatest poet can only meet with a riposte: "What makes you think so! How dare you! You hold such a logocentric, Eurocentric view!"

To a person raised on Classical literature and Greek philosophy, this is intellectual hogwash, but this hogwash is accepted today as the only form of intellectual discourse in American mass media and academia. Support for this can be confirmed by an earlier incident, in which Kelly was again involved. Back then, in 2012, however, she had the courage to insist on the existence of facts:

> [F]or all you kids watching at home, Santa is white. But this person is just arguing that maybe we should also have a black Santa, but Santa is what he is, and just so you know, we're just debating this 'cause someone wrote about it, kids [...]. *Just because it makes you feel uncomfortable doesn't mean it has to change* [...]. Jesus was a white man, too [...]. He was a historical figure, that's a verifiable fact, as is Santa. I just want the kids watching to know that.

As one might expect, a controversy followed. One could dismiss the absurdity of the discussion by saying politely that there is nothing wrong with Black people hanging pictures of their Savior as a Black Jesus, Asians as Asian, or Whites as White, or some, using Peter O'Toole's non-Semitic Irish face with beautiful and piercing blue eyes, do the same. In the realm of religious symbolism or fairy tale, pigment does not matter, and it should not. It is a private, mental, imaginary realm, and what happens in the realm of imagination does not need to agree with empirical facts. But those who attacked Kelly did not make such an argument. They responded with a statement that contradicts what Kelly claims, "Historians debate what race Jesus was." In other words, no single representation of Jesus has a privileged factual or historical position, because we don't know what the facts are, and we will never know.

All of this does not sound very serious; in fact, it sounds nonsensical.

But behind every large-scale episode of nonsense—particularly when it seizes education, employment, economy and politics—stands profound philosophical claims and cultural mutations which one needs to unwind in order to understand the world in which we find ourselves. In this case, it is relativism, which swept through America in the 1970s and 80s, and which University of Chicago Professor Allan Bloom described in his *The Closing of the American Mind.* The book incited absolute fury, and sold one million copies within the first year. Relativism was followed by "culture wars" in the 90s. We were told that we should choose among competing interpretations, competing factual statements. Today, we no longer operate in the realm of facts, but that of feelings. The apologies are not about being factually wrong (Summers used statistics, and the statistics were found "offensive"), but about not being sensitive enough to understand that others can be offended by facts. What we are witnessing is the final chapter of a book that no one has written, but whose content unfolds daily in the public square. Its protagonist is the democratic masses that Tocqueville predicted will bring down free institutions. How things will end is by no means certain, but the answer may lie in the contrast between the democratic confessions and other forms of totalitarian confessions in the past.

4.

Arthur Koestler's *Darkness at Noon* is by far the most insightful fictionalized account of the Stalinist trials and confessions. In a simple, but vivid and forceful language, Koestler shows what the trials were like, how the prisoners were compelled to admit to committing the crimes of which they were accused. After a number of vertigo-like steps on a dialectical runway, augmented by a fear of torture, the accused prisoner would come to believe that he acted against the Party and the people, either from ignorance or a simple unawareness of the nature of his actions. The speed with which dialectical thinking operates on the mind of the prisoner, leading him to have doubts about his innocence, makes the reader ponder the reality of the situation. Sometimes the reader must stop for a moment, take a deep breath, and ask himself how much Koestler invented and how much of it is real. Given what we know from history about the trials, Koestler did not invent much. The book's greatest merit lies in allowing us to understand the psychology behind the real confessions. In his ability to disentangle the intricacies of ideological thinking, Koestler exposed communist totalitarianism for what it was—namely, an attempt to lead the individual into a servitude to the collective of which the Party, armed with its ideological magic wand, was the visible representation. Attempting to undermine its authority meant death. Confession and apology were the two steps in the accused's understanding of why he deserved to be killed. Those who wished to live had to make their minds captive by understanding that history runs in an inevitable direction of disclosing the Communist future, and that a rebellion against historical necessity is futile. "There is only one proof you can give," came Gletkin's voice; "a complete confession," Koestler makes his character, the Communist interrogator, explain to the accused, Rubashov.

> We have heard enough of your 'oppositional attitude' and your lofty motives. What we need is a complete, public confession of your criminal activities, which are necessary outcomes of that attitude. The only way in which you can still serve the Party is as a warning example—by demonstrating to the masses, in your own person, the *consequences* to which opposition to the Party policy inevitably leads.

Because actions stem from thoughts, and having thoughts that are in opposition to the Party is bound to breed opposition, the purpose of confession was to send a warning to others, that they ought not to entertain any thoughts that might lead to actions that contradict the Party's ideology and the policies based on it.

George Orwell, who praised Koestler's book, also exploited the idea of confession in his *1984*. However, unconstrained by real historical events, and pursuing the logic of his own version of the totalitarian state—founded not on "love and justice," as the Communists claimed theirs was, but "upon hatred"—Orwell took a different stance on the purpose of confession.

In a manner reminiscent of Koestler's Gletkin, Orwell's O'Brian tells Winston: "There are three stages in your *reintegration*. There is learning, there is understanding, and there is acceptance." As he tortures Winston, O'Brian explains to his victim that, just as there is no truth independent of the Party, so, by implication, there is no individual independent of the collective and the state. Being an individual is an illusion, a display of insanity. Orwellian reintegration is not the process of accepting an individual into the collective, whose social glue is a collectivistic ideology, which provides "home" for the dispossessed and love for the scorned; it is a process of curing him from his own delusion that there is an individual man with an individual mind. This idea is a leitmotif of Winston's diary. The diary is a record of his own insanity: the belief in his own individuality.

One of the most misunderstood ideas in *1984* is the function of the Thought-Police. Orwellian Thought Police are there not to suppress anyone's thoughts, since no one is capable of generating them, but to ensure that no one breeds illusions. If so, truth is not truth—truth is a heresy, just like it is heretical to think that $2 + 2$ can equal anything other than what the Party declares it to be. This is not an expression of relativism. The existence of truth, to which an individual can cling and hide behind, would be tantamount to the existence of an individual. Winston's invention of the equation $2 + 2 = 4$ is his desperate effort to free himself from the collective. If there is no truth independent of the Party and its great collective, the individual does not exist.

It would be a mistake to think that Orwell's *1984* is merely a more extreme version of communism or Stalinism. To be sure, in many respects, Koestler's and Orwell's books share some similarities, but each author's understanding of the influence of ideology, and the totalitarian absorption of the individual into the collective, differs. Let's compare the endings of the two books.

> Koestler:
> He made an effort to slip his arm into his dressing-gown sleeve. But whose colour-print portrait was hanging over his bed and looking at him?
>
> Was it No. 1 or was it the other—he with the ironic smile or he with the glassy gaze?
>
> A shapeless figure bent over him, he smelt the fresh leather of the revolver belt; but what insignia did the figure wear on the sleeves and shoulder-straps of its uniform—and in whose name did it raise the dark pistol barrel?
>
> A Second, smashing blow hit him on the ear. Then all became quiet. There was the sea again with its sounds. A wave

slowly lifted him up. It came from afar and traveled sedately on, a shrug of eternity.

Orwell:
> He gazed up at the enormous face. Forty years it had taken him to learn what kind of smile was hidden beneath the dark mustache. O cruel, needless misunderstanding! O stubborn, self-willed exile from the loving breast! Two gin-scented tears trickled down the sides of his nose. But it was all right, everything was all right, the struggle was finished. He had won the victory over himself. He loved Big Brother.

The similarities are stunning, just like the borrowings. (Rubashov's diary in the "Third Hearing" is reminiscent of Goldstein's book in *1984*, which is the source of heresy, with sophisticated analyses of the past and present). But Orwell did not plagiarize Koestler's ending. Rather, Orwell wants to let the reader know that his understanding of human nature, and the resulting totalitarian rule, is different. If there are any similarities in detail, they are of a superficial nature. The presence of a portrait in both authors, the smile, No. 1 and Big Brother are parts of scenery, but irrelevant for the final moment. Rubashov is killed; Smith is not, at least not biologically, which is all that matters.

The conclusion one can draw is that the Communists did not believe in reintegration or rehabilitation, in changing the mind of a rebel. "Relapse" is not a mere possibility; it is bound to happen. And if so, the rebel must be exterminated. The idea of a rebellious human nature goes back to Dostoevsky's "Legend of the Grand Inquisitor." We are rebels by nature, and rebellion must be prevented for the sake of social order. Therefore, man needs faith—faith in edifying lies about the hereafter such that he will not rebel. Religion is a way of taming the human rebellious instinct to defy authority. Dostoevsky is by no means saying that religion—Christianity—is an edifying lie, but rather that with its superhuman demands, Christianity sets moral standards which are too high for the majority. Faced with the earthly organization of society, the Church must use a noble lie to prevent chaos or anarchy. Dostoevsky's Grand Inquisitor is an *Übermensch* who must carry the burden of the lie for the sake and well-being of the rebels.

There is no afterlife in Communist ideology, so no one will obey for the promise of future life. Fear, and fear only, can make people obey in this life. If you rebel, you will be killed, but before we kill you, we will give you an option. You can make a sacrifice for the sake of others—let your death be a warning to others not to rebel. (This is Gletkin's message to Rubashov.) Your confession and death may even be considered acts of sacrifice for the sake of humanity. Otherwise, you will die uselessly.

The final scene in Orwell, when Winston comes to love Big Brother, on the other hand, is not an act of his physical liquidation. Rather, it is his last moment of being an individual before he is reintegrated into the collective. Peace of the captive mind—both in Zamyatin and Orwell—is the final reward.[3]

Gletkin, in Koestler, is a sadist, but his sadism finds justification in the nature of the enterprise:

> My point is, one may not regard the world as a sort of metaphysical brothel for emotions. This is the first commandment for us. Sympathy, conscience, and atonement are for us repellent debauchery [...] to sell oneself to one's conscience is to abandon mankind. History is *a priori* amoral; it has no conscience.

Once again, the presence of Dostoevsky's influence is indubitable, but leads us, this time, to *The Brothers Karamazov*—the famous line from Ivan's conversation with the Devil: "If you want to swindle, why do you need the sanction of truth?" Individual conscience is a nuisance, which, if you want to make a revolution, must be abandoned for the sake of revolutionary efficiency and mankind's future well-being. To concern oneself with conscience is to put individual well-being before the well-being of the collective. In so far as individual conscience can be different from the laws of historical development, being moved by it can only lead to death.

Again, Orwell seems to have traveled further than Koestler: He makes conscience totally non-existent. Reading the scene where O'Brian torments

---

3 Whether Orwell intended it or not, one cannot resist the impression that the final moment looks like a scene from the New Testament—the return of the prodigal son, who, after a time away from home, came back to be shown the love of the loving Father.

Winston, one cannot resist the impression of his inhumanity. At no point is O'Brian moved by his victim's pain. His sadism is unbearable, and it grows each time he pushes the voltage lever higher and higher. Unlike Gletkin, O'Brian is not a revolutionary and does not concern himself with laws of history and stages of historical development. At one point he even gets irritated with Winston's slowness in understanding the real purpose of his torment. "Don't be stupid, Winston," he exclaims. His sadism is an act of wisdom and love of his victim. What greater act of love can one think of than curing someone from his delusion? O'Brian is a doctor, whose compassion extends so far that he will not hesitate to use excruciating pain to bring a sick mind to its normal healthy state. Who would not hesitate to help a schizophrenic suffer more greatly if the end of the painful procedure is his mental health, bringing him to see the world like everyone else? In a famous line from a conversation with his brother, Ivan, when faced with the question of inflicting suffering—"would you build a world on the tear of one little girl?"—Alyosha Karamazov responds, "no," but points to God who can because he himself was willing to suffer. O'Brian is God, but not the suffering Christian God, rather the God who understands that evil, not good, must ultimately triumph.

What is the difference between Koestler and Orwell's accounts of the confession? Confession, in Koestler, is public; it serves the purpose of discouraging others from following in Rubashov's rebellious footsteps. Historical inevitability does not allow for *individual* "lofty motives" (history is *a priori* amoral) independent of the collective, which marches in the same direction as designed by history. The conviction of the accused is needed only to be visually persuasive to the masses, to inspire fear in them. Interrogations, intimidation, and torture are sufficient steps in preparing the accused to make a convincing public statement.

None of this matters in Orwellian Oceania. Confession is not public, does not serve any external purpose of convincing anyone of anything, except the "thought criminal." There is no public which needs to be warned. Even the confessions of Goldstein, Rutherford, and Jones are there only to inspire more hate, which is a form of glue that assembles the masses into ever greater social cohesion. The reintegration—learning, understanding and acceptance—is to help the individual understand that he, as an individual, does not exist. Individuality is an illusion.

If so, the question is: Who is O'Brian—the most intriguing character in *1984*? Winston, like the reader, suspects him of being a member of the oppositional Brotherhood. Winston admires his intelligence, which, as he says to himself, could crush him. It is only natural that Winston thinks O'Brian must see reality his way, the true way, and be on his side. Without a moment of hesitation, he goes to O'Brian's den to reveal to him his thoughts. The crux of the book lies in the fact that O'Brian is even less an individual than the others. He, like everyone, is a member of the Oceanic Collective. He is a 20th century new-Machiavelli. His intelligence merely allows him to perfectly grasp the nature of power: He is the awareness of power itself. It is a dynamic power unconstrained, like in Machiavelli, by any moral considerations. Marxist laws of historical development imposed limits on the Party because one had to know how to read them correctly. They were also needed in designing economic policies or scientific projects. Nothing like that occupies O'Brian's mind. His mind is obsessed with power. As he explains it to Winston,

> The old civilizations claimed that they were founded on love and justice. Ours is founded upon hatred. In our world there will be no emotions except fear, rage, triumph, and self-abasement. Everything we shall destroy—everything. If you want a picture of the future, imagine a boot stamping on a human face—forever.

Only when we realize this can we understand why he feels no compassion for the suffering Winston. One cannot be understanding in regard to human stupidity. In this scheme of things, O'Brian's sadism is not evil; it is an act of compassion for his stupidity which finds justification in the belief that there is no difference between means and ends. In contrast to the Communists, who believed that ends justify means and that "sacrifices, however appalling they may appear, must be made," in Orwellian totalitarianism means are power, and power is the end. Therefore, slavery is freedom.

5.

Our democratic confessions and apologies are not made for the wrongs done to an individual person or even a group. Like in Orwell and Koestler, *they are ideological,* and they have an objective as well—namely, to send a message to the public and to transform the criminal. As in both authors, they aim at depriving man of his conscience. In Koestler, conscience is denied by the existence of historical laws; in Orwell's Oceania, the power of evil precludes its very existence; in a democracy, the individual abdicates his right to conscience. The voice of the people is one's conscience.

We know of group apologies addressed to groups: a country to a country, a nation to a nation, by a specific group of people who committed atrocities against another group. In all cases, such apologies were issued for very specific wrong-doings. They were often justified and helped to heal the wounds between neighbors and reestablish social or political relationships between countries and their peoples. More importantly, they allow us to reflect on the sources and causes of the harm done. They also have the power to make us ponder the nature of our past actions in order to prevent evil and harm from occurring again in the future. The health of a nation, just like health of an individual—though not exactly the same since a group does not have conscience—depends on our awareness of what is right and wrong, just as it depends on our ability to distinguish between true and false, and to stand up for the true and just, often at the expense of our personal feelings and political predilections.

The case in point is the situation of Nazism in Germany. The great German writer, Thomas Mann, whose books the Nazis burned, asks in his *Magic Mountain* and *Dr. Faustus* what could make one of the most civilized nations in human history go mad and commit such atrocities. After the war, Mann's fellow countryman, Karl Jaspers, published a book titled *Die Schuldfrage* (*The Guilt*), in which he considers collective guilt. Jaspers distinguishes between "criminal guilt," "political guilt" (which involves the deeds of politicians who implicate their citizens in the consequences of state action), "moral guilt" (the individual is morally responsible for all his actions, including the execution of political and military orders), and "metaphysical guilt" based on the notion of solidarity of man as man. As he asserts, "There exists a solidarity among men as humans that makes each co-responsible for every wrong and every injustice in the world, especially for crimes committed in his presence or with his knowledge. If I fail in whatever I can do to prevent them, I too am guilty."

Criminal guilt does not apply to democratic confessions at all because it requires a crime and the possibility of legal action. Political guilt requires that someone make a decision whose consequences cannot be stopped individually because they go beyond the individual's capacities as a voter. Moral guilt applies only in cases of bystanders who fail to act when they have the knowledge that their actions are, or could be, criminal—but, again, one is unable to stop them. Finally, the last form of guilt would be difficult to grasp by an ordinary person whose concerns are mundane, who thinks of daily bread, and if it is intelligible at all, it assumes a perspective of the suffering Christ looking down from the cross on the world as in Dali's beautiful painting.

Jaspers is not wrong in dividing the human moral situation into four aspects, but none of these aspects appears to be useful in explaining the democratic man's crime, and the sense of guilt that stands behind the apologies. Jasper's categories are not applicable because today's accusations are neither criminal, nor political nor moral, let alone metaphysical in nature.

As I said, our crimes fall under the heading of ideological crimes, and only an ideologue can accuse someone of ideological crimes! There are only a few historical instances where one could be accused of similar crimes: the French Revolution and communism, among them. The crimes were called "ideological deviations," "straying away from the path of progress," "going in a direction contrary to the dominant tendency of the country," "being the enemy of the people," or "the enemy of the state." All of them find counterparts in our contemporary democratic reality.

The apologies offered by Summers and Hunt go to the very heart of the matter, and the attacks against them highlight the problem more sharply than other attacks for allegedly offensive language. They pointed to the differences between men and women. Summers, who quoted statistics, merely expressed in his own words what statistics tell us and what women know, too; Hunt, on the other hand, stated in a humorous manner what the majority of women know as well: They are more emotional and sensitive than men. (Let's note, no man would take offense if he were told that men are callous, insensitive, that they do not deal with children as well as women, that they are aggressive, etc. This is because we are indeed more callous, less sensitive, we are not as caring as women, and sometimes we do act like animals.)

Why, then, the outrage? The simple answer is that in a few generations female activists (with very different social and political objectives than the suffragists of old) and self-appointed spokeswomen for all women moved away from real concerns (like universal suffrage, right to divorce, protection against a husband's physical abuse, etc.) and allowed themselves to be driven by pure ideology. Feminism is no longer an idea that aims at improving women's political or social conditions, but an ideology that makes women see the past as a product of a patriarchal system. They consider comments like Hunt's or Summers' as a form of oppression—oppression that prevents women from being scientists, computer programmers, CEOs, firefighters, soldiers, soccer players, auto-mechanics, and construction workers. By intimidating the public for about three decades, they made the case for banning inequality in all its forms and shades from public life, and now they are banning inequality from our mental universe by banning language which hides traces of such alleged domination.

The attackers are not troubled by the fact that they curtail someone's freedom of speech, that they narrow the range of topics we can talk about, or that they intimidate the passive public. Neither Summers nor Hunt did anything to women, but in saying what they said they pointed to differences between men and women and thus questioned the idea of equality. Had they said the same thing about the superiority of Christianity over Islam, Lent over Ramadan, Western Civilization over any other civilization, superiority of the Italian artistic genius over the genius of artists from other countries, or of the asserted naturalness of heterosexual relationships (which is the only form of intercourse that can lead to reproduction and the preservation of species), they would be attacked with equal fervor for the same reason: They challenged equality.

As much as the partisans of equality talk about openness and diversity, they are not at all interested in entering a debate about anything—as anyone who values freedom of speech would—let alone the idea of equality, because they are not interested in the pursuit of truth. They simply converted one system of subjugation (women by men) into another (men by women).

After Sir Tim Hunt made his humorous comment, Connie St. Louis, who directs the science journalism program at City University, London, said: "Really, does this Nobel laureate think we are still in Victorian times?" In other words, we live in different times, and unless you want to be fired, you should never suggest that men and women are different.

In 2018, James Damore, a young software engineer, was fired from Google because he dared to suggest that there are differences between men and women. What was the policy of one company is becoming a national, ideological norm which businesses are being forced to adopt. In a truly American, entrepreneurial spirit, ideology was turned into a business. On the front page of *USA Today* (May 6, 2019), Jessica Guynn told the readers that "the nonprofit venture led by diversity advocate Ellen Pao has quickly become one of the most visible efforts [to draft more women and underrepresented minorities] in Silicon Valley [...]." However, within the space of several paragraphs, "effort" became a threat. We are told that "diversity and inclusion" are going to be treated by CEOs "as they would any other business imperative, 'a must have,' not a 'nice to have.' *Setting objectives and holding people accountable for reaching them* sent a clear message to their organizations that this work is a priority."[4]

What is the objective? "They [the CEOs] work toward hitting three targets: 10% black, African American and African employees, 10% Hispanic or Latino employees and 5% non-binary, with the workforce evenly split between men and women." Let me contrast this quotation with a short fragment from Alexander Solzhenitsyn's *The Gulag Archipelago*:

> What the engineers had first seen in the October *coup d'état* was ruin [...]. How could engineers accept the dictatorship of the workers, the dictatorship of their subordinates in industry, so little skilled or trained and comprehending neither the physical nor the economic laws of production, but now occupying the top positions, from which they supervised the engineers? [...] But while their superiors demanded success in production from them, and discipline, they were deprived of the authority to impose this discipline [...]. In those conditions, what was there for the collective engineering intelligence to do—the engineering leadership of the State Planning Commission and the Supreme Council of the Economy? To submit to insanity.

4   Emphasis mine.

How different is the article from *USA Today* and the "minority's" constantly threatening lawsuits for discrimination, from what went on in the Soviet Union? It isn't! *USA Today*, which daily publishes ideologically loaded articles, sounds like the Soviet newspaper *Pravda* ("Truth").

The race and gender "objectives" remind one of the five or ten year-plans under communism. The plans were supervised not by the professional economists, but by ideological commissars who made sure that everything was done according to the logic of socialist philosophy, as Solzhenitsyn described. The new communist engineer had little in common with Tsar Nicholas of Russia's engineer, and objectives were hardly ever achieved. The failure ended with the firing or execution of the "saboteurs." Like in the Soviet Union, at no point does the author of the article consider the questions of profit and growth or qualifications of the employees. None of this is part of the economic plan. What is? Equality, which is the new economic norm.

6.

What started as a movement for a more equitable political and social reality assumed the form of a class struggle. Today's enemies, like the software engineer, Damore, and Sir Tim Hunt, are fired for their Victorian views. By "Victorian" what is meant is, of course, old or traditional views. Since history is progressive, our views should be, too, and they should be exchanged every few years for ever-newer views, like technological devices. Here again, a similarity with Marxism comes to mind. There, the obscurantists, the enemies of the people, who clung to old values were threatened by the Party with ending up in the "Dustbin of History"; now, we are threatened by the masses with ending up in the "Victorian Dustbin."

As members of Western civilization, we need to seriously ask ourselves. How many of us truly believe this ideological hogwash? And how many of us are willing to jeopardize the well-being of this civilization and future generations for the sake of equality?

Tim Hunt's discovery of "key regulators of the cell cycle" is no small matter. Nor is Einstein's theory of relativity. Only ideological zeal can blind us to measurable benefits, from which we all profit due to the existence of great minds. Yet only recently journalists, always hungry to find something discrediting in someone's past, discovered that in his 1922–23 travel journal Albert Einstein wrote about the Chinese: "industrious, filthy, obtuse people […]. It would be a pity if these Chinese supplant all races. For the likes of us the mere thought is unspeakably dreary." As one could expect, they gave their articles shocking titles, "Einstein was a racist," "Einstein's racial slurs," "shocking xenophobia," "racist attacks revealed," and so on. Some internet users organized an online boycott against Einstein. The attitude of many Chinese internet users was different, though. They retained clarity of mind and in a calm manner tried to understand why Einstein said what he did. One comment reads: "Einstein went to China at the wrong time. Hunger, war, and poverty all pressed on the Chinese. How could Chinese people at the time gain Einstein's respect?" How could the Chinese reaction be this way, whereas our reaction is one of outrage and condemnation? One simple answer might be that criticism, however unpleasant, if it can be recognized as justifiable, should make the criticized ponder his shortcomings. It is the surest way to improve. Traveling through China today, Einstein would most likely revise his views and try to understand what happened over a period of almost a hundred years. We in the West seem to have lost our critical analysis and our ability to ponder that which we encounter in our own thinkers such as Montaigne and Montesquieu.

It does not take particular skill or genius to condemn racism, sexism, homophobia, Islamophobia, misogyny, and ageism. The problem is that *not* being any of the above is *not* a guarantee of possessing the genius of Albert Einstein and Tim Hunt, to whom we owe a great deal. The attackers need to realize our Western civilization can and will fare well without them, but it will come to a halt without the accused.

We must consistently remind ourselves, using the words of Orwell, that, "Some animals are more equal than others." Accusing and expelling the Einsteins and Hunts from the farm may make us feel equal for a short time, but we can be sure that after a while the pigs will run the farm. It is unlikely that they will understand the difference between relativism and relativity.

CHAPTER 3 | THE DISSIDENTS' RIGHTS AND WRONGS: THE CASE OF JORDAN PETERSON

> The only part of the conduct of any one, for which [a member of a civilized community] is amenable to society, is that which concerns others. In the part which merely concerns himself, his independence is, of right, absolute. Over himself, over his own body and mind, the individual is sovereign.
>
> John Stuart Mill, *On Liberty*

> To offer freedom on the Cote d'Azure to a man who has been imprisoned for two years in exchange for moral suicide, you must be a pig; to believe that I could accept such an offer, you must think every person is a police spy. There are two things in this world, Sir, one of which is called evil, the other good... I don't know the future and don't know whether I will live long enough to see the victory of truth over the lie... the point is, Sir, that the value of our fight lies not in the chances of winning, but the cause in the name of which we undertook our fight.

> From a letter to the Minister of Internal Affairs by Adam Michnik, Polish dissident, imprisoned by the communist government upon the imposition of martial law in Poland.

1.

In contrast to hard totalitarianism, the soft, democratic version does not seem to create dissidents, and thereby the wider opposition that might resist it. If opposition does happen to emerge, it is quickly condemned as sexist, misogynist, racist, etc., and almost never given mass support. Communism, on the other hand, produced legions of dissidents. The names of Alexander Solzhenitsyn, Josif Brodsky, Gleb Jakunin, Andrei Zacharov, Alexander

Zinoviev, Vladimir Bukowski, Adam Michnik, Jacek Kuron, Vaclav Havel, and Milovan Dzilas are only a handful of the best-known. To them, and to those who supported them, it was obvious that they fought evil, and they were willing to sacrifice their lives to do so. Yet importantly, they knew they had the quiet or open support of the overwhelming remainder of society. It was almost an instinctual recognition that totalitarianism is evil, and it was the realization of its evil that created the opposition.

The rejection of communism was, among other things, an attempt to free one's mind from ideological enslavement in order to reclaim the idea of right and wrong, good and evil—and all this was accomplished independent of politics. Politics was thought to be subservient to values, and as things stood it was clear that politics could corrupt our understanding of what is good and right. The suffering and death of victims of the new totalitarian regime was one reason to believe that good, truth, and justice are not relative, and there was no compromise to be struck. The opposition manifested itself either as a private and quiet attitude of ordinary people, or in open and loud protests of the opponents. The level of participation depended on the courage of each individual and their willingness to take the risk. The most courageous of them became dissidents. They were admired and venerated by the quiet majority. In contrast to the masses under communism, the democratic masses are not just quiet, but seem to be almost deaf to a moral call and often act as if they reject morality altogether.

2.

According to classical Christian metaphysics, evil is privation, or lack of good; it is a force to be found in man, in his perverted will. It was understood that the role of the state is to constrain evil tendencies in man; or, as the Greeks believed, the task of politics was to create the conditions for the development of virtue. As Aristotle wrote in the *Nichomachean Ethics*, "The function of a lawgiver is to make citizens good."[1] Such an understanding

---

1   Aristotle was not the only ancient thinker who thought so. We find the echo of this idea in Plato's account of the trial of Socrates when one of the accusers asks the philosopher whether he agrees that the purpose of the laws is to make citizens good.

of evil and the role of the state was rejected by the liberal thinkers.[2] The writings of John Stuart Mill, probably the most representative of the liberal doctrine, are peppered with the word "evil." However, the reader quickly realizes that its meaning departs from the traditional—classical and Christian—understanding of it. Hundreds of sentences in which the term "evil" occurs in Mill's writings allow the reader to infer that evil is of a social nature and is the result of unequal distribution of power. The terms "fairness" and "social justice," which definitively entered socio-political vocabulary in the 1950s, made this a reality. "Fairness" and "social justice" came to signify the situation in which no one has more power than anyone else; that one person does not have more goods than another. Even elevating people out of poverty to an unprecedented level of material well-being and limiting abuses of the judicial system are not enough for those who think of evil the way Mill conceived of it.

The shift from a metaphysical conception of evil to a social one stems from the liberal understanding of power. Power, as Mill famously remarked in his argument for freedom of speech, is *illegitimate*, and therefore evil. Thus, for example, "[The power] of the aristocracy in the government is not only no benefit, but a positive evil." Similarly, the power of husband over wife, of parent over child, etc., are evil as well. Good, on the other hand, is what diminishes the political power and social authority. The purpose of

---

2   Just as the Greek or Christian view of good and evil was reflected in many thinkers' visions of what the purpose of the state and its institutions is, so the liberal notion of evil redefined the function of the state. Its purpose was no longer to shape man's moral character, as Aristotle would have it, nor to constrain evil tendencies in man's nature, as Hobbes would have it. The state and its institutions in the liberal perspective is an instrument of oppression which arrests the progress and development of the expressive powers of the individual. Accordingly, anything that is conducive to diminishing the power of the state must be denied authority because it is evil. This was Mill's attitude from the time of his earliest publications. Thus aristocracy, like in the passage quoted above, in so far as it is a political institution that wields political power and authority, is "evil." So is religion, the Church (of England) and its teaching, Christian religion, the old metaphysics, and custom, which Mill famously said to be despotic. In short, national history, tradition, education, reverence for the past and authority, and the whole realm of human historical experience is inimical to the liberal mind.

diminishing authority is to expand equality; and because progress is part of a historical process, as history develops so does the scope of equality. At the end of this historical process, as Mill says in the conclusion of his *Utilitarianism*, we will witness a slow death of aristocracies of race, sex, and color. Looking at things from today's perspective, Mill must be given credit for understanding the consequences of his own doctrine. He predicted that as long as there is still a single minority "left behind," to use contemporary vocabulary, the fight against authority will continue. And it does.

However, socializing the idea of evil turned out not to be without serious consequences. In his discussion of fairness as an ethical principle, Erich Fromm notes that the principle of fairness

> is the ethical principle governing the life of the marketing personality. The principle of fairness, no doubt, makes for a certain type of ethical behavior. You do not lie, cheat or use force [...] if you act according to the code of fairness. But to love your neighbor, to feel one with him, to devote your life to the aim of developing your spiritual powers, is not part of the fairness ethics. We live in a paradoxical situation: we practice fairness ethics, and profess Christian ethics.[3]

Nothing could be further from the truth. Today, sixty-five years after Fromm wrote these words, we hear the leaders of Christian churches and Reformed Jewish synagogues announce the same message about social justice and hardly a word about our individual responsibility for our next-door neighbor. The answer to the question of how we reached the point of turning away from the individual man and his responsibility within a social collective, toward impersonal help in the form of high taxation, can be traced to Mill's writings.

Mill's understanding of the nature of the historical process is similar to that of Marx and Engels, according to whom "the history of all hitherto existing society is the history of class struggles." In Marx, it is the class of the capitalists who oppress the workers, whereas in Mill the oppressed classes are

---

3   Erich Fromm, *The Sane Society* (Greenwich, Conn.: A Fawcett Premier Book, 1955), p. 155.

minorities. Once we accept such a view of history, we must come to the conclusion that the goal of politics is to end inequality. Accordingly, those who either attempt to slow down or stop the progress of equality are perpetrators of evil. In other words, those who fight authority (of whatever kind) fight oppression, and are therefore on the side of good and right, whereas those who uphold the *status quo* are oppressors who are on the wrong side, the side of evil and wrong.

The idea that authority is evil must sound strange to someone who thinks of evil as a destructive or corruptive moral force to be found in man. But this is what Mill rejected. He *socialized* the moral right and wrong, and in doing so Mill denied them their former metaphysical validity, rendering right and wrong instruments of politics. To put it simply, what is good is what promotes equality; what is bad is what prevents its implementation. The consequence of this socialization of good and right, of evil and wrong, is that the words "evil" and "wrong" could no longer be applied to the partisans of progress and equality. Progress and equality are by definition good, and those who are on the side of progress promote the good. In such a conceptual-linguistic framework, the term evil might be legitimately applied only to those who defend authority, or who fight the desired social and political changes.[4]

A perfect illustration of this process of socialization of good and evil is the position of almost all of the Democratic presidential candidates in 2020. In the words of Beto O'Rourke, "Religious institutions like colleges, churches, charities—they should lose their tax-exempt status if they oppose same-sex marriage." A similar attitude concerning different ills experienced by the LGBTQ community was expressed by Corey Booker, Elizabeth Warren, and Kamala Harris! All of them see the use of political force to support progressive causes, however unrealistic or insane they may be, as normal. There are no economic, social, or other kinds of problems; everything

---

4   Given the progressive nature of the historical process, there is no room for the idea of metaphysical moral evil in history, as it was in the case of the theodicies of Milton, William King, Leibniz, Dostoevsky, and Hegel. The last of these figures made his philosophy of history an attempt to explain the role moral evil plays in the nature of historical process by using the traditional Christian metaphysics. However, unlike Mill, Hegel was acutely aware that history is a "slaughter bench," and even though it is progressive, it stands condemned from the point of view that traditional moral categories do not apply to it.

comes down to fighting discrimination, that is, to bring about more equality. No one voices concerns that such policies are intrusive, undesirable in some respect, or as a violation of individual conscience. The reason is that the aim of politics, according to them, is total submission of conscience to politics. And if this requires war against Christianity, as represented by churches of all the different denominations, then so be it. Biblical teaching regarding right and wrong, people's commitment to national culture, transcendence, and conscience do not matter. Their views are simply wrong. And we know them to be wrong because they run counter to the ethics of social fairness.

Let me substantiate my claim by invoking one of the most recent legal cases. On October 2, 2019, the United Kingdom Employment Tribunal Ruled that the biblical view of the sexes is "Incompatible with Human Dignity." The tribunal in the United Kingdom ruled against a Christian doctor who alleged that the Department of Work and Pensions (DWP) breached his freedom of thought, conscience, and religion pursuant to the Equality Act. Disability assessor Dr. David Mackereth claimed discrimination after the DWP failed to accommodate his refusal to use pronouns which did not correspond with the biological sex of clients. In its decision, the panel stated that Dr. Mackereth's belief that "the Bible teaches us that God made humans male or female" was "incompatible with human dignity." [...] In June 2018, about a week after being hired, Dr. Mackereth attended a training course for assessors, including on DWP's policy to refer to transgender clients by their preferred name and title. Dr. Mackereth said "As a Christian, I cannot use pronouns in that way in good conscience [...]. I am a Christian, and in good conscience I cannot do what the DWP are requiring of me."

The ruling, no doubt, runs counter to biblical teaching and common sense. But above all, such a ruling amounts to a violation of individual conscience on the part of the State. However, given that liberalism did away with the transcendent view of right and wrong, what the tribunal declares must be right. Thus it is not religion that is found is on the side of right and wrong, but the *feelings and claims* of the LGBTQ community.

In this, the minorities act like the communists of old who threatened their opponents and made them abandon their values for the sake of equality. Lack of acquiescence to the new or socialist morality means one is destined to end up in what the Marxists called the "Dustbin of History."

3.

The acceptance of such a socialized view of right and wrong ejects the individual who dares to adhere to a different ethical code than that of fairness from the social collective. It also explains why dissent in liberal democracies is extremely rare, and why when it happens the dissenters are attacked and condemned as perpetrators of "social injustice," and, naturally, are being labeled as sexist, racist, misogynist, homophobic, xenophobic, and ageist—that is, as those who oppose "progress." Almost nothing else is evil or wrong except being one of the above. Dissent means disagreement with progressive causes and is viewed as an implicit attempt to restore authority, to roll history back, to return to the oppressive past, to impose old-fashioned and obsolete moral standards of behavior on others, or to attempt to increase the power of the state (or "power structure") over the individual.[5] Hardly ever is dissent thought of as an attempt to stop or slow down changes perceived as socially undesirable and sometimes dangerous, or as an attempt to restore a sense of national pride and a return to virtue, sanity, the renewal of moral rectitude, or the promotion of decency.

Once we accept a new understanding of evil, everything is decried as fascist. Mussolini and Hitler were fascists, but so was Aristotle because he endowed the *polis* with considerable authority over the individual. But even if we leave aside the political projects of classical philosophers, the absurdity of such reasoning does not disappear. After the collapse of communism in Russia, it was natural for the formerly oppressed countries to ponder what post-Soviet reality should look like. One of the voices in the debate was that of the former arch-dissident, Alexander Solzhenitsyn. He offered a program of moral regeneration for his country by looking to the past. Soon after, Solzhenitsyn, who spent decades in a gulag for his opposition to communism, was accused by liberal critics (Cathy Young in the *Boston Globe* and Zinovy Zinik in the *TLS*) of being "the theoretician of Putin-style authoritarianism and even a quasi-fascist."[6] Such accusations leveled against

---

5 It is a paradoxical situation that progressives see the state as a "power structure" that needs to be dismantled, on the one hand, and yet on the other wish to use the state to enforce their own rules through judicial processes.

6 "The Moral Witness of Aleksandr Solzhenitsyn," *First Things*, 2009.

former anti-communist dissidents and members of former anti-communist opposition have become almost a norm in today's liberal West.[7]

In the October 2018 issue of *The Atlantic Monthly*, Anne Applebaum, a well-respected journalist, historian, and author of several books including the excellent *Gulag: A History*, wrote a long article titled "A Warning from Europe" as part of *The Atlantic's* larger section: "Is Democracy Dying?" In it, she devoted considerable space to Poland and Hungary, addressing the rise of authoritarianism, intolerance, and other ills in these countries. The culprit is of course the past and its defenders, organized into political parties whose policies allegedly threaten democracy. The paradox that emerges while reading articles about former communist countries, written by and large by liberal commentators, is that many of those who represent the parties which supposedly threaten democracy are the former members of anti-communist opposition. Given the anti-totalitarian credentials of the new "totalitarians," one wonders how credible the claim is that the former anti-totalitarian fighters have become destroyers of the freedoms they fought for, and, consequently, whether such a reading of political life in Poland, Hungary, and Trump's America, is correct.

Such claims can be true only if one measures the health of democracy by today's standards of the socialized right and wrong. Thus, democracy in Hungary and Poland is threatened because of a firm commitment to the tradition and religious values that helped the nation to survive forty-four years of communism and the German occupation that wiped out one-fourth of the population, or by strict immigration rules from Muslim countries. The disastrous effects of friendly immigration policies of people from countries whose cultures and religions are hardly compatible with Western values can be observed in the countries that received them. Any attempt to resist such demands is perceived as anti-democratic, intolerant, or evil.

---

7   One can mention here Ryszard Legutko's case. Legutko, a philosophy professor at Jagellonian University in Krakow, Poland, is a conservative member of European Parliament, and was the editor of an anti-communist, underground magazine *ARKA* in the 1980s. In 2016 he published a book *The Demon in Democracy*, which was followed by invitations to give a lecture in a number of American universities, including Middlebury College. However, upon his arrival at Middlebury, the lecture was canceled because of student protests against his views. See his "The Demon in Middlebury" (*First Things*, August 2019).

4.

Lenin once remarked that he wanted "to purge Russia of all the harmful insects." Such an attitude was responsible for the gulags, murders, brutal interrogations, merciless persecution of dissenting voices, fear, and intimidation. The prime example of such policy exercised today is the case of the Canadian psychologist, Jordan Peterson. Peterson made a name for himself in 2016, during the debate concerning Bill C-16 in Canada. The bill's intention was to advance human-rights law by expanding "gender identity and gender expression." As Peterson argued, such a law would violate free speech because of the way the 'transgender' and so-called 'non-binary' people use pronouns such as 'they' (for singular). The Ontario Human Rights Commission concluded that if public institutions (workplace or schools) refuse to refer "to a trans person by their chosen name and a personal pronoun that matches their gender identity," it could be a violation of non-discrimination principles. Peterson refused and said: "I am not going to be a mouthpiece for language that I detest. And that's that."

It would appear, one would think, to every commonsensical person that the debate was over nothing or was simply silly. Singular cannot be Plural! Yet Peterson's obstinacy caused a social explosion and the psychology professor was soon the most persecuted man in North America. His public pronouncements about the use of pronouns may have triggered a reaction among some, but it is an unlikely explanation of why the attacks have continued for years and never stopped. An explanation should instead be sought in his views, which he laid out in his *12 Rules for Life: An Antidote to Chaos*. The book is what it says it is, but it is also a well-presented case against enforcing equality of outcome, as well as ideological brainwashing; and it is a defense of hierarchy. Let me use a few quotations to illustrate Peterson's position:

> What such studies imply is that we could probably minimize the innate differences between boys and girls, if we were willing to exert enough pressure. This would in no way ensure that we are freeing people of either gender to make their own choices. *But choice has no place in the ideological picture*: if men and women act, voluntarily, to produce gender-unequal outcomes,

those very choices must have been determined by cultural bias. In consequence, everyone is a brainwashed victim, wherever gender differences exist, and the rigorous critical theoretician is morally obligated to set them straight. This means that those already equity-minded Scandinavian males, who aren't much into nursing, require even more retraining. The same goes, in principle, for Scandinavian females, who aren't much into engineering. Such things are often pushed past any reasonable limit before they are discontinued. What might such retraining look like? Where might its limits lie? [...] *Mao's murderous Cultural Revolution should have taught us that.*[8]

And:

A shared cultural system stabilizes human interaction, but it is also a system of value—a hierarchy value, where some things are given priority and importance and others are not. In the absence of such a system of value, people simply cannot act. In fact, they can't even perceive, because both action and perception require a goal, and a valid goal is, by necessity, something valued.

What Peterson says, if an additional explanation is needed, is that contemporary progressives—just like the former communist architects of the gulag—are trying to force an ideological vision on people by turning them into what they think the people should be, by training them to act as they "ought to." None of it is done with any concern for their individual well-being. Its most likely effect will be what the history of communism was—utter brutality. The second fragment states it clearly: Hierarchy is a fundamental part of healthy human existence. It is the scaffold without which the world would plunge into chaos, and therefore, the liberal position, according to which all values are equal, is actually morally destructive. One might go further and say that living according to *ad hoc* whims, by which the progressive liberals want to organize private and public life, is a recipe for chaos. This is what the book is trying to prevent.

8   Emphasis mine.

One should also add that the book is rich in serious philosophical reflections, references to Christianity, Jesus (who is referred to as Christ!), poets, and philosophers. Even though it is a book written by a clinical psychologist, it has an incredibly broad humanistic scope. Clearly, it is a work by someone who deeply cares for his fellow man. His *12 Rules* is not a personal statement or confession of his religious beliefs, nor is it a book about religion, but Peterson does not hide his sympathy for Christianity. This in itself, one can suspect, may be a reason why he caused such an uproar. But, more importantly, it explains why he is so difficult to destroy. He was persecuted by his colleagues who wanted his removal from his university post at the University of Toronto. Yet Peterson refused to give in and bow to ideological dictates that would compromise his moral stance. During the unfortunate two years of attacks against him, he gained many followers and admirers, adding more fuel to the old controversy.

In the *Wall Street Journal* (January 25, 2018), Peggy Noonan wrote the following:

> Mr. Peterson is called "controversial" because he has been critical, as an academic, of various forms of the rising authoritarianism of the moment—from identity politics to cultural appropriation to white privilege and postmodern feminism. He has refused to address or refer to transgendered people by the pronouns "zhe" and "zher." He has opposed governmental edicts in his native Canada that aim, perhaps honestly, at inclusion, but in practice limit views, thoughts and speech […]. This is unusual in a professor but not yet illegal, so I bought his book to encourage him. *Deeper in, you understand the reasons he might be targeted for annihilation.*[9]

Noonan is right on two counts. First, screenings of the new documentary about Peterson in Toronto and New York were recently canceled, signifying that some desperately wish for the public to forget about Peterson.

> ShapeShifter Lab, an event space in Brooklyn, has canceled a screening of the newly-released Jordan Peterson biopic because

9   Emphasis mine.

of staff complaints. The New York cancellation mirrors a similar incident in Toronto, where a scheduled week-long theatrical run of *The Rise of Jordan Peterson* was canceled after some members of the staff vented their displeasure with the film.

Noonan's prediction about annihilating him was, no doubt, prophetic. However, the idea that one can *understand* why anyone should "be targeted for annihilation" simply for refusing to use personal pronouns in an incomprehensible and ungrammatical manner, is truly mind-boggling. But perhaps not so much if one keeps reminding oneself that Peterson's case is not an isolated incident.

In August of 2017, a young software engineer James Damore was fired from Google for circulating an internal memo in which he suggested that the disparity in employment between the sexes may be due to biological differences. Here is a fragment from an article he wrote for *The Wall Street Journal* (August 11, 2017):

> I was fired by Google this past Monday for a document that I wrote and circulated internally raising questions about cultural taboos and how they cloud our thinking about gender diversity at the company and in the wider tech sector. I suggested that at least some of the male-female disparity in tech could be attributed to biological differences (and, yes, I said that bias against women was a factor too). Google Chief Executive Sundar Pichai declared that portions of my statement violated the company's code of conduct and *"cross the line by advancing harmful gender stereotypes in our workplace."*
>
> My 10-page document set out what I considered a reasoned, well-researched, good-faith argument, but as I wrote, the viewpoint I was putting forward is generally suppressed at Google because of the company's "ideological echo chamber." My firing neatly confirms that point. How did Google, the company that hires the smartest people in the world, become so ideologically driven and intolerant of scientific debate and reasoned argument?
>
> [...] Echo chambers maintain themselves by creating a shared spirit and keeping discussion confined within certain

limits. As Noam Chomsky once observed, "The smart way to keep people passive and obedient is to strictly limit the spectrum of acceptable opinion, but allow very lively debate within that spectrum."

Mr. Damore became an instant celebrity, but his fame did not last for very long. His case, like Jordan Peterson's, is symptomatic of how liberal-democracies operate and punish people for their convictions. Neither Damore nor Peterson were sent to a gulag, but the former suffered the highest punishment that the dissidents can suffer in a democracy: losing a job, becoming a social pariah and being decried as an enemy—the enemy of equality! We may never have communist-style gulags, but then again we do not need them. Ideological training, reminding people that there is no right and wrong independent of the *social* context, and that Biblical teaching is wrong, and that the 'good' is what diminishes authority and expands equality, is all that is needed. And the American educational system is doing just that.

What we all seem to know, but are too afraid to say clearly and openly in public, is that we fear "being purged like insects," the way Mr. Damore was, and that we are being intimidated daily by the Leninist policies of minority groups instigated by a class of egalitarian ideologues. Those who insist that anyone should use "zhe" and "zher," (or "comrade," as was spoken under communism, or "citizen," as used during the French Revolution), or that we attend various "trainings" to learn the *new* norms (unless we want to be fired), are political terrorists. We should all admit that the new progressive terrorists have hijacked public life in America, Canada, and elsewhere in the Western world, and that America and Canada are not much different from the Leninist State.

Let us also note that policies that require mind-transformation and stifling free speech, thought, and actions, are not the work of the right, ultra-right, white-supremacists, or nationalist parties. These policies stem from the liberal ideological dictates. It is enough to compare eastern European countries, such as Poland and Hungary—described by liberal journalists as places where democracies are dying—and the United States, Canada, and the United Kingdom, and ask: In which of the above countries does one find greater freedom, and which parties or segments in their respective societies impose ideological rules on others? Or, to put it differently, which of the above countries are closer to being totalitarian?

Anne Applebaum's article is symptomatic of the perception of danger. Such a perception, if accepted by a large number of people, may miss the real threat to the existence of democratic institutions. She sees one side of the problem and ignores the other—namely, the rise of totalitarianism in America, which poses a greater danger to the health and preservation of a democracy than anything else. The expansion of equality which can only be done if the state forces the entire population to accept certain views while ruling contradictory beliefs illegal as was done in the UK (whose tribunal ruled biblical teaching wrong) will transform democracy into a totalitarian system. Even if we agree with her that some of the policies and laws (or, attempts to establish them) in post-communist countries are restrictive and misguided, they are, and always were, simply part of a normal political game: the struggle for influence and power, conflict between social and political claims, competing visions of a nation's future, all of which stem from normal human motivations.

What one cannot say about politics in those countries is that the parties propagate mind-enslaving ideology as the Democratic Party does in the United States, or like such publications and news outlets as *The New York Times, Washington Post, USA Today, CNN, MSNBC,* and *NPR*. Right-wing or conservative magazines exist in Poland and Hungary, just as they do elsewhere, but their influence is limited to a small group of readers who have a certain way of thinking and are hardly an outlet for ideological brainwashing. Neither Poland nor Hungary has a Canadian-style Bill C-16, the United Kingdom's 2006 "Racial and Religious Hatred Act" (or the 2016 M-103), sensitivity and sexual harassment training, mandatory ideologically driven courses for students, the De Blasio American bill—which threatens people with a fine of 250,000 dollars for the use of the term "illegal alien"—or a bill that prohibits students in New York schools from eating meat on Mondays. Polish and Hungarian languages are still in good shape in contrast to the American Newspeak which insists on certain phrases and prohibits others, such as requiring the use of "maintenance hole" instead of "manhole." What is more important, unlike the Delaware Regulation 225 which says that "all students enrolled in a Delaware public school may self-identify gender or race" without consulting their parents, Polish and

Hungarian parents have control over the mental well-being of their children. No political party in those two countries worries about parts of the population following Sharia law, and the biblical teaching that there are only two natural sexes is accepted by the overwhelming majority of the population. Absence of such regulations, laws, and views leaves the population of those two countries a considerable degree of freedom, something one cannot say about America and Canada, which embody Lenin's ideal of the state.

5.

Whence came such similarities between the former Soviet Union and North America? Liberalism and Marxism operate according to the same principle: Both view history as teleological, moving in a definite direction. Its aim and end are *known*: the ultimate realization of equality through man's liberation from the shackles of oppression which in liberal ideology is equated with authority and hierarchy. Opposing any progress toward equality is tantamount to opposing the inexorable march of progress. The individual is helpless to stop it, nothing can be done to redirect its course. The conviction that "nothing can be done" and that the notions of good and evil, right and wrong, belong to the discarded dictionary of past historical formations forced many people to resign themselves and accept communism. But it also allowed the totalitarians to keep the atrocities they were committing from occupying their minds. Their moral numbness and dismissal of the idea that they did anything wrong can be explained by their exclusive focus on bringing about more equality. Progressive interpretation of history provided them with absolution for destroying those who opposed progress toward equality, or who had little or no faith in it.

However, it was not the communists who invented the idea of equality. In his *Gods will Have Blood* (*Les Dieux ont soif*), the French writer Anatole France gives a fictionalized account of the French Revolution, which he had written long before the rise of fascism and communism.

> Did you know, Louise, that this Tribunal, which is about to put the Queen of France on trial, yesterday condemned to death a

young servant girl for shouting "Long live the Queen!" She was convicted of malicious intent to destroy the Republic.

And:

"You must be more careful, Citizen Brotteaux," he began, "far more careful! There is a time for laughing and a time for being serious. Jokes are sometimes taken seriously. A member of the Committee of Safety of the Section inspected my shop yesterday and when he saw your dancing dolls, he declared they were anti-revolutionary."

Anatole France's description of how the revolutionary spirit operates aptly renders the atmosphere in today's America, where the Barbie doll—her color and size—became a matter of serious controversy, and the Oreo cookies—black on the outside, white on the inside—found themselves in the midst of an ideological whirlpool.

Communism is gone, and ironically it was brought down by those who retained the belief that truth, right and wrong, good and evil, are neither man-made categories, nor the product of a historical process. They are objective and transcendent standards in which private and public life should be grounded. Only then can human existence, individually or collectively, be fully experienced.

Peterson's *12 Rules for Life* is not a silly 12-step program for dummies. It is an attempt to return an insane world, where subjective whims create our own personal and collective destinies, standards for right and wrong, and strange personal pronouns according to which one person can be many, to normalcy. It is a book about the human psyche, God, politics, culture, society, human decency, and compassion for the weak. In this respect Peterson, as a psychologist, can be put in the same category as one of his great predecessors, Carl G. Jung—a man of infinite compassion for human frailty and understanding of man's place in the universe. Like Peterson, Jung understood the danger of totalitarian systems. If there is an explanation for why Peterson is still around, it is because of his unwavering commitment to values, religion, hierarchy, and decency. That is probably why he is so difficult to destroy and why he infuriates his foes.

The experience of brutality and death, as in the Soviet Union, made communism a fertile ground for breeding opposition and dissidents. The absence of brutality and death in soft-totalitarianism makes it more difficult to perceive the evil of equality. However, the other reason why dissent grew under communism was a strong sense of moral right and wrong taught by religion. The communists, despite their efforts, did not succeed in entirely socializing right and wrong, and where they did, the opposition was weak, as in Bulgaria or Romania, because religiosity was weak. In Poland, on the other hand, where the Church was strong, ideological opposition was unprecedented.

Given the different faces of opposition in communist countries, one can say a few things with confidence. A rapid decline in religiosity among Americans may be one reason why the country is becoming totalitarian. Young Americans' sense of right and wrong seems weak, and if it is strong it is often limited to students who graduated from religious, predominantly Catholic, schools. One can also add that the weak perception of evil may stem from the fact that Americans have not experienced the atrocities that other nations have; they don't even know about them. Furthermore, the high standard of living also contributes to the changes in perception of what real evil is.

The infusion of ideology into education, which is partly responsible for moral weakness, is truly unprecedented. There is no point in drawing any parallels between communism and today's America because one could not find such parallels. The young American's sense of right and wrong comes from schools and training, college orientation meetings where students are being told about new sexual rules, the use of proper pronouns, and being addressed by their "chosen" names (Peter can choose to be called Molly, and Barbara can be called Roger). If one adds to this a number of courses, some of which are mandatory, stuffed with ideological content, the picture of the young American mind is terrifying. For example, "feminist philosophy" might be equivalent to a seminar on Kant, Descartes, Plato, Hume, etc. There are other courses, such as "environmental justice," "racial justice," "social justice" and the like. History and sociology classes are often simply about slavery, white privilege, or the discrimination of minorities. Not much time is left for real education. By comparison, the one and only class students under communism had to take—that is, "Foundations of Marxism and Leninism" offered only to students at a university level—makes socialism look like an educational paradise of orgiastic free-thought.

All of the above is destructive intellectually, but also morally. If, as Peterson claims, human beings need a sense of values to act, *socialized* norms of what is good and evil, right and wrong, can become a substitute for a real moral compass. But there is a danger in this. Today's social morality can become tomorrow's instrument for the destruction of others. A temporary moral *ersatz* is unlikely to build a community of moral beings responsible for each other due to a lack of a sense of commitment to the transcendental reality in which human life is inscribed. All such an *ersatz* can provide is a sense of temporary belonging to a collective, which over time produces its own leaders who will always ultimately demand mind subjugation. All of that sounds like what we know from fascist Italy, Nazi Germany, the communist Soviet Union, Mao's China, and the Kims' North Korea. We may not have a single leader, but a strong, frustrated desire to implement ideology can cause social unrest and generate the need that *someone* do something. This was Tocqueville's prediction.

One may not expect great moral courage from ordinary people whose preoccupation is daily bread. But one would absolutely expect such commitment from intellectuals, academics, or generally 'men of letters.' They, however, have turned out to be most cowardly, and it is they who planted among ordinary people the seeds of moral destruction. They committed what Julian Benda calls the betrayal of truth in his classic work. Persecution of Jordan Peterson by his university colleagues makes Benda's *The Great Betrayal* as relevant today as it was when it was published a hundred years ago. Peterson's survival says something further. It is a testimony that dissent in a democracy is possible, but given the isolated nature of it one is bound to wonder: Is Jordan Peterson the only man in North America who knows and has courage to say, "this is right and this is wrong"?

CHAPTER 4 | AMERICAN NEWSPEAK

> Literature must become Party Literature [...] Down with non-partisan literatures! Down with superman literature! Literature must become a part of the general cause of the proletariat, "a small cog and a small screw" in the social democratic mechanism, one and indivisible—a mechanism set in motion by the entire vanguard of the whole working class. Literature must become an integral part of the organized, methodical, and unified labors of the Social Democratic Party."

Lenin, *Novaia Zhizn*, November 1905

1.

An insightful observer of today's political and social reality cannot but notice the similarities between socialism and liberal democracies. The two systems are like twin brothers that were raised separately, who did not like each other when they met, but who in their mature years act as if they came from the same genetic stock. A recent book by Ryszard Legutko, *Demon in Democracy: Totalitarian Temptations in Free Societies*, explains many of those similarities. There is one topic, however, which Legutko left out—namely, *language*, without which totalitarianism is impossible.

George Orwell's greatest insight was to realize the indispensable role that language plays in creating a totalitarian reality. In fact, it is impossible without an appropriate language. Language, like everything else in totalitarianism, must be subject to rules and regulations. It is not merely an instrument of daily communication but is a reality of its own. We are born into a language just like we are born into a world. Words, syntax and grammar are the scaffold, and style is its façade. It is a home in which we live, but it can become the most oppressive prison. Listening to today's American English, one quickly realizes that liberal democracies create a specific pattern of speech which is totalitarian. Comparing it to socialist Newspeak, all the differences notwithstanding, one quickly notices that today's American Newspeak is fundamentally totalitarian. By accepting it, using it, we not only get caught in the totalitarian unreality, but we become its accessory cofounders.

2.

One reason for the need to create a new language is that totalitarianism requires that the entire population share a uniform vision of reality, which can be accomplished only through uniformity of thought. Totalitarian language cannot reflect the world. The opposite must happen: The world, which is not given, which is not an objective fact, must reflect the thought that we express through language. However, this requirement is only a necessary, and not sufficient, condition. My vision of the world, different from that of others, makes my vision no more or less valid than anybody else's vision. Therefore, to give my vision legitimacy and make it real, the second condition must be met: My language must be shared with others who understand and see reality in the same way. This can be accomplished only if we *speak the same language*.

Thus, for example, an invasion of another country might mean liberation of that country. This is what happened, for example, in Eastern European countries after World War II. Imposition of the communist rule was not an act of depriving those countries of political sovereignty, or national independence, but an act of liberation from the oppressive capitalist and bourgeois system that existed there before the war. President Reagan's decision to land in Grenada to prevent it from communist takeover was heralded in the communist mass-media as an act of "American invasion and imperialism," whereas a similar intervention by the Soviet Union and the political take-over would be heralded as a "great victory of progressive forces" or something similar. Liquidation of multiple political parties by absorbing them into one party (socialist or communist), was called "democratic centralization." Since democracy is associated with multiplicity of views, opinions, etc., by preserving the word *democracy* in the term "democratic centralization," one could make an entire population believe that democracy became even stronger by being centralized. In fact, it meant that democracy had been destroyed. East Germany, under the leadership of

Honecker, was more oppressive than any of the Soviet satellite countries; yet it did not compel its leadership to consider changing the name from German Democratic Republic to something else, despite the fact that it was neither federal nor democratic.

Communists had a real allergy to the word "crisis"—both in politics and economics. Crisis, we were taught, was caused by overproduction. Since shortages of apartments, furniture, cars, food, clothes, or toilet paper were commonplace, it could not be a result of crisis, i.e., overproduction. Crisis was exclusively a property of capitalist economies. Crisis in a socialist economy was the proverbial *contradictio in terminis*. However, since the inefficiency of productive powers in a socialist economy could not be admitted (because socialism was a "superior" system), communists came up with a different explanation for the cause of the shortages. They blamed either speculators or saboteurs, the "undesirable elements," as they were called.

Orwell captured this idea in his *Animal Farm*: "'Comrades,' [Napoleon] said quietly, 'do you know who is responsible for this? Do you know the enemy who has come in the night and overthrown our windmill? SNOWBALL!' Whenever anything went wrong it became usual to attribute it to Snowball." The communists had their Snowballs, too, but there were other reasons as well—for example, wrong attitudes of the higher echelon of factories' governing bodies, CEOs, and social parasites. The latter, instead of working, would litter the streets, while the honest workers toiled—sometimes more than one shift—like Orwell's Boxer. They were building socialism, and for their superhuman effort they were awarded "socialist worker's medals." They were called shock-workers. (Andrzej Wajda's influential movies *The Man of Marble* and *The Man of Iron* show very well the parody of the socialist reality, and everyone who tries to understand it should watch them.) Even shortages of vodka, a product the communists tried to supply ceaselessly so that people could drown sadness and desperation,[1] could be explained by pointing to parasites who were drinking too much, not leaving enough for the (socialist) workers.

Occasionally, during the moments of real crises (every decade or so), it was even members of the Polit-Bureau and their misguided politics who

---

1 Anyone interested in understanding socialist reality should read Alexander Zinoviev's *We and the West* and *Homo Sovieticus*.

were to blame. To keep socialism going, they invented the slogan: "socialism, Yes, distortions, No." Distortions, often a result of "ideological deviations," resulted from sabotage of the real spirit of socialism by the corrupt Party leaders, who forgot in whose name they were governing the country (like Emanuel Goldstein in *1984*). During each time of crisis, the communists would exploit the situation by calling on the workers to "tighten up the ranks," to fight speculators, saboteurs, corrupt CEOs, laziness, inefficiency, to look out for thieves, who, by stealing whatever one could steal from a factory, were stealing what belonged to everybody, and since there was not enough for everybody to steal, the popular mood would turn against people who, for example, stole a piece of wire to fix a fence at home because they could not buy it. The list of absurdities, accompanied by invention of language, was endless. But the Party was never to blame (the Party's problems, corruption, deviations etc., were the Party's internal affair).

Responses to such social mobilization calls did not bring about the desired effects, and the workers, again dissatisfied with their economic situation, would go on strike. Here, the communists displayed linguistic ingenuity. Since "the means of production" were state owned, one could strike against the private owner, but in a socialist country, a strike would mean a rebellion against socialism or the Party. So instead of using the word "strike" in the media, they would say that the workers are on "a break from work."

Every few years or so, the workers would take "breaks," while in reality they were on strikes, rebelling against socialism. However, they were only half-aware of it. The idea of socialism (without "distortions") was still appealing. In so far as they adopted the Party's newspeak, they were unable to make an ultimate break from socialist reality. Even the glorious Solidarity period in Poland was not anti-socialist. The language of the demands for reforms was semi-socialist, or it was a compromise. This was partly a question of political realism (not to go openly against the socialist state and be crushed by a Soviet invasion, the way Hungary and Czechoslovakia were in 1956 and 1968) and partly a result of vague language which made a clear-cut break impossible. One demanded the changes that could neither heal the country politically nor economically.

After the imposition of martial law in 1983, the underground opposition did a world of good by clearing up the language from the socialist newspeak sediment. The translation of the writings of F. von Hayek, M.

Friedman, L. von Mieses, R. Scruton, A. Besançon, and several others contributed greatly to the purification of the language of economics and political science. We regained clarity of vision. The final moment was inevitable and arrived in 1989 when communism was forced to end its life. When it collapsed, socialist newspeak likewise disappeared.

In the meantime, the Party would coin new vocabulary and slogans to patch up holes in socialist reality, of which "The Workers with the Party and the Party with the Nation" was probably the best sounding and most socially effective, but also the most pernicious. It combined the idea of the Party and socialism with the idea of the nation, and the nation with the working people. The Party was the link between the workers and the nation, and whoever was against the Party was, implicitly, against the workers and the nation. And since the workers were the nation, whoever was against either the Party or the workers was against the nation, which meant: If you stand up to the Party, the Party has a right to crush you, and it will do it in the name of the nation, which stands behind it.

The Party was also the official guardian of national history, which meant that it could change or adjust history to the current political needs. Of course, it was always in the interest of the workers. The last part was a milder version of Orwell's "Who controls the Present controls the Past, and who controls the Past controls the Future." Orwell's second observation is also true. "Oceania was always at war with Eurasia," or "Oceania was never at war with Eurasia"—just like Russia was never at war with Poland, in spite of the 1920 war, and earlier in 1795 when it partitioned Poland for the third time, erasing it from the map of Europe for 123 years.

Orwell was, no doubt, a very acute observer and aware of the fact that changes in language constitute the core of social consciousness, and that if it is weak, a return to normalcy is impossible. One of the saddest moments in *1984* is Winston's realization that the proles, who are most free from the Party's supervision and who would, one would suspect, be most likely to rebel, never will.

> It was not desirable that the proles should have strong political feelings. All that was required of them was a primitive patriotism which could be appealed to whenever it was necessary to make them accept longer working hours or shorter rations. And

even when they became discontented, as they sometimes did, their discontent led nowhere, because being without general ideas, they could only focus it on petty specific grievances. The larger evils invariably escaped their notice.

There were plenty of other words and terms that the communists would use to manipulate the public. The following are probably the most glaring. Under a one party system, "justice" could, and did, mean injustice—brutality, unequal application of regulations to different people, and a hopeless lack of recourse to the Rule of Law. The Ministry of Justice had as much to do with the administration of justice as the Ministry of Truth had to do with truth in Orwell. The Ministry of Economy was in reality probably closest to the Orwellian Ministry of Plenty. It dealt with fictitious economic statistics, very much like in Orwell ("it was one piece of nonsense substituted for another piece of nonsense," as Winston realized), whereas reality in the stores and on the streets would tell you that shortages and poverty were rampant. One could say a similar thing about the Department of Education. However, one needs to add that the case varied in different countries, different times, and to greater or lesser degrees. In its ideal form, which did not exist under communism in the Soviet Union nor in Eastern European countries (but exists in North Korea today, and existed, and to a lesser degree still exists, in China), it would have been more proper to call it the Ministry of Indoctrination.

One should add parenthetically here that with the exception of the most ideologically driven times, the prevalence of ideology in education has never reached the current level of brainwashing in America. This topic is so vast that it would require a separate chapter.

A striking thing about the language that communist totalitarianism created is that it disappeared almost overnight. The former denizens of socialist paradise displayed incredible ease in abandoning former Newspeak, almost as if it were never their "first" language. If they used it, it was only in an official capacity, so to speak, but their minds were never truly affected by it. If so, was Orwell wrong? Not necessarily. His *1984* totalitarianism is an extreme form of communist totalitarianism, imposed from above. The Orwellian Newspeak could operate only so long as the fear of the state persevered. When the political power disappeared, so did the language.

Language was a convention to keep reality going, and only those who played serious roles on the stage of socialist reality bought it, selling their souls and mind. It was mostly intellectuals, writers. The process of the transformation of one's mind was described by Czesław Miłosz in *The Captive Mind*—by far the best book on how ideology can impress itself and make a mind captive. However, this process of enslavement worked mostly on intellectuals, while ordinary people seemed relatively unaffected by it. Orwell's fantastic vision of language manipulation seems to apply much better to today's America and American Newspeak, which is omnipresent, operating like the first and only language of the masses.

3.

The dawn of political correctness, which we can trace back, more or less, to the mid-eighties, corresponds to changes in American English. It started in a rather innocent way—with the introduction of "he or she" in lieu of the traditional and generic "he". In contrast to communism, the change was not dictated by the Polit-Bureau of the American Socialist Party, or any power from above, and that is why it is difficult to understand how ideology can spread in a democracy. There were no educational commissars or language police from the Department of Education who would make journalists, politicians and educators speak in the new way. The changes were gradual, piecemeal, and rather quiet. Over time, however, different scholarly associations, such as AMLA, American Philosophical Association, American Historical Association, and others, would send brochures with new "writing guidelines." By the mid-nineties, "he or she" made inroads into the way Americans spoke. Almost everybody tacitly accepted it as a new norm in communication. A moment of hesitation to say "he or she" was immediately greeted with faces of minor disapproval. It was almost like a digestive reaction to bad food that one could see on people's faces. Using the generic "he" on television in the company of women was thought of as excluding the women with whom one spoke on the panel. By the beginning of the new millennium, all, except the most obstinate would use "he or she."

"You know, it is not such a big deal," my friends would say when I expressed surprise at their choice. For me, a former denizen of a socialist paradise and someone who learned English by absorbing grammatical rules from serious books, it was a very big deal. Like Hamlet's "To be or not to be," the situation was existential. As I learned under socialism, one little compromise leads to another little compromise, and several little compromises lead to the loss of integrity. To say "he or she" was a pact with the devil himself (or herself).

But it was not just that I was stubborn, or merely unwilling to adapt to the new linguistic reality. There are serious problems with the new use. First, it is ungrammatical. Here is an example, "If a reader doesn't understand something, it is *his* fault because he did not pay attention." This is how we would speak in the past. The sentence is also grammatically correct. The word "reader" in the sentence is singular, and the possessive pronoun for singular must be singular, too. One could also say: "If a reader doesn't understand something, it is *his* or *her* fault because *he* or *she* did not pay attention." The problem here is that the sentence with two *he*'s and two *she*'s sounds robotic and doubling pronouns is superfluous. Today, the "correct" way to say this is: "If a reader doesn't understand something, it is *their* fault because *they* did not pay attention." It is obvious grammatical and logical nonsense (and grammar usually follows logic), but the nonsense is not seen, heard, let alone corrected by teachers of English. In fact, it is what American students are taught in schools. They are taught ungrammatical English for ideological reasons, which I will explain later.

In most languages which have nouns divided by gender (masculine, feminine and neuter) the problem would not arise because the nouns would dictate the gender of the possessive pronouns. But English is a language without gender, except in some cases. Gender of some nouns in English was inherited from Latin—for example, a ship is referred to as a "she," as are cars and pieces of machinery, since *machina* in Latin is feminine. Church, in Latin *ecclesia*, in British English is feminine, and the British refer to the church as "she." A linguistic fact was turned into an ideological problem. Using "he" rather than "he or she," became an incendiary issue. Feminists, followed by the rest, claimed that the use of "he" means exclusion of women. This is not true and one can easily demonstrate it.

The word "reader" means a female reader or a male reader, just like the word "friend" can mean a boy or a girl (like in Latin: *amicus* and *amica*), and if we use "he" instead of "she," we simply adopt the traditional, centuries-old way of speaking to avoid the repetitive use of "he or she." However, today's language police refuse to accept such an argument, not because it is grammatically incorrect, but on account of their interpretation of the past. It is their understanding of the past that demands changes to language. It claims that the traditional use of the pronoun "he" is an expression of "patriarchy," "male domination," "oppression," and by using a "he" one perpetuates patriarchy, domination, and oppression. Thus, to end patriarchy, one has to eliminate the use of "he" by changing people's habits. So, the teachers, publishers, journalists, editors—including publishers of prestigious magazines—remove traces of patriarchy by changing pronouns.

This interpretation of the past, however, creates logical and historical problems. First, what shall we say of all past women—the Brontë sisters, Jane Austen and others, for example—who were great stylists and used "he" instead of "she" or "he or she"? Did they, too, support the oppressive patriarchal system? For example, a famous 18th century poet, classicist and translator of Epictetus' *Moral Discourses* (1758), Elizabeth Carter, writes the following in the introduction to her translation (which, due to the high quality of the translation, is still admired today): "But then, where was the use of their favorite doctrine, that a wise *man* must always be happy? Might not a person, determined to follow *his* own inclinations, very reasonably object 'What is that to me if I am not, or to anybody else if no one ever was, a *wise man?*'"

Carter uses both *man* and *his* in a generic sense. "Man" means man and woman, and "his," as the context makes abundantly clear, means "his" or "her," depending on whether a man or a woman is the reader. Wisdom—as in "wise man"—accordingly, is attributed here to men and women. Today, the standard answer to why Carter uses a "he" would be that women were oppressed, brainwashed, or both, by men, and used pronouns without knowing that they exclude half of the human race. It is laughable to think that Carter, a distinguished poet, philologist, translator, and member of the Bluestocking Circle had no control over the proper use of language. Of course, the idea of distinguished women in the past who ran literary salons whilst brainwashed, or unaware of what the proper use of language should be, runs counter to what we know they accomplished in the intellectual realm. Moliere's *Les femmes savants* (*The Learned Women*) is one of the greatest testimonies to the intellectual significance of women as early as the 17th century.

To translate Carter's sentence into contemporary jargon, the sentence should say: "But then, where was the use of their favorite doctrine, that a wise *person* must always be happy? Might not a person, determined to follow *their* own inclinations, very reasonably object 'What is that to me if I am not, or to anybody else if no one ever was, a *wise person?*'"

As the sentence is now free of the traces of patriarchy, what makes it unattractive to the ear is the jarring sound of the word "person" three times and the lack of agreement between the singular noun and the plural possessive. Employing the word "person" three times makes the sentence sound flat, robotic, almost like the sound of a hammer. It is also unimaginative. One can almost be certain that Mrs. Carter was aware of it because her one time use of the word "person" (in "Might not a *person*, determined to follow *his* own inclinations [...]") breaks the monotony that the repetition of the word "man" would introduce. To avoid this repetition, Mrs. Carter inserted "person" in a place where "man" would be even more appropriate. She did it to avoid repetition.

A few sentences from an introduction written in prose may not show how barbarous this process of language manipulation can be. The best way of showing how to destroy language is to apply it to poetry. In a memorable conversation about the 11th edition of Newspeak Dictionary, Syme explains to Winston with an open fascination the progress that the changes will affect:

> By 2050—earlier, probably—all real knowledge of Oldspeak will have disappeared. The whole literature of the past will have been destroyed. Chaucer, Shakespeare, Milton, Byron—they'll exist only in Newspeak version, not merely changed into something different, but actually changed into something contradictory of what they used to be.

Take a poem, "Playwright," by Shakespeare's contemporary, Ben Johnson (1573–1637), who once wrote:

> Playwright, convict of public wrongs to men,
> Takes private beatings and begins again.
> The kinds of valour he doth show at once:
> Active in 's brain and passive in his bones.

And now, let us apply today's Newspeak principles to it:

Playwright, convict of public wrongs to men *and women,*
Takes private beatings and begins again.
The kinds of valour he *or she* do show at once:
Active in 's *or 'r* brain and passive in his *or her* bones.

Let us use another word—individual—with which today's politically correct English speakers try to bypass the generic "man."

Playwright, convict of public wrongs to individuals,
Takes private beatings and begins again.
The kinds of valour *they* doth show at once:
Active in *their* brain and passive in *their* bones.

It is only 2021, not 2050, but as the above examples show, rewriting old poetry in Newspeak is damaging enough. Thirty years from now, this poem will mean the opposite of what it originally said. Style and sound matter, but only to people who know language. The unimaginative, ideologically driven use of words which make reality flat and ugly, and without the vibrancy which poetic meter requires, make it sound like the bad American prose language one hears in every classroom and on television: "You know [...] it's like—you know what I mean. What I meant was, it's like [...]."

We should be wary, remembering that following proper rules, and breaking them when one knows when and how, creates conditions for freedom; shrinking it can have only the opposite effect: slavery can mean freedom. This is what the 11th edition of Orwell's *Newspeak Dictionary* teaches.

4.

One might still try to argue that language is one thing and content another, and that content is what matters. This is not so. Evelyn Waugh and Vladimir Nabokov would vehemently disagree: Language is everything. A survey of 20th century poetry does not point to any distinguished poet whose language was shaped by ideology, and whose poems were great at the same time. Vladimir Mayakowsky, Wladyslaw Broniewski, Pablo

Neruda, and several others were great poets; each lent a helpful hand to communist ideas in their poems. However, if they succeeded in remaining great poets rather than conveyors of ideological messages, it was due to their exceptional mastery of the language. But when both language and content are subjugated to ideological dictates, then we can be pretty sure that we are recreating a kind of American Socialist Realism. This is not a matter of some remote future; it has already happened. Last year, on July 24, the editor of one-time prestigious and oldest American magazine, *The Nation,* wrote the following:

> *The Nation* and its poetry editors, Stephanie Burt and Carmen Giménez Smith, made this statement about the poem below, which contains disparaging and ableist language that has given offense and caused harm to members of several communities:
>
> As poetry editors, we hold ourselves responsible for the ways in which the work we select is received. We made a serious mistake by choosing to publish the poem "How-To." We are sorry for the pain we have caused to the many communities affected by this poem. We recognize that we must now earn your trust back. Some of our readers have asked what we were thinking. When we read the poem, we took it as a profane, over-the-top attack on the ways in which members of many groups are asked, or required, to perform the work of marginalization. We can no longer read the poem in that way.
>
> We are currently revising our process for solicited and unsolicited submissions. But more importantly, we are listening, and we are working. We are grateful for the insightful critiques we have heard, but we know that the onus of change is on us, and we take that responsibility seriously. In the end, this decision means that we need to step back and look at not only our editing process, but at ourselves as editors.

Here, once again, a parallel with communism comes to mind. Those who are familiar with Soviet and Chinese history (particularly the period of the Cultural Revolution) should recall the crawling and growling of pet-poets and pet-writers, betraying their friends, renouncing what they wrote, and condemning the past. Instructive in this context is the case of Yevgeny Zamyatin, the author of the first totalitarian novel *WE*, the prototype of Huxley's *Brave New World* and Orwell's *1984*. In 1929, the Russian Association of Proletarian Writers (RAPP) took control of literary output in the Soviet Union. Those who wanted to publish had to conform by bending to the politically correct orthodoxy. As Mirra Ginsburg, the translator of Zamyatin's *WE* wrote: "There was a wave of suicides among writers and poets. Recantations became epidemic. Endless non-party writers, theirs spirits broken, publicly repented of their sins and came into the fold, repudiating and rewriting their own works." In the same year, Zamyatin's friends and colleagues denounced him. (The only writer who stood by him was Bulgakov, author of *Master and Margarita*.) Zamyatin resigned from the Writers' Union. "I find it impossible to belong to a literary organization," he wrote, "which… takes part in the persecution of a fellow member." Thanks to Maxim Gorky, a convert to communism and a Stalinist, who intervened on his behalf with the Great Leader, Zamyatin was allowed to leave Russia. The history of communism is littered with stories like this. In fact, it is the history of communism itself.

How different is the behavior of the *Nation's* editors from that of RAPP? It is not. In fact, much of American history of the last 30 years is a mirror image of what happened under communism. Their apology is an outright denunciation of the poet Anders Carlson-Wee. He, too, however, offered an apology: "To all who have voiced questions and concerns about my poem in *The Nation*: I am listening closely and I am reflecting deeply. I am sorry for the pain I have caused, and I take responsibility for that." Bravo!—one wants to exclaim. This is the real spirit of Stalinism without Stalin, the Cultural Revolution without Chairman Mao. American poets and writers do not have a leader. They *listen* to the voice of *the people*, and when the people get angry or voice their dissatisfaction, they offer sincere apologies. We do not even have to wonder what the new poetry will look like. It was written by D-503—the protagonist in Zamyatin's *WE*.

Eternally enamored two times two,
Eternally united in the passionate four.
Most ardent lovers in the world—
Inseparable two times two [...]

The fear of public disapproval in America is not limited to the last thirty years when political correctness took sway over the American mind. It was prominent from the inception of the country. "If America has not as yet had any great writers," Tocqueville wrote, "the reason is given in these facts; there can be no literary genius without freedom of opinion, and freedom of opinion does not exist in America." The problems of literature in America are not new, and they are linked to the very idea of democracy, which does not allow for freedom of thought, and an unuttered thought is bound to die if it is not shared with others. Paradoxically, in many respects, despotism seems to be more conducive to prose and poetry, to the arts in general, than democracy. The history of Russian literature is the best example. Russia, whose statehood goes back to the 10th century, had no great literature before Pushkin (b. 1799), but within half a century or so it became a literary giant which made the czars fear and admire the poets;[2] whereas America, with its alleged freedom and the First Amendment, produced individual writers, but no American Literature *per se*. The rise of great writers in the 20s and 30s creating a literary milieu and scene by Edmund Wilson, can be considered a great period in American literary history, yet the problem persisted. In 1930, a hundred years after Tocqueville published his work, Sinclair Lewis was awarded a Nobel Prize in Literature. In his lecture before the Swedish Academy, he said:

> Fortune has dealt with me rather too well. I have known little struggle, not much poverty, many generosities. Now and then I have, for my books or myself, been somewhat warmly denounced—there was one good pastor in California who upon reading my *Elmer Gantry* desired to lead a mob and lynch me, while another holy man in the state of Maine wondered if there was no respectable and righteous way of putting me in jail. And, much harder to endure than any raging condemnation, a certain number of old acquaintances among journalists, what in the

2   A very interesting account of the relationship between political power in Russia and writers is Mikhail Shishkin's piece from *The New Republic* (July 1, 2013), "Poets and Czars. From Pushkin to Putin: The Sad Tale of Democracy in Russia."

galloping American slang we call the "I Knew Him When Club," have scribbled that since they know me personally, therefore I must be a rather low sort of fellow and certainly no writer. But if I have now and then received such cheering brickbats, still I, who have heaved a good many bricks myself, would be fatuous not to expect a fair number in return.

[…] There is in America a learned and most amiable old gentleman who has been a pastor, a university professor, and a diplomat. He is a member of the American Academy of Arts and Letters and no few universities have honored him with degrees. As a writer he is chiefly known for his pleasant little essays on the joy of fishing. I do not suppose that professional fishermen, whose lives depend on the run of cod or herring, find it altogether an amusing occupation, but from these essays I learned, as a boy, that there is something very important and spiritual about catching fish, if you have no need of doing so. This scholar stated, and publicly, that in awarding the Nobel Prize to a person who has scoffed at American institutions as much as I have, the Nobel Committee and the Swedish Academy had insulted America.

The case of *The Nation* and Mr. Carlson-Wee follow the same trajectory that Lewis happened to have traveled—"the people" felt offended. However, the problem of the last thirty years adds an entirely new dimension to the problem of the majority versus minority opinion. The influence of religion in America, and its dictates on what to publish, is no longer a problem. The problem is new: In America, ideology has replaced religion. In an ideological framework, language is no longer subject to evolutionary changes, nor is the subject of literature a matter of indifference.

5.

The next stage of the development in Newspeak took place in the second decade of the 21st century. To avoid the use of a "gender loaded" language, in which people are identified as "she" or "he"—that is as women and men— the new reformers insist—in a similar quest for inclusion—that they be called "they," instead of "he" or "she." The use of "they" to refer to a single person (!) because "he" or "she" is oppressive, discriminatory, and non-inclusive—non-inclusive of persons who do not identify as men or women. They are the non-binary, sexually non-conformist individuals who are neither men nor women. They are neither and/or both at the same time, and we need to change grammatical rules to include the non-binary non-conformists by referring to them as "they" when we talk to "them"—that is, to a single person. In short, if one does not feel one is a woman or a man, others should refer to him or her as "they." If you think it is illogical to refer to a single person as "they," you missed the point: "They" is more "inclusive!" If you refer to a single person as a man *and* a woman, you are more inclusive than if you were to refer to him or her as a man or a woman only.

If you want to follow the logic of this reasoning to its ultimate conclusion, you would have to conclude that there are no men and women. And you are right. This is what is implied. The late-eighties and early-nineties were the times of the great new social theories, of which the predominant conclusion was that men and women are "social constructs." This is outright nonsense, and everybody who has a cat or dog, as I do, knows the sex of his cat or dog, and if they could talk, they would likely be offended at the thought that someone "constructed" them. They are naturally born male or female, as are we, and the language reflects this reality. (My dog is a girl not because she was "conditioned" to play with dolls, and dressed in pink, as human girls often do; nor did my tomcat play with cars or hammers which conditioned him to be aggressive—as human males often are.) But here is an important point: American newspeak does not reflect reality, it reflects the content of one's mind, and if the mind becomes sick, the language becomes sick, too. "They" is, and always will be, plural, just like third person singular is singular. Gender is a grammatical, not a social, category, and if you claim a plural third person pronoun because you feel you are both a woman and a man, what you are saying is an expression of a troubled psyche.

6.

One could argue that an ideological mind is by definition a troubled mind. It is troubled because it refuses to accept reality as it is, and instead of seeking gradual improvements, it invents global methods of changing the world. Such solutions to political and social life are not different from what we know about the communist tactics. However, the tactics to bypass reality by inventing a new language can never work. Ideological explanations, as Leszek Kołakowski wrote,

> purport to offer solutions not only to particular social issues or particular grievances, but to all the important questions of human life [...] they purport to be all-embracing *Weltanschauungen* [...]. It seems at first glance that ideologies enjoy the same privilege of immunity to facts and the same proficiency in absorbing them, since the frame of meaning they give to human destiny is unfalsifiable as the meaningful order of the world in the believer's perception. If I decide that the whole of history consists of acts of class struggle, then there is no way in which this principle could be conceivably refuted [...]. If for any reason the life of the country is deteriorating in some aspects, the doctrine is born out: the exploiters are oppressing the toiling masses in order to seek profit [...].[3]

This is the classical "doctrine of the enemy," and such language expresses frustration over the world which does not lend itself to molding, as if it were a piece of clay that can be shaped according to the ideas in our minds. The "enemy doctrine," which worked so well in explaining why things went wrong under socialism, but did nothing to quell the workers' misery, operates exactly the same way in liberal-democracies, and not surprisingly relies on the very same linguistic trick.

Let's take the word *inclusion*. We are being constantly reminded there are not enough women, blacks, or Hispanics, for example, in the tech industry. The explanation for this is "exclusion"—that is, discrimination. And because it would be politically incorrect and highly offensive to suggest any other explanation, we run in a circle. The explanations might be numerous, but they are never seriously entertained because it would cast doubt on the idea of equality. First, women *statistically* score lower than men in math

---

3   "Why an Ideology Is Always Right," in Leszek Kołakowski, *Modernity on Endless Trial* (Chicago: The University of Chicago Press, 1990), pp. 232–33.

and are less interested in engineering than men. Therefore, there cannot be as many women to make the employment equal. What about blacks, or black men in particular? The same commonsensical rule could apply. Because the graduation rate among the black student population is lower, because they go to schools where the level of education is lower than in other schools attended by whites, and, thirdly, because a great many black children come from homes where there is no father (to discipline the boy and supervise his homework), the number of qualified black men who could apply for such jobs is *statistically* lower. Finally, the Hispanic population. It has always been the case that immigrant groups are poorer and their primary concern is survival in their new country. Interest in education, which is a long process, comes later. Because the masses of immigrants themselves are often uneducated, they care much more deeply about vocational skills for their children, which would help them quickly contribute to their family's expenses and become independent. It is only in the second or third generation, when immigrants catch up with a higher educational level, that the opportunity for high-paying jobs manifests, let alone jobs in the humanities and classical music. *Ergo*, the relative absence of Hispanics in certain professions, proportional to their population in the U.S. must be *statistically* lower. The same explanation, the reasons for which I gave above, applies to women and blacks.

Because ideological thinking is impervious to empirical facts and deaf to any non-ideological explanation, the reasons why the inclusion of minority groups has nothing to do with the actual groups, or their characteristics and social predicaments, is never considered: It must be discrimination and exclusion! What else could it be? It is the white males who prevent minorities from advancing. What happens in this situation in today's America is what happened under socialism—short of killing people. One fires the critics (for example, James Damore from Google) and forces employers to hire minorities so that a company has a "dressing window" from which it can show minority employees. They are as important to have as the product a company produces.

Interestingly, what I said is not new, and there are women and black men who think and say it, too. Among them are Supreme Court Justice Clarence Thomas and a Hoover Institution resident scholar Thomas Sowell. Both gentlemen are black, so it would be difficult to accuse them of racism. However, they are never promoted in the liberal media. Again, the American media is not different from its past counterpart in the countries of real socialism. Instead of blaming socialism for misguided policies, deaths, brutality and misery, the Party blamed the saboteurs and wrong attitudes. No one saw them, but the belief in their existence was enough. What other explanation could there be? Ideology, as Kołakowski wrote, is always right.

7.

Anyone who has read Ludwig Wittgenstein, a very important philosopher who shaped rigorous philosophical thinking at British and American universities in the 20th century, will know about the relationship between objects "out there" and the language that reflects them. Today, there is no world "out there" to which I attach words by means of which I understand reality outside of me. There is only nonsense in my head, according to which I adjust reality, all while forcing my sick perception of it on others.

Of course, one could reply, few people take it seriously because this nonsense is so striking that no one who has skipped college would ever believe it. But if that is the case, the question arises, "why bother thinking or writing about it?" My response would be that ideas have consequences, and bad ideas have bad consequences. Forcing others to live by bad ideas is to introduce chaos and disorder into people's lives, and thus to destroy society. If this is done by institutional means backed up by legislation increasing the power of the state to make people abide by nonsensical rules and regulations, then we are contributing to the creation a totalitarian state. We should be acutely aware of what is happening around us and resist it.

Here is an excerpt from a newspaper in July 2019:

> Legislators in Berkeley, California, voted Tuesday to ban some gender-specific words in its city code and replace them with gender-neutral options.
>
> Berkeley's municipal code will no longer feature words like "manhole" and "manpower," and instead say, "maintenance hole" and "human effort" or "workforce." The measure passed unanimously Tuesday and replaces more than two dozen terms. Gender-specific references to job titles, like "policeman" and

"craftsmen," will also be changed in the code, to "police officer" and "craftspeople" or "artisans." "Sorority" and "fraternity" would change to "collegiate Greek system residence." And the use of gendered pronouns, like "he" and "she," would be replaced with specific titles, like "the attorney" or "the candidate."

8.

The communist newspeak was, by and large, of an economic and political nature. Its aim was to falsify political reality so that people would believe that democracy was not done away with—that in fact it was a *higher form* of democracy. That free elections took place, even though the socialist party would always win; that economy existed despite the fact that bureaucrats set the prices, which reflected nothing, and any changes in them made no difference for the fundamental economic principle of supply and demand. The socialist language was a façade whose real goal was to introduce a sense of normalcy into the abnormality of political and economic existence, whereas the real game was about political power, either within the countries of real socialism or Soviet expansion.

As long as the linguistic rules were either accepted or believed by the overwhelming majority of the population, the Party had no reason to worry. The population was occupied, tired and unlikely to abolish the system. Creating a new language was important for another reason: It made one think that socialism is possible.

Yet, the collapse of communism showed that the newspeak did not do much damage. Possibly because communism was like religion in that it required an act of faith and the appropriate vocabulary, but when it turned out that there was no god behind the façade, one disposed of the communist newspeak. Once again, the language started reflecting reality—namely, reality of the free market economy, private property, politics, and the struggle for power. Invasion of Ukraine by Russia means invasion, not liberation of the Ukrainians from anything, and the occupation of Crimea is not a "brotherly union with Big Brother." In such a world, one can negotiate changes in reality. In a world where words have lost meaning, empirical reality does not exist.

What is striking about the American Newspeak is that following its proper linguistic rules is a very serious matter. One cannot joke about them by breaking them. Making a joke about women, gays, racial minorities, etc., can get you fired the same day. Using an incorrect form, like "he," instead of "he or she," is of paramount importance. It is a demonstration of one's dissension from inclusion and equality—equality of all sexes, orientations, and preferences. Omitting a "she" can make, for example, part of an audience leave a lecture hall, causing protests, speakers to be shouted down, or might even initiate student riots; referring to "him" or "her" (singular) as "he" or "she" rather than "they," if that is how the single person wishes to be referred to, can cause very serious repercussions (as is the case of Jordan Peterson).

In contrast to Communist Newspeak, American Newspeak is not concerned with political power *per se*—that is, who the holder of power is (which Party)—but with politics as a method of enforcing an ever-wider range of egalitarian rules. Political machinery is of interest to the enforcers only in so far as it can institute policies which safeguard the progress of equality. They do not seek to "centralize democracy" because democracy for them is not a system that can counteract despotic oppression, but because it is a despotism in pure form—exercised collectively. The progress is defined in one way only: It is expansion of equality—be it inclusion of minorities or different "lifestyles."

To understand why the American language is changing, we need to realize that *the ultimate social goal is the abolition of social hierarchy in order to abolish privilege.* This is the process that started in 1776 and which was completed in 1789. The first event, cessation from the Crown, was a way of leaving the English hierarchical political order. The year 1789 was more consequential as it marked breaking away from tradition and the past. No text mirrors it more profoundly and describes its violent character more precisely than Tocqueville's *The Old Regime and the French Revolution.*

> The French made, in 1789, the greatest effort that has ever been made by any people to sever their history into two parts, so to speak, and to tear open a gulf between their past and their future. In this design, they took the greatest care to leave every trace of their past condition behind them; they imposed all kinds of restraints upon themselves in order to be different from their ancestry; they omitted nothing which could disguise them.

The French Revolution acted, with regard to things of this world, precisely as religious revolutions have acted with regard to things of the other. It dealt with the citizen in the abstract, independent of particular social organizations, just as religions deal with mankind in general, independent of time and place. It inquired, not what were the particular rights of French citizens, but what were the general rights and duties of mankind in reference to political concerns.

It was by thus divesting itself of all that was peculiar to one race or time, and by reverting to natural principles of social order and government, that it became intelligible to all, and susceptible of simultaneous imitation in a hundred different places.

By seeming to tend rather to the regeneration of the human race than to the reform of France alone, it roused passions such as the most violent political revolutions had been incapable of awakening. It inspired proselytism, and gave birth to propagandism; and hence assumed that quasi-religious character which so terrified those who saw it, or, rather, became a sort of new religion, imperfect, it is true, without God, worship, or future life, but still able, like Islamism, to cover the earth with its soldiers, its apostles, and its martyrs.

It must not be supposed that all its methods were unprecedented, or all the ideas it brought forward absolutely original. On many former occasions, even in the heart of the Middle Ages, agitators had invoked the general principles on which human societies rest for the purpose of overthrowing particular customs, and had assailed the constitution of their country with arguments drawn from the natural rights of man; but all these experiments had been failures. The torch which set Europe on fire in the eighteenth century was easily extinguished in the fifteenth. Arguments of this kind cannot succeed till certain changes in the condition, customs, and minds of men have prepared a way for their reception.

The so-called "inclusive" language is a means to an end, the end to extinguish *all* privilege, and, paradoxically, including the privilege of speaking properly. As language is becoming more and more egalitarian—more inclusive—it becomes self-destructive. It is an instrument of anti-culture. Even within the confines of the language itself, we see the same degenerative process taking place: all accents, dialects, ungrammatical jargons, jive and Ebonics, are equally valid forms of language. None, including former highbrow BBC English or Queen's English, is higher on the scale, since there is no scale.

The same process can be observed in plastic arts, literature, and music. Self-expression means everything. The idea of correctly applying old rules disappeared. Rules, we are told, were oppressive. It is enough to be a "minority" painter, sculptor, writer, or singer to have an exhibit and have a review published in *The New York Times* (its Arts section leads the way), if your minority group has not yet received recognition. And the review is always positive because it *must be.* A negative review would be taken to mean an attack on the minority artist (on his race, sex, or sexual preference), not his work. His work is shielded from criticism because it was never of interest; what was of interest was that there was a minority member who made art. Such a situation creates an atmosphere of self-admiration and coterie. The only people who can be criticized and attacked are the whites, who are either looked upon with suspicion or, at best, tolerated.

Occasionally, the liberal-democratic newspeak uses semi-Marxist terms, which come in handy—for example, *power-structure.* Marxism, too, wanted to abolish the old regime (capitalism) and create a more egalitarian society. But Marx and Marxists had a vision, and the vision was, it was believed, unfolding itself according to the strict rules of historical development. The liberal democrats do not have such a vision, they have no philosophy of history, and the term "power-structure" is an accidental borrowing that is useful because it points in the direction of a structure that is perceived as a bastion of the old hierarchy, which slows down the march of equality. It might be a grading system in schools, SAT tests for students applying to college, it may even be a different lab-coat worn by a novice and an accomplished doctor (Johns Hopkins hospitals abolished the system which differentiated between doctors). Perfect equality requires that all distinctions be abolished.

Socialist Newspeak was created for the purposes of maintaining political power and imperialist expansion. Even its economic part was important only in so far as it served politics. American Newspeak is an *ad hoc* creation of a liberal-democratic ideology, and it creates even more strange words and grammatical rules as the movement discovers new hierarchical obstacles on the way. To many such rules and changes seem absurd, but the world without hierarchy is absurd, and we should awaken to it. Hierarchy is an essential component of excellence, nobility, virtue, and the good life. In a word, hierarchy is the highest aspiration of *human* nature. As Aristotle put it, philosophical or intellectual life is possible in so far as there is something divine in us. Without it the world looks like an open and flat terrain. It is vast but uninteresting. So is newspeak. Language that does not reflect the wide world, which is diverse and therefore interesting, cannot be beautiful, either. It is, as it is in Orwell's *1984*, an instrument of an ideological oppression.

There is nothing new in saying it: Democracy is the most oppressive form of government because there is nowhere to hide. In a hierarchical system of government there are many places where one can escape oppression. Unlike monarchs, who, as Tocqueville noted, want your body, democracy wants your soul, your freedom. Good, rich, clear and proper language is the best safeguard against tyranny. Winston Smith discovered it, and we should re-discover it.

One should also add that these changes to language are fundamentally barbaric in nature. The liberals believe that the changes based on the idea of inclusion expand the realm of freedom by limiting "patriarchy" and so on. They do not seem to realize, however, that the intervention into the linguistic tissue is an act of violence committed on the body of the language and tradition which developed over centuries, and which carries with it the wealth and treasures of Western civilization. It is a destructive process and attack on European civilization.

Winston Churchill was once asked about the rule of not using a preposition at the end of a sentence. In response, he said: "This is the kind of nonsense I would never put up with." We should all take Churchill's advice. The liberal-democratic Newspeak is the kind of nonsense we should never put up *with*.

CHAPTER 5 | BLIND SPOT PSYCHOLOGY AND THE NEW "ROAD TO SERFDOM"

The technological malaise seems to have been much less acutely felt in the United States. Individuals such as Aldous Huxley, Paul Tillich, and Erich Fromm, who have raised their voices in protest, are of European origin and received their education in Europe. Technolaters such as Professor B. F. Skinner of Harvard and most other American professors represent the familiar type of the American intellectual caught in an ecstatic technical vertigo…

Robert K. Merton, Preface to Jacques Ellul's *The Technological Society*

The whole idea that one can 'design' a better society on a scientific basis appeals to many who earlier might have been socialists. Did not Marx, too, want to design a better society. Did he not call his brand of socialism 'scientific' in contrast to 'Utopian' socialism… Moreover, Skinner's theory rings true, because it is (almost) true for the alienated man of the cybernetic society.

Erich Fromm, *The Anatomy of Human Destructiveness*

1.

One would think that the day when communism collapsed in Eastern Europe and the Soviet Union would go into the annals of history as the official date when the socialist idea was buried for good, and that Karl Marx's philosophy would be unlikely to seduce anyone again. Yet Marx is back, and his grip on people's minds appears stronger than ever. This time, however, Marx's domain is not economy or politics, but psychology, and his *modus operandi* is called the Implicit Association Test (IAT). It is designed to measure one's "biases."

The test is widely disseminated in psychology courses in American universities, and is easily accessible on-line. One can even see people in cafés testing their level of prejudice. Its inventors are two psychologists: Mahzarin R. Banaji, from Harvard, and Anthony G. Greenwald, from Washington University (also a graduate of Harvard). They are the authors of *Blindspot: Hidden Biases of Good People*. The two professors are rock stars of American psychology, and the idea behind the test they invented may already have had a bigger impact on the American mind than B. F. Skinner's behaviorist theory.

Banaji and Greenwald's work deserves attention not because of the originality of their idea, but because of the danger which it creates. The premise on which the IAT is based is a direct reformulation in psychological language, of Marx's theory of "false consciousness." The concept of "false consciousness" lies at the root of the philosopher's concept of class struggle and the withering away of the state—reminiscent of the contemporary jargon of the Left's call to dismantle the "power structure."

Banaji and Greenwald do not hide their Leftist agenda. In fact, they espouse their views openly. Given the Marxist provenance of the theory of implicit bias and everything we know from history about mixing science and ideology—including Hitler's scientific establishment's attempts to provide a justification for purging "undesirable elements" from his future Reich—one should be deeply apprehensive about theories that can easily be used and exploited to implement dangerous social policies.

Let me begin by invoking a very well-known incident. After two black men were arrested in a Philadelphia Starbucks in April 2018, the company rushed to announce that it would conduct "anti-bias training." To assure everyone that the problem of unconscious biases among its employees was taken seriously, Starbucks closed down *all* its stores nationwide for several hours to train their employees. No one protested against the training, or even questioned the validity of such an idea. Millions of docile employees, mostly young people who probably never suspected themselves of having biases, underwent the training. Not much was said about the circumstances of the arrest or the manager's decision to call the police. It was decided that the incident was racially motivated. The media's coverage of the event made it look like a great day of national solidarity, while millions of customers impatiently waited for Starbucks to reopen. The day was reminiscent of the

May Day parade of solidarity with the "oppressed workers" of the world in former socialist countries.

Around the same time, Nike, too, announced that it was going through an executive "shake-up." The shake-up was not caused by a racial incident. It aimed instead at fighting the company's "misogynistic culture." It brought down a few members of the highest executive echelon. Again, the coverage made it sound like another day of solidarity against social injustice.

These are only two major recent cases, but they are symptomatic of the general tendency in the U.S. to explain virtually *all* social, political, and economic problems as a result of prejudice or bias. *No alternative diagnosis or explanation*—individual or group behavior—of any problem seems to exist. Sooner or later, everything comes down to a problem of bias.

Was the closing of all stores and the training of millions of employees justified because of what happened in a *single* Philadelphia location? Doubtful. But to appease social justice warriors and defend oneself against the accusation of being racist, sexist, homophobic, or xenophobic, we seek a solution which is consistent with the predominant belief that all problems are reducible to the existence of biases. Our efforts must, therefore, focus on finding a way of identifying and getting rid of them. This explains why Banaji and Greenwald became the two most talked about psychologists.

Their work came to the larger public's attention in 2005, when Shankar Vedantar, a reporter for the *Washington Post*, published a story about the IAT, and invited a gay activist to take the test. As it turned out, she was biased against gay people. A similarly surprising result was the case of a writer, Malcolm Gladwell. Despite having a Jamaican mother, he turned out to be "slightly biased against black people." The two instances reveal to us that, our best intentions notwithstanding, we cannot assume an objective, unbiased point of view. Our lack of awareness of the biases' presence is our "blind spot," which works the same way that an outside mirror on a car works. We may believe we do not suffer from prejudices, yet they hide from us, like a vehicle that is there but for a split second goes unseen.

Where does the blind spot come from? In a nutshell, we are prisoners of history, culture, education, religion, and political and social institutions, and as long as they exercise their hidden influence on us, we are doomed to discriminate, not always in a conscious way, against people who are unlike us.

Although the two authors do not advocate any specific way of curing these biases, in so far as the test passes for a *scientifically verifiable* form of measurement, one can easily imagine a number of ways in which their research can be turned into a dangerous political tool. Recently, Dr. Peter Simi, a professor of sociology at Chapman University, California, published an article in which he identifies *hate* as an "addiction." The idea was seized by National Public Radio, which gave Dr. Simi a public forum to propagate his views. And this is what we find in his paper:

> The process of leaving deeply meaningful and embodied identities can be experienced as a struggle against addiction, with continuing cognitive, emotional, and physiological responses that are involuntary, unwanted, and triggered by environmental factors. Using data derived from a unique set of in-depth life history interviews with 89 former U.S. white supremacists, as well as theories derived from recent advances in cognitive sociology, we examine how a rejected identity can persist despite a desire to change. Disengagement from white supremacy is characterized by substantial lingering effects that subjects describe as addiction.

Reading Dr. Simi's paper, one very quickly realizes that this is not a scientific analysis: It is ideological gobbledygook that pretends to be scientific. But Dr. Simi deserves mention, because he made "hate" the exclusive property of white people and turned it into a semi-medical category.

The appearance of such ideas, dressed in the language of science, creates a danger. As more people give credence to such absurdities, the public will seize them and demand that politicians do something. We can imagine that "hate addicts" will be treated the way that drug-addicts are—sent to specially designed "medical" facilities, or treated as social "undesirables" who need to stay separated from the rest of the society, in some kind of semi-penal institutions, until they are cured. Their release will be contingent on how un-biased their psyche is. German history in the 1930s provides us with disturbing examples of the dangers of pseudo-science. Castration of "idiots" and racial "measurements" were not conceived in Hitler's mind. Desperation, the social mood of the country, and the urge to find a solution to its problems, helped to create an atmosphere in which one would believe anything, including pseudo-science, and this Hitler exploited.

Given the very strong scientific orientation among Americans—much stronger in the U.S. than in any other Western country, but in some respects similar to that of Germany of the 1930s—one cannot exclude the possibility that this kind of pseudo-scientific jargon will resonate among the American public, and will subsequently take over the public realm. In fact, it already has. It expresses itself daily in such phrases as "According to new research," or "A new study shows"—the two most frequently heard phrases in support of social policies, always based "on scientific studies." Once "hate" is considered to be a "social health issue," we can justifiably declare "war on hate," just like we declared "war on cancer," "war on drugs," "war on obesity," "war on smoking," "war on trans-fats," and so many others. They are all the present-day enemies of the American people and are presented by the media as such. Such language can be easily translated into policies—like meatless Monday, which was recently declared in a bureaucratic capacity, with no public consultation or, for that matter, opposition. Policies which are deemed important for national security are supported by the Surgeon General, Federal Drug Agency, Department of Education, and other institutions.

The idea of implicit bias easily inserts itself into such an ideological climate. Imagine now a clinical psychologist measuring your "hidden biases." He will tell you that your psyche is "mal-aligned,"[1] which implies that you are prejudiced against women (if you are a man), blacks or browns (if you are white), gays (if you are straight), "transgendered" individuals (if you think your birth sex is natural), foreigners (if you are a U.S. citizen), and older people (if you are young). In other words, you suffer from sexism, misogyny, racism, homophobia, xenophobia, transphobia, and ageism.

Banjaji and Greenwald's method is so popular because it provided a "scientific" backing to confirm a prevailing suspicion—namely, that our social and political structure is geared toward favoritism of certain groups

---

1   "Today," wrote Erich Fromm in *The Sane Society*, in 1955, "the function of psychiatry, psychology and psychoanalysis threatens to become the tool in the manipulation of men. The specialists in this field tell you what the 'normal' person is, and, correspondingly, what is wrong with you; they devise the methods to help you adjust, be happy, be normal."

(whites) who enjoy "privilege" and discriminate against others, (blacks and browns). This is what constitutes "systemic racism." The question why other cultures lag behind is never asked, and if it is, the explanation is "colonialism" and "white supremacy." The simplicity of such explanations meets the demands of the wider public, along with social activists and politicians, who now know that some people remain poor and uneducated, and are thus prevented from advancement, never by their own faults, habits, failed traditions, or their culture's slow adaptation to modernity. Their disadvantages are always a result of the existence of unjust "power structures" and the domination of white men and Western culture.

2.

Every student of history and philosophy can recognize the Marxist roots of the IAT. In *The Communist Manifesto*, Marx and Engels explained that "The history of all hitherto existing societies is the history of class struggles. Freeman and slave, patrician and plebeian, lord and serf, guild-master and journeyman, in a word, oppressor and oppressed." The struggle could continue indefinitely, but since history, according to Marx, develops in a definite direction following several stages of development, from less advanced to more advanced, at some point it reaches a level where the opposition between the oppressors and the oppressed intensifies and results in a revolution. The revolution puts an end to class struggle, in fact, to history itself, only to return man to his true nature as a "social being." Accordingly, the dismantling of an unjust power-structure ends oppression, injustice, and inequality.

Marx's entire historical scheme rests on the distinction between man as an alienated being and man as a social being. To turn the former into the latter, Marx advocated the removal of alienating forces or factors that prevent him from seeing himself in proper—non-antagonistic—social relationships to others. In his 1844 "Paris Manuscripts," he identifies seven factors or sources of alienation: "religion, family, state, law, morality, art, science." They exercise a hidden influence on us in the way we think. They express the dominant group's hidden interests, of which the members of the group are not always aware. Thus, law, for example, built into the judicial system, is not the expression of a universal idea of justice, but serves class interest, just like political or state structures are there to protect the interests—economic, financial, educational, etc.—of the dominant class or classes. These seven sources create what Marx called "false consciousness." It is, to put it simply, an unawareness of our own motives, and the recognition that state and social institutions are also forms of oppression, imposed by one class on another.

One can easily see in this Banaji and Greenwald's theory of the blind spot: Marx's alienated man corresponds to their prejudiced, or biased, man, and Marx's "false consciousness," unawareness of the operations of alienating forces, is what the two psychologists call a "blind spot." In so far as Marx believed that his diagnosis of social ills was correct, he did not want his discovery to remain a theoretical insight. He proposed to overturn the entire system by abolishing capitalism—the base upon which all seven sources of alienation rest—and to thereby return man to his true nature as a social being. Much of the 20th century is a demonstration of Marx's ideas put into practice on a global scale. Millions of people whose consciousness remained "false" were either killed or subjected to gruesome punishment. Banaji and Greenwald never cite Marx, nor do they acknowledge him as their source of inspiration. Reading their book, one gets the impression that, while writing it, the authors got caught in a Marxist blind spot without being aware of it, and simply repeated the lesson of false consciousness in contemporary, psychological language. The reader who is interested in psychology will be disappointed if he is looking for a serious discussion of how they formulated their ideas.

Their book is mostly an exercise in statistics, and, in so far as it claims to be a work in the field of psychology, it is a total failure. It suffers from a lack of theoretical assumptions. It does not ask how we acquire biases, does not explain the cognitive processes that accompany their acquisition, let alone whether biases contain valuable knowledge, without which we might not survive. Further, there is not even a reference to deductive or inductive reasoning, and the authors seem to be oblivious to the selection of eminent philosophical literature which treats the subject. The name of Karl Popper, whose works in the field of the theory of knowledge cannot be avoided (at any rate not by a serious student of the idea of what makes scientific theory), is not mentioned. Even Freud's name is mentioned only twice, and only in passing. His masterpiece *Group Psychology and the Analysis of the Ego*, which would be invaluable in this context, is ignored outright. The references to other founders of their discipline are nonexistent.

Particularly in the context of *social* psychology, to which the book claims to be a contribution, the reader would expect to find at least the names of social psychologists, such as Karen Horney, Erich Fromm, and Carl G. Jung. Fromm's contribution to the field of social psychology (and his works on Marx and psychology) cannot be overestimated, and Horney's thesis about culturally determined linguistic concepts, through which we understand psychological states (including neurosis), could yield pivotal results in the context of their work.

3.

For example, as Horney wrote in *The Neurotic Personality of Our Time* (1937): "Today, for example, if a mature and independent woman were to consider herself 'a fallen woman,' 'unworthy of the love of a decent man,' because she had sexual relationships, she would be suspected of a *neurosis* [...]. Some forty years ago this attitude of guilt would have been considered normal." Contrary to Freud, for whom our reactions were reducible to physiological determinants, according to Horney, it is the "average attitude" within a culture and a historical epoch which determines the sense of "normal"—the deviation from which causes neurosis.

Following Horney's general line of reasoning, one could argue that neurosis consists in the experience of a discrepancy between the private psyche (shaped by cultural patterns, rather than by biology alone; or at least not always, as Freud would have it) and the public or "common" perception of reality through concepts to which our psychic states refer. Thus, for example, we might be appalled by something, or condemn something, or simply find it unacceptable, whereas members of another culture would have different—even positive—reactions to the same thing. Now, one could imagine a situation where a conflict arises within the same society—divided into two groups, more or less equally—with respect to its members' perception of the same "form of behavior," just like in a situation of two individual members of different cultures. According to Horney's classification, such a conflict could be classified as neurosis. Thus, group behavior, not unlike individual behavior, could be said to be neurotic.

Here is a difficult but important question. Classifying individual behavior as neurotic could easily be done, since it can be measured against the "statistical average," just like the example of a woman who considers herself to be "a fallen woman" in a society in which ninety-nine percent of women are fallen by the standard of the past. However, if a society is divided more or less equally, how would we know which part of the society is neurotic? All examples given by Horney in her work refer either to the contrast between the past and present (within the same society), or the contrast between cultures which display different attitudes vis-à-vis the same situation or objects (e.g. menstruation, death, work, etc.). Can one determine neurotic behavior against something else—say, an idea? Nothing in Horney's reasoning excludes such a possibility.

Let's take several concepts—sexism, misogyny, racism, homophobia, etc.—that we term as biases (and which some claim to be mental illnesses). Today, these concepts are no longer understood as individual attitudes. For example, in the past "fear" of homosexuality could be as "terrifying" as the primitive tribal fear of the menstruating woman. At present, due to complex cultural mutations over a long period of time, they became socio-political categories. How did this happen? The answer, I suggest, is that the idea of equality brought them to the fore of political discourse.

Consider slavery, for example. Contrary to what is taught in the university, it has been widely implemented across time and cultures. Hardly ever was it questioned. It was only with the famous French and American announcements—"All men are born equal" and "All men are created equal"—that slavery became a problem, whereby a moral language was generated, through which the human psyche began to express itself in a way unprecedented. If one wonders why neither Plato nor Aristotle, Hobbes, or even Montaigne (who was critical of European "superiority") condemned slavery, it is because they did not think much of equality.

However, once, in the post-Enlightenment period, equality began to dominate our political and social language, slavery became a problem. It is only against the background of "equality" that such categories as sexism, misogyny, homophobia, xenophobia, ageism, etc. could make their political claims.

An egalitarian mind has only one eye. It can only look for traces of discrimination, hence the preoccupation of today's social activists and journalists; one must not wonder why they no longer see the difference between news and propaganda. What passes for news in America today always revolves around those few concepts, in the service of which 24/7 coverage is organized.

As the chasm between the egalitarian psyche and public reality—the existence of political, social, and educational structures still rooted in the past hierarchy—grows, neurosis grows as well, and it manifests itself in group behavior. Such groups which insist that every private attitude functions as a fully legitimate social attitude are frustrated over the existence of biases which they see as barriers to absolute equality. Discriminatory biases are, as the contemporary social jargon would have it, embedded in "power-structures" (called "white privilege" in America) that social activists and reformers strive to abolish. Not only is their attitude *not* different from that of Marx: It is the exact application of Marx's theory, which claimed that false consciousness will continue to operate for as long as the base—capitalism—remains in effect. It is no wonder why those who believe in the pernicious power of biases are the same people who display an anti-free-market attitude and call for the abolishment of educational standards.

The *perceived*, rather than real, lack of equality appears to be a catalyst for group neurosis. Its emergence and growth are not due to someone's negative private attitude toward *me*, but this person's *suspicion* that I may not be in favor of full equality. Therefore, I may have never displayed a negative attitude against another sex, race, sexuality, religion, etc., yet I stand condemned when I am unwilling to pledge public allegiance to the idea of equality. As long as I resist there is always a hidden possibility that I may commit an evil act in the future. We find a confirmation of my suggestion in Freud's *Group Psychology*: "We have found that what neurotics are guided by is not ordinary objective reality but psychological reality [...] and the sense of guilt in an obsessional neurosis is based upon the fact of *an evil intention which was never carried out.*" As we know from the examples of different groups, be it ordinary gangs or ISIS, killing someone can be a rite of passage, a way of demonstrating commitment to the cause. Here, the commitment may be less bloody, but is even deeper: It requires aligning one's mind to ideological dictates, just like under communism.

The cases in point are the frequent public protests, and the display of the rainbow coalition flags in all kinds of places (churches, cafés, offices of university professors, bumper stickers and mugs). Most people who participate in pro-gay, pro-abortion, pro-transgendered, anti-racist, protests are neither gay nor transgendered nor black; nor have most of them had abortions, or even the attributes that presuppose such a choice, and they are usually young. The question arises: Why do they participate in rallies that, quite often, make them behave as if they lost their minds, or as if they saw the second coming of Christ? The answer is that they unleash their neurotic frustration, not because any specific decision limiting their freedom has been made, but because they believe that as long as there is still someone, somewhere, who refuses to believe without reservation in the idea of equality, their dream of a perfect egalitarian utopia is in danger.

This is what the recent hysteria over "white supremacy" appears to have as cause. Incidents of "white supremacy" are extremely rare. Most Americans have never seen a "white supremacist" (save for on television), and if extremely rare incidents happen, they concern groups whose numbers, for political purposes, are totally irrelevant. In individual cases of shooting, common in America, people who call themselves supremacists are—every sane person would agree—mentally unstable. They seem to be lost, disconnected from social reality, and would subscribe to any ideology to regain a sense of existential purpose. If there was a Satanist political group, they would join it too, just like those who joined a chiliastic climate change ideology. White supremecy's opposite, the Antifa groups, are instead very real, operate often throughout the country (especially on college campuses), and yet they are not met with any condemnation by the liberal media.

"White supremacy" in America is like a ghost that few people saw, but which everybody talks about. The reason is that the ideology of "white supremacy," or any supremacy, is in principle against equality, whereas Antifa, despite their brutal methods and hatred, is, at least in theory, for equality.

In commenting on Hitler's methods, Aldous Huxley wrote, "Opponents should not be argued with; they should be attacked, shouted down, or, if they become too much of a nuisance, liquidated." It is not entirely surprising that those who permit one party to beat members of another party do nothing about it. They believe that the former are on the "right side," perhaps even on the right side of history. As Erich Fromm, who devoted *Escape from Freedom* to understanding and explaining the psychology of fascism, wrote: "freedom is not less endangered if attacked in the name of anti-fascism than in that of outright fascism."

Let's notice that what we term biases were not frustrating *on a large-scale* decades or centuries ago, but recently they have become increasingly so. Those who would be inclined to say that they existed but were suppressed in the past by the dominant culture that oppressed minorities miss a very important point. It was not the suppression of dissenting voices that prevented equality, but the opposite: Equality, as we know from history, is not a universal idea, nor is it a historical constant. It is an intellectual product of the modern mind. However, once articulated our mental demand for equality grew, and our frustration over unequal relationships grew as well. The anger that the proponents of egalitarianism unload in the form of public protests and violence seems to be an expression of *their* ever-growing neurotic personality—the lack of alignment of their wishes with historically given social and political structures.

If so, it may very well be the case that it is not the sexists, misogynists, racists, homophobes, and similar types who individually may suffer from neurosis, but their opponents. In all likelihood, their egos' mental life, which has been shaped by an abstract idea of equality, is, to use Banaji and Greenwald's language, misaligned, and fails to understand that hierarchy is inscribed in the nature of social and political institutions.

Extending equality beyond its logical limits is likely, as Plato predicted in book VIII of his *Republic*, to produce anarchy and social chaos. None of this should surprise us: It is only with the emergence of two egalitarian systems in the 19th century—communism and liberal-democracy—that anarchy has become one of the greatest problems of our times. Communism prevented the masses from sliding into it by making the individual totally subservient to the state; individualist liberal-democracies seem to have two mechanisms to prevent anarchy—namely, a fascist takeover, *à la* Mussolini or Hitler, or mounting legislation. The outcome is likely to be what it was under communism: The private realm, under the pressure of legislation, is bound to disappear, as it has in the U.S. and Europe. Regulating every aspect of one's life will deprive man of privacy, and will render him totally transparent, easily traceable, manipulated, mindless, as a result of a unified educational system and methodology, and subservient to the bureaucratic state machinery operated by millions of robot-like security officers. Individual freedom will be something totally unknown.

In explaining how fascism came about, and the psychological factors which made its emergence possible, the great social psychologist Erich Fromm has a word of warning for those who play with fire:

> The principles of economic liberalism, political democracy, religious autonomy, and individualism in personal life, gave expression to the longing for freedom, and at the same time seemed to bring mankind nearer its realization. One tie after another was severed [...]. The First World War was regarded by many as the final struggle and its conclusion the ultimate victory from freedom. Existing democracies appeared strengthened, and new ones replaced old monarchies. But only a few years elapsed before new systems emerged which denied everything that men believed they had won in centuries of struggle.

If equality is not an eternal political or social fact, then hierarchy must balance it. The extent of a hierarchical order can be debated, but not its recognition. The existence of limits can be frustrating, but a healthy ego should be able to recognize it.

In his insightful and succinct work, *The Undiscovered Self* Carl G. Jung talks about prejudices as well, but considers them to be individual and moral, not statistical problems. The danger that this great and compassionate man saw in statistical analyses is that "the individual is bound to be a function of statistics and hence a function of the State." None of this seems to matter to Banaji and Greenwald, whose idea of aligning the psyche is not about the individual, even if he suffers from biases. Their purpose is to offer a method that would allow for "more egalitarian relationships." Thinking of Nazi science and the Nazi doctors' practices, one should be frightened by the promise of being cured. Such a cure can only result in the loss of individuality.

Now, imagine Marx as a medical doctor in a white lab coat, telling you that, after reviewing your test, it is obvious that your psyche is misaligned; you suffer from biases against women, homosexuals, transgendered individuals, foreigners, old people, blacks and browns; in short, you suffer from sexism, misogyny, homophobia, xenophobia, ageism, sexism, and racism. All of them are mental illnesses, as we hear from some corners of the new scientific world.

Here is the danger of their new method. It is one thing for *me* to say:

I, like everyone else, have some biases; I am prejudiced on the basis of my experiences with people, but I exercise the virtue of civility, restraint, and kindness toward those against whom I am prejudiced. It is quite another thing for a doctor, an educational counselor, a state official to tell me, as some say, that biases are a mental illness that should, or even *must* be taken care of, so that one may become a well-adjusted member of society and the work-force. Thus, what began as an innocent exercise in furthering our knowledge of the human psyche can be turned into a powerful weapon. In the political realm, calling those who are biased "deplorables," may be a political suicide if they constitute 51% of the nation's population. However, if the number of "deplorables" sinks below 50% of electoral votes, such a statement can be taken to mean an open call to violence against them, or to have them cured, just as D-503—the protagonist in Zamyatin's *WE*—underwent lobotomy only to realize that he was an enemy of the One State's happiness. An unhealthy political climate, animated by ideological zeal, has proved historically to breed all kinds of "scientific" nonsense that can support social policies required by the state. Hitler's Germany is the case in point. What guarantee do we have that the ideas propagated by those like Banaji, Greenwald, and Dr. Simi will not be used in the (near) future to hunt political deplorables? We don't.

Given that the last several years witnessed the imposition of training (sensitivity, cultural awareness, and sexual harassment training) into most institutions in the U.S., while non-discriminatory algorithms are already applied by loan lending companies—the justice system may be moving in this direction as well—we can easily imagine the same done in the psychological realm.

Mandatory anti-bias testing—for all students (ages 5–21 yrs.) and employees of all ages, including members of Congress—will be our new *soma*. Then the only fitting slogan for the gates to the American Brave New World will be what the great Italian poet Dante wrote on the gates of hell: "*Lasciate ogni speranza, voi ch'entrate*"—abandon all hope, ye who enter.

CHAPTER 6 | SEXUAL LIBERALISM

> *Hook-up* is my generation's word for having sex (or oral sex) or sometimes for what used to be called "making out." The hook-up connotes the most casual of connections. Any emotional attachment deserves scorn and merits […] without embarrassment, [the idea that] there cannot be any surrender. We can only hook-up. Our sexual landscape is already soaked in the language of betrayal before we've even begun.
>
> Wendy Shalit, *A Return to Modesty: Discovering the Lost Virtue*

1.

"'For instance,' she [Linda] hoarsely whispered, 'take the way they have one another here. Mad, I tell you, absolutely mad,'" says one of the female characters in Aldous Huxley's *Brave New World*, referring to the "old ways" of having sexual encounters with one person. "Once a lot of women came and made a scene because their men came to see me. *Well, why not?*" This fragment comes as close as possible to what we call today "consensual sexuality"—sexuality based on mutual agreement divorced from feelings. *Brave New World* was published in 1933, and if we wonder what the reactions among Huxley's original readers were, we should compare them to dialogue in the 1930s movies touching on the subject of sex. They are silent in this respect, and if they *allude* to "it" at all, the characters are likely to blush.

The 1930s readers must have been amused by the way Huxley's characters think and act, probably for the same reason we are amused by the old science-fiction books, or the movies about man landing on the moon or Mars, wearing regular clothing and breathing oxygen. "We get the point!" We know the author created the situation and characters to push the boundaries of our imagination, but "we don't really buy it." It isn't real because there is no oxygen on the moon, or Mars! Being plausible does not make it real. So, we brush aside such scenarios with an ironic smile. The original reader of *Brave New World* most certainly brushed aside the possibility of consensual sex divorced from emotions. Poetic license is one thing, reality of human nature and relationships is another—and if women in Huxley's novels do not blush it is because they are human robots.

Whether a technetronic utopia requires exactly the kind of sexual relationships as Huxley described is by no means certain, but he seems to have indicated that lack of strong emotional bonds is the premise on which totalitarianism rests. His state is the administrator and dispenser of sexual pleasure and the psychological well-being of its citizens in the form of a mood-regulating drug called *soma*. Huxley was not the only one to realize that emotions and sex are problems for utopian politics. He and George Orwell got the ideas for their respective novels from the Russian author Yevgeny Zamyatin's *WE* (1923), whose fear of a totalitarian future goes back to Fyodor Dostoevsky's predictions in *Notes from the Underground* (1864). There, with his typical visionary power, Dostoevsky warned us that a society composed of people who act according to strict scientific or rational rules, whose actions can be "calculated and tabulated," is bound to create a community of individuals without individuality, and whose form of personal identification is a number. He called them "cyphers" or "piano keys" (on account of the predictability of their respective sounds).

In matters of sex, the One State in *WE* allots a certain number of hours to pleasure. This is the way it is done:

> O was to come in an hour. I felt pleasantly and beneficially excited. At home I stepped hurriedly into the office, handed in my pink coupon, and received the certificate permitting me to lower the shades. This right is granted only on sexual days. At all other times we live behind our transparent walls that seem woven of gleaming air—we are always visible, always washed in light.

Both Huxley and Zamyatin stripped their characters of genuinely human reactions, but Zamyatin, likely taking the idea from Dostoevsky, goes even further than Huxley: He strips them of their names, too. His characters are numbers, like I-330, or the female lover of the protagonist, named D-503. Orwell, on the other hand, in order to assure that the state's control is absolute, and there is no pleasure independent of the Party, in a memorable fragment that sketches mankind's future with a boot on the human face, makes O'Brian explain to Winston that the Party will eliminate orgasm as well. Sex will be a formality, serving the purpose of procreation.

The characters in *WE* and *Brave New World* are robots, for whom the depth of human experience—expressed and recorded in classical literature, art, music, paintings—is non-existent and cannot touch their souls because they do not have any. Their human soul has been taken away from them *by the author of the fictional reality* who created them. Eighty-eight years after the publication of *Brave New World*, ninety-six after *WE*, and seventy-one after *1984*, we can say with considerable certainty that the literary imagination is not the only place where human beings can be manipulated to achieve fictional perfection. American reality is quickly catching up with fiction.

2.

"Consent is Sexy" and "Sex without Consent is Rape" are two slogans with which every American student is familiar ("You Can Withdraw Consent at Any Time!" is a third supplementary slogan). Knowing how to go about finding sexual pleasure is as important as knowing one's class schedule or where the gym is. Notices that would have been considered indecent and outrageous thirty years ago wallpaper university hallways, so that you know that the most intimate part of your life is no longer yours. Sex is now subject to regulations, and if you break them you might be accused and arrested. The slogans are hammered into the minds of college freshmen by counselors, harassment experts, and guest speakers at orientation sessions (like in Huxley's "elementary sex" classes or "Aphroditeum Club"). More and more American students show up in classes with T-shirts or with pins (the size of a hand-palm) on which it is written: "Consent is Sexy" (worn mostly by young men) and "I love Female Orgasm" (worn by young women). They are made to participate unconsciously in an ideological campaign, whose emotionally detrimental effects for their lives they are completely unaware. Knowledge of "how to do it," taught by the "sex-masters" with college degrees, is a new rite of passage with which colleges send their graduates to the workplace. There they deepen their initiation into the American Brave New World by taking mandatory "sexual harassment training" and "sensitivity training."

Passing "training," administered yearly, is a condition of employment and participation in the workforce in today's America. To make things as though we were in a futuristic novel, raising the new totalitarian generation begins in kindergarten. Several years ago, we learned about two six-year-old boys—H. Y., from Canon City, Colorado and M D., from Aurora, Colorado—who were accused of sexual harassment. H.Y. was accused of kissing a girl (his age) on the hand; M.D. for singing a line from an LMFAO song, "I'm Sexy and I Know It," to a female classmate while waiting in the lunch line. The cases were considered to be of national importance judging by the fact that they were reported in *The Washington Post* and on national radio.

If you think this is crazy, hold on! Victoria Brooks, lecturer in law at the University of Westminster, rushed to defend Samantha against inhuman treatment when several of her fingers were broken. Samantha, it turns out, is a sex doll who "worked" in a brothel in Barcelona. Human rights activists now want sex-dolls to be endowed with a consent chip. "It is a step toward a consent-oriented approach to sex dolls."

3.

Now, this insanity can be explained. Sex gains legitimacy through consent of the two parties, just like any commodity trade, except that in this case the commodity is sexual pleasure. It is a peculiar *ménage à trois*: me, you, and the state which provides a legal framework in the form of guidelines for students and employees and sexual harassment training, all embedded in "Title IX." If things "go wrong," I can file a complaint with my employer, my college counselor, or the police.

In the midst of great social rebellion and sexual revolution, on April 4, 1969, *LIFE* magazine asked on the cover: "How Far is Far Enough?" And in a timid fashion, the editors responded: "Once again, a society built upon certain values was testing the limits. How far is far enough?" The language makes you think of parents watching children in a kindergarten sandbox, wondering whether they should permit their kids to have more fun. The real question pertained to limits of sexuality and sex's relationship to the public sphere. Should sex be dictated by social norms, that is, the Protestant puritanism that for centuries influenced American social and moral standards? The sexual revolution of the sixties (just like the sexual "experimentations" in Protestant Holland and Scandinavian countries a decade earlier) was indeed a reaction against Protestant moral heritage, which for its part was a rebellion against the sinfulness of carnal pleasure.

The new approach to sex has nothing to do with the rejection of a religious tradition, nor is it an extension of anti-puritanical rebellion. (In fact, not too many people, including parents, would think that it is wrong to have "too much pleasure.") *It is a war over privacy and individuality*, and as such it is an offshoot of a totalitarian *Weltanschauung*, or, more precisely, the liberal ideology that wants to socialize sex, to take sexuality out of its moral and emotional domain, and to make private morality public. What is public is subject to regulatory power of the state.

Liberalism is interested in sexuality because it sees the private realm as an extension of political realm. It considers *all* forms of relationships—private and public—to be legitimate if, and only if, they are based on consent (as in "the consent of the governed"). The underlying assumption of such a view is the equality of the parties entering the contract. In this case, it is the *equality of sexes*—neither should (subconsciously or by nature) "succumb" to the other, like in the scenarios of seduction described in *Les liaisons dangereuses*, *Princes de Clèves*, Richardson's *Pamela* and countless other great works of literature that explore vulnerability, of which love is an expression and aspect.

The absurdity and paradoxical illiberality of the liberal view becomes clear when we realize that we do not consent to fall in love; we happen to fall in love. It is the yearning of the soul, not regulations, that creates a bond and rules that unite people. Even the propagators of "free love" of the 1960s had no intention of doing away with love, and the following two decades of the 70s and 80s are saturated with hundreds of songs about love. The lyrics of John Paul Young's "Love is in the Air" (1976) captures the spirit of the epoch well:

Love is in the air
Everywhere I look around
Love is in the air
Every sight and every sound
And I don't know if I'm being foolish
Don't know if I'm being wise—

But it's something that I must believe in
And it's there when I look in your eyes […]

Or, take a female singer, Barbara Streisand's hit, "Woman in Love":

But down inside
You know we never know why
The road is narrow and long
When eyes meet eyes
And the feeling is strong
I turn away from the wall
I stumble and fall
But I give you it all
I am a woman in love
And I do anything
To get you into my world
And hold you within
It's a right I defend
Over and over again

One of the reasons why songs like this seized the hearts of millions of people is because they are *genuine*. They touch our souls; they say something about us. Those who wrote them knew that songs—like poetry—appeal to emotions, and if a song is to touch you, it has to put ideology aside. Only propaganda follows ideological dictates.

The partisans of consensual sexuality prefer not to talk about vulnerability ("I stumble and fall/But I give you it all") because it would lead them back to nature and the differences between the sexes. Today's liberalism is dismissive of love and emotions because they do not fit its consensual or contractual framework. Young or Streisand might even be accused of promoting a "wrong attitude." Instead of reflecting on the nature of emotions and love in great novels, the scholars influenced by new trends forget (or never learned) that one of the reasons why literature exists is because it sheds light on human motivations and actions. Instead of explaining this, they made it their business to look for traces of misogyny or sexism in literature. The results are predictable. As one critic observed, what we find in *Pamela* is a "sexual harassment problem in the work-place"! They operate on the assumption that in so far as one sex—particularly women—is or can be more vulnerable, the sexes are *unequal*, and our effort must focus on eliminating inequalities by rendering men powerless. In order to do that, we enact sexual rules which indirectly give the state more power than it ever had before.

The perversion of such reasoning leads one to see seduction as an attempt to "exercise power" over another. And power in all its forms and manifestations, as John Stuart Mill, the father of the liberal idea, taught us, is "illegitimate." This is partly the reason why the feminist critics prefer Ibsen's character Nora in *Doll's House* over Tolstoy's *Anna Karenina*, despite the similar maternal and marital predicament in which the two women find themselves. Nora is celebrated as a "strong and independent" woman who asserts her independence from her husband and marital bond (no longer considered to be sacramental, but contractual), whereas Tolstoy's Anna is a foolish woman who falls victim to her vulnerable *feminine* nature. In 1861, eighteen years before Ibsen's *Doll's House*, John Stuart Mill published his most ideologically driven work, *The Subjection of Women*. Interestingly enough, of all literary heroines, probably none fits Mill's idea of the *new* woman better than Ibsen's Nora.

The idea that only women are vulnerable is not necessarily true, either. Consider Prevost's *Manon Lascaut* where love of a manipulative woman makes a man a total fool, or Vladimir Nabokov's *Lolita*. Great literature is the best place to see how men and women's emotions create the world of eroticism, sex, and love, and the last thing the great writers confirm is that we can direct, let alone legislate, emotions. In so far as politics can direct our sexual behavior, it must exclude emotions and become an instrument of political power that can create a totalitarian reality. Huxley could create his characters to have "consensual sex" with many partners because he denied nature its right to direct the characters' actions. *Brave New World* is possible only because sex in such a reality is divorced from love, eroticism, and the mystery of giving birth—of which the women in *BNW* are appalled.

Liberal ideology wants to destroy all of that. It claims to have the power to redeem and correct nature's mistake by establishing the equality of the two sexes, where sex is negotiated not through feelings but consent. In subscribing to the liberal view, we relinquish our sacred right not just to emotions, but to privacy and intimacy.

Just as in political and social life, liberalism is inimical to the old ways (tradition, aged institutions, custom, laws, and religion) such that traditional sexual morality is seen as a hindrance *that invades* the private realm (the last bastion of privacy), which explains its hostile attitude toward religion and Church teaching. According to the old moral code, in the private realm shame, chastity, love, craving to be united with one person, and the need to be seduced in order to give in, all reign supreme. All of them—explicitly or implicitly—stand condemned by today's liberal ideology. They are viewed as expressions of the patriarchal system, a male-dominated world, a power structure, or simply false consciousness. The last term, taken from Marx's dictionary, operates in the form of a religious morality. Accordingly, chastity is not something objectively positive or grounded in a woman's natural reactions, but is a result of the religious brain-washing of a chaste woman to stay chaste for the benefit of her man. Once she understands that she was ensnared by religion in the form of teaching by a male priest, pastor, or rabbi, she will become autonomous and freed from traditional constraints. That's certainly true, given that according to recent statistics, the rate of marital betrayal by women since the early 90s went up by forty percent.

Democratic-liberalism requires that political and social interactions be transparent, and demands the same form of transparency in private or sexual matters. "There is nothing shameful about it; it is all about your pleasure, provided it is consensual." This is a normal phrase with which sexual harassment counselors in America address young people. The media—particularly National Public Radio stations—are seconding the effort to spread the message of consent: "Consent is sexy!" In Spain, in the Extremadura region, several years ago, the socialist government introduced masturbation classes for girls and boys (age 13 and older). To make it sound truly sweet, it was titled: "Pleasure is in Your Own Hands." Sex liberated from shame can be appealing, but because it is transparent it deprives you of privacy—that is, individuality.

There is more to it, though. Consensual sexuality precludes moral evaluation, which, once again, is consistent with the liberal idea that sees one's behavior as the creative expression of one's self. If consent is all that matters when approaching sex, then there cannot be anything wrong if I have sex with seven different people in one week. Those who disapprove of my actions are guilty of being judgmental and intolerant. What is more, they prevent me from becoming self-confident. This kind of attitude backed by a psychology of self-esteem can be easily turned into political ideology, which creates semi-formal social and political structures that demand institutions stop discriminating against any kind of sexual self-expression. Those who support or participate in such movements see sexuality not as a private affair but a political program, and the state is an arm of their sexual politics, whose purpose is to defend them against "offensive" language and the judgmental attitudes of others.

Clearly our politicians, journalists, activists, educators, the Department of Education, and hundreds of institutions—whose handbook is "Title IX," and whose language is that of the politically correct orthodoxy—bought the idea too, since no other view of sexuality is even considered, and those who dare oppose it are called "bigots." But they've got it wrong on all counts: They've got it morally, emotionally, aesthetically, legally, and politically wrong. And so the question arises why no one, including those who are suspicious of the new sexual morality, asks a commonsensical question: Why do those who impose the new sexual norms think that it is the business and duty of secular institutions and the state (which, let's emphasize, has no moral authority) to propagate this view of sex, let alone teach youngsters about it?

The fact that the outrageous case of accusing six-year-old boys of sexual harassment did not make us reflect on how our approach to sexuality is wrong, or that it did not cause any changes in legislation, is proof that what hides behind new sexual politics is not anyone's protection, but the imposition of ideological rules that mean to destroy privacy and intimacy, and if it requires that six year old children be sacrificed by branding them sexual harassers or predators, so be it. It appears that it is easier for politicians to impose meatless Mondays on children in all schools in New York, as did Mayor de Blasio, than protect children from the adults' ideological insanity.

Most recently, universities started offering a phone app for students to send out alerts when one is experiencing sexual violence, *or is made in any way to feel uncomfortable*. It is not difficult to predict what will happen: The "university sexual squad" will be intervening daily, arresting male students. Such a scenario brings to mind the scene of Julia and Winston's final moment together in *1984* when the squad barges into the room to arrest them.

If you are puzzled—as you should be—as to why colleges are interested in young people's sexual lives, instead of encouraging sexual modesty or simply staying out of their private lives, leaving the matters to parents and religious institutions, here is the answer: Colleges are the Meccas of liberal ideology, and their mission is to make students think *and* act in a certain way. They neither educate them nor provide them with a truly moral vision of the world. Sexual re-education is a *part* of the project of the Great Liberal Transformation *à la* Huxley. In so doing, they destroy the young people's emotions and individuality before there is any chance to develop them during the educational process by exposure to something beautiful or sublime.

Because they politicized human sexuality, they had to invent and impose new rules and norms. Those norms make your life transparent, and transparency means there is no way to escape the state's scrutiny. No political regime in history went that far. Not even the communists, Nazis, or the fascists succeeded in appropriating the most intimate realm. The old totalitarians were not interested in citizens' sexual lives unless one slept with an ideological or state enemy. But even then, one's sexual life was of interest to the state only in so far as it could sabotage politics.

The reason why there is no serious opposition to what is happening and why the liberal ideologues succeeded thus far is twofold. First, consensual sex with "seven people a week" escapes moral evaluation because it is a form of explicit agreement to exchange pleasure for pleasure. Also, no one can be called "names" any longer nor pass judgment on what I do because I did it according to the rules of consent. Second, we have been seduced by the idea of easy sex—easy because it does not require a very complex moral, aesthetic, emotional and erotic game, like the one we find in great works of literature. Not a single student I asked in recent years has read Stendhal's *On Love, Charterhouse of Parma*, Tolstoy's *Anna Karenina*, Goethe's *Sufferings of Young Werther*, or Flaubert's *Sentimental Education*, let alone Ortega y Gasset's *On Love* and Octavio Paz's *The Double Flame: On Love and Eroticism*. Like everything else in America, even the most profound reality must be made simple.

There is *The Complete IDIOT's Guide to Amazing Sex* and *Sex for Dummies*. Both had four editions, which makes one wonder how simple the fourth edition must be compared to the first one. The eleventh edition will probably be as simple as the eleventh edition of Orwell's "Newspeak

Dictionary." The analogy is not as crazy as it may appear at first sight. The language of love, like regular language, is an expression of the way we communicate with the opposite sex, who we are as human beings, and how we relate to each other. If our love vocabulary shrinks as do the words in Orwell's Newspeak, our humanity will be robbed of what is precious, and we will begin to "engage"—as Huxley predicted.

The consequences of the new education are already visible. No one, including young people, talks about being in love, and very few new singers sing songs about love. Love is no longer in the air; Love evaporated from the atmosphere. Ask students the question and they will look at you with incredulous eyes as if you spoke to them in Arabic. Those who are in love, are most likely to be religious and see love as a path to sex at some point, but not this Friday when everyone, as in Huxley, will be doing it. Of course, it is not going to be an emotional experience followed by a conversation about being together in the future. Even at eighteen they are too cynical and emotionally destroyed to believe that they can experience what Abelard and Heloise or Tristan and Isolde did. It will be like sweating and moaning in the gym, rather than a way to form a moral bond that keeps people together. Their moral world has been destroyed by the ideology of transparency propagated by the new class of sex experts and counselors whose job it is to provide "safe spaces" for young people to satisfy their animalistic instinct.

Those who either do not see the danger of consensual sexuality, its anti-aesthetic and anti-moral dimension, and prefer it to the old rules of intimacy and privacy, should consider using consensual phone devices for protection from legal danger. It could be called Con-sex. The device has not been built yet, but such an idea is not beyond the horizon. It could use authorization passwords in the form of voice, fingerprints, or a social security number. Those who will use it may feel safe now but should be aware that Big Brother will keep the electronic record forever. One day in the future it will destroy your life.

Never before, it seems, was intimacy so dangerous. In fact, never before was being *oneself* so dangerous.

CHAPTER 7 | FROM THE BOOK OF GENESIS TO THE GULAG: A COMMENT ON ZAMYATIN AND ORWELL

> Thus the mind itself is bowed to the yoke: even in what people do for pleasure, conformity is the first thing thought of; they like in crowds; they exercise choice only among things commonly done; peculiarity of taste, eccentricity of conduct, are shunned equally with crimes: until by dint of not following their own nature, they have no more to follow: their human capacities are withered and starved: they become incapable of any strong wishes or native pleasures, and are generally without opinions or feelings of home growth, or properly their own. Now is this, or is it not, the desirable condition of human nature?

John Stuart Mill, *On Liberty*

1.

Three years before the publication of his *1984*, in a review of Yevgeny Zamyatin's *WE*, published in "Tribune," on 4th January 1946, George Orwell wrote: "It is this intuitive grasp of the irrational side of totalitarianism—human sacrifice, cruelty as an end in itself, the worship of a Leader who is credited with divine attributes—that makes Zamyatin's book superior to Huxley's." Huxley never acknowledged his debt to Zamyatin, but neither did Orwell after he published his novel. Kurt Vonnegut, speaking about his *Player's Piano* in an interview with *Playboy* Magazine, said, "I cheerfully ripped off the plot of *Brave New World*, whose plot had been cheerfully ripped off from Yevgeny Zamyatin's *WE*."

The list of similarities between and borrowings from *WE* in Huxley and Orwell could fill pages. Such pages, however interesting they might be in their own right, would almost certainly miss an important point. Given that Zamyatin's book is inferior to *Brave New World* and *1984* in its literary qualities, the question should be: What did Orwell and Huxley discover in *WE* that made them 'rewrite' the Russian author's book? A simple answer is: Zamyatin discovered two sides of totalitarianism—hard and soft—which the English writers, so to speak, split between themselves and produced works in which each shows how soft and hard totalitarianisms operate and what happens to man under each of them.

Brave New World explores Zamyatin's vision of a future "glass paradise"—a ratio-technological utopia in 2600 A.D. Orwell, on the other hand, as he states in his review, took interest in totalitarianism's dark and brutal side. Brutality and control are the premises of his *1984* totalitarian state, which also underlies *WE*.[1] There is a difference, though, between Orwell and Zamyatin. Unlike Orwell, Zamyatin made explicit (which is what makes his work important) that the ideology behind totalitarianism is anti-Christian and therefore anti-Biblical. This is what seems to be missing from both *1984* and *Brave New World*: an explanation that tells the reader how a state can become totalitarian. Neither author seems to be particularly troubled by how the totalitarian mind came about; they seem to assume that the world "is what it is," rather than worry about why it became totalitarian.

What we come to understand in reading Zamyatin is what lies only hidden below the surface of *Brave New World* and *1984*: "'We' is from God, and 'I' from the devil," writes D-503, the protagonist, in an entry of his book, that he, like Winston, writes for the future generations. His reference to God and the devil is not an off-the-cuff rhetorical device, but an explicit allusion to the Bible. And later, we find a statement that could have been written by Nietzsche: "But we anti-Christian, we..." But the "We" does not mean the simple plural form of 'we', nor is it Nietzsche's We—a race of supermen. It means the new *collective*, the new totalitarian state in which there are no more individuals, no one different from another:

1   The best collection of essays on Orwell's *1984*, to my knowledge, is *1984 Revisited*. Edited by Irving Howe. New York: Harper and Row, 1983. The essays included by Howe deal with many aspects of insights in Orwell's book. I am not aware, however, of a similar collection devoted to the analysis of Huxley's *BNW*.

But our table of Hours! Why, it transforms each one of us into a figure of steel, a six-wheeled hero of mighty epic poem. Every morning, with six-wheeled precision, at the same hour and the same moment, we—millions of us—get up as one. At the same hour, in million-headed unison, we start work; and in million headed unison we end it. And, fused into a single million-handed body, at the same second, designated by the Table, we lift our spoons to our mouths. At the same second, we come out for a walk, to the auditorium, go to the hall for Taylor exercises, fall asleep [...].

Zamyatin was not totally original either. He took the ideas for *WE* from Dostoevsky. The "glass paradise," which for Huxley is his *Brave New World*, goes back to *The Notes from the Underground*, where Dostoevsky launched a penetrating critique of rationalism, and in an almost identical form expresses what Zamyatin thought the new totalitarian "we" would be like. In chapter VII of *The Notes*, we read:

Consequently, we have only to discover these laws of nature, and man will no longer have to answer for his actions and life will become exceedingly easy for him. All human actions will then, of course, be tabulated according to these laws, mathematically, like tables of logarithms up to 108,000, and entered in an index; or, better still, there would be published certain edifying works of the nature of encyclopedic lexicons, in which everything will be so clearly calculated and explained that there will be no more incidents or adventures in the world. Then—this is all what you say—new economic relations will be established, all ready-made and worked out with mathematical exactitude, so that every possible question will vanish in the twinkling of an eye, simply because every possible answer to it will be provided. Then the "Palace of Crystal" will be built. Then [...] in fact, those will be halcyon days. Of course, there is no guaranteeing (this is my comment) that it will not be, for instance, frightfully dull then (for what will one have to do when everything will be calculated and tabulated), but on the other hand everything will be extraordinarily rational.

The juxtaposition of the two passages leaves little room for doubt that the totalitarian 'we' is a creation of Rationalism. An absolutely rational mentality is totalitarian and sick. This is what Huxley took over from Zamyatin, on which he built his utopian brave new world. What gave the Russian author the idea for calling his world "Glass paradise"—a mirror image of which is Huxley's *Brave New World*—is "Crystal Palace," to which Dostoevsky refers in the above passage, and which he talks about in his *Winter Notes of Summer Impressions*, after his visit to London. The new architectural structure symbolizes human technological progress, and the rational organization of society which one cannot but accept.[2]

However, the new age will be built in opposition to, and on the ashes of, the story of man's Fall described in the biblical Book of Genesis. The rules of rationality derived from scientific laws will replace the old, religious moral code. The new code—the enslaving precepts of science, telling man what to do, what to eat, how to act, how to think, how to 'engage' with the opposite sex (just like in *WE*), will free him from the unpleasant need to choose—from freedom. Rational decision, which is one and the same in all of 'us'—as read in the above passage—is the only decision man can make. There cannot be any doubt as to what course of action to choose because laws of nature do not allow for exceptions. Rationality and technology are the pillars on which a future glass utopia rests.

2   "Yes, the Exposition is striking. You feel a terrible force that has united a single herd; you become aware of a gigantic idea; you feel that here something has already been achieved, that here there is victory and triumph. You even begin to be afraid of something. No matter how independent you might be, for some reason you become terrified. 'Hasn't the ideal in fact been achieved here?' you think. 'Isn't this the ultimate, isn't it in fact the 'one-fold'? … You look at these hundreds of thousands, these millions of people humbly streaming here from all over the face of the earth—people who come with a single thought, peacefully, persistently, and silently crowding into this colossal palace—and you feel that here something final has been accomplished, accomplished and brought to an end. It is a kind of biblical scene, something about Babylon, a kind of prophesy from the Apocalypse fulfilled before your very eyes. You feel that it would require a great deal of eternal spiritual resistance and denial not to succumb, not to surrender to the impression, not to bow down to fact, and not to ideolize Baal, that is, not to accept what is your ideal." Chapter 5 ("Baal").

2.

In the "Legend of the Grand Inquisitor," Dostoevsky explores the same idea, but this time the justification for taking away man's freedom of choice finds a different source. The Grand Inquisitor, standing in front of the magnificent Medieval Gothic Cathedral in Sevilla, announces that man is too weak to carry the burden of freedom. According to the Inquisitor, the old world—the world which came about because of Jesus' teaching—relies on a misreading of human nature: Jesus' belief that man can and will follow the dictates of conscience. Accordingly, conscience—man's ability to discern right from wrong, and to follow its dictates—made the need for law superfluous in many respects. Yet this is not so, says the Inquisitor. What if man has no conscience? As Dostoevsky famously announced, then everything is permitted. This is the point he explores in the chapter in which Ivan Karamazov converses with the Devil.

By rejecting earthly authority and endowing man with freedom of conscience, Jesus unleashed the devilish part in human nature, which makes man follow the Devil's temptations rather than moral precepts. Accordingly, by giving man freedom, he also gave him the freedom to disregard moral rules which govern the social and political realm. In fact, Jesus allowed the Devil to claim the political domain. The Inquisitor—the representative of the New Order—is bound to correct Jesus' error.

3.

The discovery of totalitarianism deals with the problem of bringing the dark side of human nature into agreement with the requirements of a perfect society. Such perfection is possible only through ideological transformation, and that is what makes totalitarianism different from utopia. This is what both Orwell and Huxley accomplish in their respective novels. The question for both authors is the same: Does politics have a redemptive mechanism that can solve the problem of building a perfect society by using *individual*, that is *different*, human beings? In Huxley's view, the answer lies in a rational organization of society. The individuality (which is not the same as imperfection) entails private—that is, individual—desires and emotional disturbances that follow from dissatisfaction. Huxley, following Dostoevsky from the *Notes*, eliminates them by transforming irrational, individual desires into 'rational,' commonplace desires. Rationality is a filter through which our desires must pass, and once they have been sifted, they are the same in all of us. The filter of rationality turns millions of individuals into 'We.'

In the event individual desires resurface and bring about unwanted mental or emotional disturbances, the citizens of *Brave New World* take *soma*, a mood-regulating drug. By bringing people's moods to a socially desirable norm (same for all citizens), *soma* makes the population docile *and* happy.

In Orwell, on the other hand, the state extinguishes individuality—rebellious human nature—by fear and force. Its amplitude, however, is much higher greater in any previous political philosopher, including Machiavelli or Hobbes. When fear reaches its highest point, in order not to break under its pressure, the mind creates the needed conditions for accepting the official truth. However, either to minimize the use of force or to dispense with its unnecessary use, the state uses propaganda. It consists in the repetition of slogans until one's perception of reality is completely altered. Thus, slavery can mean freedom, and war can mean peace. The goal of propagandistic brainwashing is to bring about a sustained condition of hypnosis. It takes the mind captive, but also leaves it reconciled and peaceful. In such a state, there are no more contradictions, conflicting interests, desires to rebel, or, most importantly, to be an individual. Acceptance brings peace, and peace is a form of liberation of the individual from his own self, his desire to be different.

In Zamyatin, the sudden awakening of the protagonist, whose realization that he has a soul terrifies him: "But why, why suddenly a soul? I've never had one, and suddenly... Why... No one else has it, and I...?" Soul is called sickness. D-503 is cured of it at the end of the novel. He is reintegrated into the collective, just like Orwell's Smith, who comes to love Big Brother.

All the obvious differences between Huxley and Orwell notwithstanding, propaganda in *1984* is the equivalent of *BNW*'s *soma*. In both cases, man is returned to his blissful state of innocence, in which for the last time he remains in the biblical garden of Eden. All three works fall under a category which one might call *Utopia of Integration*. It brings man back to a child-like, paradisiacal freedom, to a condition preceding his knowledge of good and evil. But only in Zamyatin do we find an explanation for the need to be (re)integrated.

4.

Not long before his death, when asked about the future, Orwell quoted a sentence that he wrote and, apparently, came to like: "If you want a picture of the future, imagine a boot stamping on a human face—forever." Out of the context in which it originated, the sentence appears to be a terrifying prediction, and Orwell's personal vision of the future of mankind in general. But the vision of such a world developed against biblical soil. We find it in Zamyatin, from whom Orwell retrieved it, and to which he added an intriguing twist. In a conversation with D-503, R-13, the "versifier," says the following:

> You see [...] the ancient legend about paradise [...]. Why, it's about, about today. Yes! Just think. Those two, in paradise, were given a choice: happiness without freedom, or freedom without happiness. There was no third alternative. Those idiots chose freedom, and what came out of it? Of course, for ages afterward they longed for the chains. The chains—you understand? That's what world sorrow was about. For ages! And only we have found the way of restoring happiness [...]. No, wait, listen further! The ancient God and we—side by side, at the same table. Yes, We have helped God ultimately to conquer the devil—for it was he who had tempted men to break the ban and get a taste of ruinous freedom, he, the evil serpent. *And we, we've brought down our boot over his little head, and—cr-unch!* Now everything is fine—we have paradise again. Again, we are as innocent and simple-hearted as Adam and Eve. No more of that confusion about good and evil. Everything is simple—heavenly, childishly simple. The Benefactor, the Machine, the Cube, the Gas Bell, the Guardians—all this is good, all this is sublime, magnificent, noble, elevated, crystally pure. Because it protects our unfreedom—that is, our happiness. The ancients would begin to talk and think and break their heads—ethical, unethical [...]. Well, then. In short, what about such paradisiac poem, eh? And of course, in the most serious tone [...]. You understand? Quite something, eh?

In a perverse way, the trampling on another man's face means to be on the side of God, to sit at the same table with him. Once again, Zamyatin's idea has a precedent in Dostoevsky, in his "Legend of the Grand Inquisitor." The Legend is an imaginary monologue of the Grand Inquisitor—the highest representative of the Catholic Church—who challenges Jesus, who has come for the second time. The Inquisitor points out that, contrary to what Jesus taught man centuries ago,

> Nothing has ever been more insupportable for a man and a human society than freedom. [...] They will be convinced, too, that they can never be free, for they are weak, vicious, worthless and rebellious. Thou didst promise them the bread of Heaven, but, I repeat again, can it compare it with earthly bread in the eyes of the weak, ever sinful and ignoble race of man? And if for the sake of the bread of Heaven thousands and tens of thousands shall follow Thee, what is to become of the millions and tens of thousands of millions of creatures who will not have the strength to forgo the earthly bread for the sake of the great and strong. [...] No, we care for the weak too. They are sinful and rebellious, but in the end they will become obedient. They will marvel at us and look on us as gods, because we are ready to endure the freedom which they have found so dreadful and to rule over them—so awful it will seem to them to be free. But we shall tell them that we are thy servants and rule them in Thy name [...]. There are three powers, three powers alone, able to conquer and to hold captive forever the conscience of these impotent rebels for their happiness—these forces are miracle, mystery and authority. Thou hast rejected all three [...].

The Grand Inquisitor is many things. He is a political realist who understands that the Church, in so far as it is also an earthly institution, must combine Caesar's power and spiritual might. Caesaro-papism, as this mix is called, is not in his eyes a matter of choice, but necessity. He points out that a hungry man is oblivious to spiritual values. In fact, he has no need for them. Only a few men do. He is weak and, if he is hungry, he will lay down his freedom—freedom to live by conscience—in exchange for a loaf of earthly bread. The Grand Inquisitor is an 'earthly organizer'—the baker of earthly bread. This interpreter and official guardian of Jesus' own doctrine, ironically, feels forced to explain to Jesus that, contrary to his own teaching that "man does not live by bread alone," man does not live by conscience or freedom alone. In so far as man inhabits the earth, he values bread more than he values freedom. The task of politics is not to make a man free, but to make bread to keep order, to keep man happy. Jesus, on the other hand, rejected the Old Law in favor of a Christian spiritual 'bakery' that claims love to be sufficient to sustain social order.

But above all, the Grand Inquisitor is Jesus' nemesis. He is a devil himself, the same devil who spoke to Jesus in the New Testament.

> I don't want Thy love, for I love Thee not. And what use is it for me to hide anything from Thee? Don't I know to Whom I am speaking? All that I can say is known to Thee already. And is it for me to conceal from Thee our mystery? Perhaps it is Thy will to hear it from my lips. Listen then. We are not working with Thee, but with him—that is our mystery.

The Devil/Inquisitor is the first totalitarian who not only wants man's total obedience, but claims that the only political arrangement is one in which man abdicates his right to be free and that Christian moral principles do not apply to politics.[3] Freedom was never originally a divine gift, rather it was the Devil's, and so depriving man of freedom now appears to be done according to God's will. "We"—that is, the state with its Thought Police or the Guardians, the Benefactor or Big Brother or the Controller Mustapha Mond—are God. God created man unfree but happy. So now,

3 See a very interesting article by Leszek Kołakowski, "Politics and the Devil," in *Modernity on Endless Trial* (Chicago: The University of Chicago Press, 1990, pp. 175–90.) See also an interesting conversation about the devil in politics in George Urban in a conversation with L. Kołakowski, "Devil in History," in *Encounter*, January 1981. Republished in George Urban, *Stalin and Stalinism: Its Impact on History and the World* (Cambridge: Harvard University Press, 1982), and Leszek Kołakowski, *My Correct Views on Everything* (South Bend: St. Augustine's Press, 2004).

after centuries of pain, labor and exile from paradise, 'We' offers him happiness (in exchange for his freedom). One cannot be happy and free at the same time. This is the message of all four authors: Huxley, Orwell, Zamyatin, and Dostoevsky. Not surprisingly, both Huxley and Orwell's novels imitate the structure of the "Legend," in which their Grand Inquisitors, each in his own voice, explain to their interlocutors—the rebels—what Dostoevsky's Grand Inquisitor explained to Jesus: One cannot be free and happy.

In his tirade in which he explains the problem of social organization to Winston, O'Brian admonishes: "Winston don't be stupid." His words bring to mind the Grand Inquisitor's irritation with Jesus, who did not understand that man's nature must be restrained. Like the Grand Inquisitor, O'Brian is not disturbed by the evil of what he is doing to Smith because he does not have a conscience. Mustapha Mond, in the final chapters (XVII and XVIII) of *Brave New World*, implies the same. His interlocutors—Bernard, Helmholtz and John Savage—like Jesus, miss the point. The Controller explains patiently and in considerable detail to them how the new world works, including the fact that scientific progress had to be arrested as well. Deception is the Inquisitor's noble lie. Analyzing these works from a structural point of view, both Huxley and Orwell end their novels with a remake of the Grand Inquisitor's explanation—rewritten according to the logical demands of each author's version of totalitarianism—for why the rebellion must be extinguished by the earthly authority. Let me quote a few passages here.

Orwell:
"We are not like that [the Nazis, the Russian Communists]," says O'Brian. "We know that no one ever seizes power with the intention of relinquishing it. Power is not a means; it is an end. One does not establish dictatorship to safeguard a revolution; one makes a revolution in order to establish the dictatorship. The object of persecution is persecution. The object of torture is torture. The object of power is power [...]. And remember that it is forever. The face will always be there to be stamped upon. The heretic, the enemy of society, will always be there, so that he can be defeated and humiliated again."

Huxley:

"What?" said Helmholtz, in astonishment. "But we're always saying that science is everything [...]."

"Yes; but what sort of science?" asked Mustapha Mond sarcastically. "You've had no scientific training, so you can't judge." I was a pretty good physicist in my time. Too good—good enough to realize that all our science is just a cookery book, with an orthodox theory of cooking that nobody is allowed to question, and a list of recipes that mustn't be added to except by special permission from the head cook. I'm the head cook now [...]."

"Why don't you let them see *Othello* instead?"

"I've told you; it's old. Besides, they couldn't understand it."

Yes, that was true. He remembered how Helmholtz had laughed at *Romeo and Juliet.* "Well then," he said, after a pause, "something new that's like *Othello*, and that they could understand."

"That's what we've all been waiting to write," said Helmholtz, breaking a long silence.

"And it's what you will never write," said the Controller.

"Because, if it were really like *Othello* nobody could understand it, however new it might be. And if it were new, it couldn't be like *Othello*."

"Why not?"

"Yes, why not?" Helmholtz repeated. [...]

"Because our world is not the same as Othello's world. You can't make flivvers without steel—and you can't make tragedies without social instability. The world is stable now. People are happy [...]."

5.

If we bear in mind the Christian dimension of Dostoevsky's "Legend" and apply it to Orwell and Huxley, in whose works religion is not even mentioned, we realize that both forms of totalitarianism—hard and soft— were born out of an anti-Christian rebellion and must be understood as such.[4] The new, post-Christian political vision does not merely consist in a simple replacement of one worldview by another, but in introducing a totalitarian vision in lieu of a religious view of politics. To be sure, Christianity may have a problem of explaining how politics can be Christian, but the Christian moral code for centuries introduced an important corrective to politics—the perspective from which one could pass judgment on the world. Whatever the critics may say, this vision made societies gentler, less cruel, and more humane. All pre-Christian societies—it is enough to think of Greece and Rome—were based on cruelty unimaginable to us today, and it is thanks to Christian teaching that human relations softened, adopting a more merciful character.[5] It may have taken Christianity centuries to live up to what it preached, but it was hardly Christianity's fault. Totalitarian politics does not provide for such a corrective.

6.

In each novel, anti-Christianity triumphs and must triumph, either through the use of brutal force to "crunch" rebellious human nature, the 'devil' in us as in Orwell, or by sedation in the form of *soma*. In Huxley, there is the promise of material security and comfort that turns a society into a collection of idiots who believe they are free because they make rational choices. In Dostoevsky's "Legend," this triumph assumes the form of a noble lie about a future reward in Heaven in exchange for happiness.

> Too, too well they know the value of complete submission. [...]
> They will marvel at us and will be awe-stricken before us, and

---

4   Huxley was more than aware of his debt to Dostoevsky. The last two pages of his *Brave New World Revisited* end with his rewrite of Dostoevsky's "Legend" in the contemporary language of democracy.

5   One can point in this context to the popular idea of "social justice" and dignity of man that today's secular reformers use daily. In the economic realm, the former goes back to the end of the 19th century. It was expounded with full force by Pope Leo XIII in his papal encyclical *Rerum Novarum* (May 15, 1891). The notion of human dignity goes back to the Italian Humanist Pico della Mirandola's *De hominis dignitate* (*Oration on the Dignity of Man*), 1486, published in 1496.

will be proud at our being so powerful and clever, that we have been able to subdue such turbulent flock of thousands of millions. They will tremble impotently before our wrath, their minds will grow fearful, they will be quick to shed tears like women and children, but they will be just as ready at a sign from us to pass to laughter and rejoicing, to happy mirth and childish song. Yes, we shall set them to work, but in their leisure hours we shall make them like a child's game, with children's song and innocent dance. Oh, we shall allow them even sin, they are weak and helpless, and they will love us like children because we allow them to sin. We shall tell them that every sin will be expiated, if it is done with our permission, that we allow them to sin because we love them, and the punishment for these since we take upon ourselves. [...] There will be thousands of millions of happy babes, and a hundred thousand sufferers too, who have taken upon themselves the curse of the knowledge of good and evil. Peacefully they will die, peacefully they will expire in Thy name, and beyond the grave they will find nothing but death.

Dostoevsky predicted what a totalitarian state will require, and in this sense, he went further than any political philosopher before him. Hobbes' *Leviathan* is sometimes thought of (as Alexander Solzhenitsyn argued in his "Harvard Address") as a prototype of an all-powerful or totalitarian state. This is hardly the case. His *Leviathan* is not a totalitarian utopia, but a place where political realism plays itself out. The Hobbesian man is by nature amoral: He does not have an inborn sense of right and wrong. He recognizes what is "right and wrong" only as part of his political life, when he left the state of Nature. In so far as the Hobbesian man can be turned into *zoon politikon*, his first lesson of political existence is to teach him to recognize the punitive character of the law. The law in Hobbes does not contain any intrinsic component of good or evil. Good is only 'good,' and evil is only 'evil.' They are not moral, but political categories, more or less like the traffic rules which make 'political traffic' possible.

If *Leviathan* is oppressive, it is only because Hobbes allowed it to amass considerable power to keep the desired level of order to prevent violence and anarchy. But its power is not totalitarian because it does not need to be. All Hobbes wants for his state is enough power to curb man's violent nature. The Hobbesian Leviathan does not use fear as a means to 'integrate' man into the collective for the sake of bringing about a more perfect or utopian society; nor does a Leviathan care about how well 'integrated' he is, as long as he displays *external* signs of conformity. At minimum, fear of the laws is what is necessary to make political life possible; at maximum, a certain amount of fear is what makes citizens obey the rulers.

Dostoevsky was not a political philosopher, but an ingenious writer and thinker who discovered that the essence of totalitarianism lies in violation of conscience. His discovery goes beyond a simple realization that the state, in order to make man social and curb his violent nature, must amass considerable power to maintain order. Hobbesian Leviathan, as I said, is powerful, but not totalitarian. Dostoevsky understood *why* the new state has to amass more power than any before. He grasped that to claim man's soul the state must destroy his conscience—that is, the entirety of man's social, political, and *private* existence. There is no private life in a totalitarian state, and lack of privacy is a sign that the state—whatever we believe it is—is totalitarian. But would a man who does not know what privacy is, know that he has no privacy, no soul? It is a devil's trick. Dostoevsky knew it when he wrote the conversation between the Devil and Ivan, the former making the latter believe anything he wanted.[6] If the state, like Dostoevsky's devil, can enter your mind, be it through fear or rational organization of your life, as in *WE*, totalitarianism triumphs.

The problem raised in the "Legend"—and indirectly in Zamyatin, Huxley, and Orwell—is absolutely unique, but its uniqueness can be fully appreciated only if we remember that it is built on the Devil's script—the conversation between Jesus and the Devil, which we find in the New

6   The ideological mind manipulation—wherein two contradictory statements can be reconciled—is very well described by Leszek Kołakowski in his story about a guide in the Hermitage museum, who, on two separate occasions pronounced two lies, believing in the truth of what he said each time. See his "Totalitarianism and the Virtue of a Lie," in *My Correct Views on Everything*. *Ibid.*, pp. 66–76. See also his "From Truth to Truth," and "Why an Ideology Is Always Right," in *Modernity on Endless Trial*.

Testament Gospels.[7] If totalitarianism is the Devil's work—regardless of whether it manifests itself as a boot trampling on a human face, the Surgeon General's dietary recommendation, the UN ban on trans fats, secular social activists' claim that men and women are "social constructs," or similar absurdities—resistance is unlikely to succeed unless we rekindle the spirit of biblical religion. Upholding the Judeo-Christian values of our civilization does not mean, as some secular activists would like the public to believe, going back to persecutions, bone-breaking beat-downs, and burning witches at the stake. As things stand, it is sanity and individual conscience—not Galileo—that are at stake.

7   Matthew 4:1–11: "Then Jesus was led up by the Spirit into the wilderness to be tempted by the devil. And after He had fasted forty days and forty nights, He then became hungry. And the tempter came and said to Him, 'If You are the Son of God, command that these stones become bread.' But He answered and said, 'It is written, MAN SHALL NOT LIVE ON BREAD ALONE, BUT ON EVERY WORD THAT PROCEEDS OUT OF THE MOUTH OF GOD.' Then the devil took Him into the holy city and had Him stand on the pinnacle of the temple, and said to Him, 'If You are the Son of God, throw Yourself down; for it is written, HE WILL COMMAND HIS ANGELS CONCERNING YOU; and ON THEIR HANDS THEY WILL BEAR YOU UP, SO THAT YOU WILL NOT STRIKE YOUR FOOT AGAINST A STONE.' Jesus said to him, 'On the other hand, it is written, YOU SHALL NOT PUT THE LORD YOUR GOD TO THE TEST.' Again, the devil took Him to a very high mountain and showed Him all the kingdoms of the world and their glory; and he said to Him, 'All these things I will give You, if You fall down and worship me.' Then Jesus said to him, 'Go, Satan! For it is written, YOU SHALL WORSHIP THE LORD YOUR GOD, AND SERVE HIM ONLY.' Then the devil left Him; and behold, angels came and began to minister to Him." Cf. Luke 4:1–13.

CHAPTER 8 | ORIGINS OF TOTALITARIANISM: FROM DOSTOEVSKY TO HUXLEY, ELLUL AND FROMM

> But I repeat for the hundredth time, there is one case, one only, when man may consciously, purposely, desire what is injurious to himself, what is stupid, very stupid—simply in order to have the right to desire for himself even what is very stupid and not to be bound by an obligation to desire only what is sensible. Of course, this very stupid thing, this caprice of ours, may be in reality, gentlemen, more advantageous for us than anything else on earth, especially in certain cases. And in particular it may be more advantageous than any advantage even when it does us obvious harm, and contradicts the soundest conclusions of our reason concerning our advantage—for in any circumstance it preserves for us what is most precious and most important—that is, our personality, our individuality.

> Dostoevsky, *Notes from the Underground*

1.

There is a straight line from Fyodor Dostoevsky's prophesies in *The Notes from the Underground* (1864) about the danger of scientific rationalism in man's understanding of himself to Aldous Huxley's *Brave New World* (1931), Jacques Ellul's *The Technological Society* (1954) and to Erich Fromm's *A Revolution of Hope: Toward a Humanized Technology* (1968): Each sends us a warning how rationalism can turn a healthy human psyche into a schizophrenic public mind. All of these authors are concerned with the question of the relationship between science and the resulting ascendance of the new totalitarianism. All four authors are in agreement that the new version of it is not going to be the brutal and explicitly ideological system that we know from the past, but a mind-enslaving, scientific thinking that can destroy the human psyche. Huxley's *Brave New World* is a mind-boggling approximation of what sort of world a purely rational organization of society must produce. However ingenious, his novel merely explores Dostoevsky's insight about the danger of elevating reason to the position of highest authority.

Huxley explores the idea that links happiness and reason which goes back to the Enlightenment and its philosophy of rationalism, heralded and welcomed by virtually every major thinker of the epoch, including Immanuel Kant. Kant saw the Enlightenment as the dawn of mankind, the moment when man left a state of infancy, when irrational and superstitious religious beliefs finally gave way to reason that might serve as ultimate guide to social and political organization. Naturally, the philosophy of history became a popular and powerful branch of study which teaches man about his own historical growth. Hegel, Thomas Buckle (with whose conception of history Dostoevsky spars in his *Notes*), Marx, Mill, and others, created grand historical narratives that present history as a highway on which man drives higher and higher to reach ever newer levels of rationality. As he progresses, he is also leaving behind his bloodthirsty nature and irrational impulses. The man who emerges from this historical process is rational, and as history is still in the making one can expect that in the near future his irrational desires will altogether disappear. The end of history will be a triumph of reason.

Many found this appealing. For instance, John Stuart Mill, who published his essay *On Liberty* the same year Dostoevsky published his *Notes*, recognized representative government to be a fitting form of political organization only for a rational and civilized man who has lost the desire for spilling blood, and who can listen to a reasoned argument without resorting to force. Despotism, as he famously remarked, is a legitimate way of governing barbarians.

One might wonder, how far can one travel on the highway of rationality? As Dostoevsky suggested in his *Notes*, the road ends exactly where *Brave New World* begins:

> We have only to discover these laws of nature [...] life will become exceedingly easy for him. All human actions will then, of course, be tabulated according to these laws, mathematically, like tables of logarithms up to 108,000, and entered in an index [...] men still are men and not the keys of a piano, which the laws of nature threaten to control so completely that soon one

will be able to desire nothing but by the calendar [...] he will at once be transformed from a human being into an organ-stop or something of the sort; for what is a man without desires, without free will and without choice, if not a stop in an organ?

However, since no man would knowingly abandon freedom to become "a stop in an organ," as Dostoevsky calls him, one had to create for man a powerful illusion of freedom. This illusion required that man remain convinced that his choices stem from *his* desires, and that his desires are rational. It was the Devil's trick, and today's America is a case in point.

Our daily slogans are: "A new study shows" or "new research says." And since 'study' and 'research' have the flair of scientific objectivity, it follows that in so far as I am a rational person, I should live my life according to the new study or research, which says that what is good for others is good for me too. For example, I may have never had a desire to drink green tea, but now under the influence of new research, shown on national news as propaganda cloaked in scientific objectivity, I develop a desire to drink green tea. Similarly, even though I never drank red wine after dinner, now, after reading a Surgeon General announcement that red wine dissolves fat from the meal I just ate, I develop a desire to have a glass of red wine after dinner. It works just like a piece of syllogistic thinking: "What is good for man is good for me because I am a man." Such a scientific formula translates "what I want" into "what I ought to want."

Today's America, the country in which science took hold of the population's collective mind, is a fulfillment of the Russian author's prophesies, and Huxley's vision. All restaurants in America are required by law to have a list stating the number of calories in each meal. The same goes for virtually every other product in a grocery store, from a bagel to mineral water. All products carry labels with a list of chemicals and calories contained therein. Comprehending them without a degree in nutrition is impossible, and the only way to compensate for the lack of knowledge is to listen to the people who are competent enough to tell you what to eat and drink, as well as what to avoid. Mass media—television, radio, newspapers (or the internet, which reproduces such articles)—plays such a role, and as new research trickles down to the public, it becomes a caricature of the original and introduces ever more confusion into our eating and living habits. And as science progresses almost daily, so, too, do recommendations and warnings change, and with each announcement we update official public policy. Such announcements do not have any legal force, but often become a *de facto* policy which governs our lives. The recently introduced "meatless Mondays" in California and all New York City schools and bans on certain products (as in the announcement of World Health Organization to ban trans-fats all over the world by 2024) are the outcome of the way of thinking that Dostoevsky predicted would pave the way to a totalitarian Brave New World.

The campaign against meat started a decade ago and was limited to red meat only. We were told not to eat it more than once a week. The choice was left to us. Within a decade, we moved from red meat to all kinds of meat, and we moved from recommendations to interdictions—presently we prohibit ourselves from eating meat once a week. The same goes for fats and other products. We are moving from recommendations to interdictions. For example, smokers of today are looked upon as if they were lepers, and it is not the proximity to someone who smokes that causes a reaction among non-smokers, but his very existence. It is not the smoke that people run away from, but the undesirable habit, which is no longer a reaction of the body, but of the mind, now intolerant of the existence of someone who dares not to cultivate scientifically or rationally shaped habits. In a decade, the meat eaters will be looked upon the same way, just like two decades ago women who wore fur coats had to be careful that no one would splash paint on them. One can be quite sure that vegetarianism is the way of the future, provided that no "new study" disproves the former study. If this happens, we will have a massive social movement composed of the very same people who advocated vegetarianism, but the opposite direction.

All this makes Dostoevsky's predictions and Huxley's description of the new world rather frightening. Our desires, and the choices that stem from them, have been socialized and turned into politics through public policy recommendations. Each year America looks more and more like Brave New World, and Americans who live and think according to strictly rational precepts look like the characters we find there. Huxley's novel is no longer a warning or a description of a *future* society, but describes the one in which we live. It is a world in which individual choices, traditional norms and rules of acting have been destroyed in the name of scientific rationality. It is also a world in which real people, like Huxley's characters, are devoid of passions, feelings, and common sense. As Dostoevsky predicted, everyone who would think otherwise, who would stick to the old ways, is decried as "obscurantist" and "mad," like John Savage, raised in the reservation, which is the world of old values and habits.

It would be a mistake to believe that what Dostoevsky saw was simply a conflict between the old and new, between reason on the one hand and tradition and a religious world view on the other. On a more fundamental level the conflict is about man's soul, individuality, freedom and moral responsibility, as opposed to his enslavement to the promise of happiness. Dostoevsky writes:

> You see, gentlemen, reason is an excellent thing, there's no disputing that, but reason is nothing but reason and satisfies only the rational side of man's nature, while will is a manifestation of the whole life, that is, of the whole human life including reason and all the impulses. And although our life, in this manifestation of it, is often worthless, yet it is life and not simply extracting square roots. Here I, for instance, quite naturally want to live, in order to satisfy all my capacities for life, and not simply my capacity for reasoning, that is, not simply one twentieth of my capacity for life.

No literary text, however imaginative, can do justice to the real human experience. There is a difference between a real person deprived of emotional life and a character in a novel who acts according to reason only. Such characters, as in Huxley's novel, may act a bit like human robots, and, as characters, they might even be interesting and occasionally amusing. In real life, however, taking *soma* (a drug which induces happiness by making us oblivious to problems around us) would produce a society of hallucinatory drug-addicts, who think the world is beautiful, but are unable to function in professional, social and private settings. Depriving a real person of emotions, on the other hand, would not result in the increased level of rationality which in theory could make one's choices and actions better calibrated. Rather, it would turn a healthy human being into a schizophrenic, or a depressed paranoiac.

This is how Erich Fromm saw it in 1968. Commenting on Pascal's

famous remark—"Le Coeur a ses raison que la raison ne connait point"—
Fromm writes:

> Reason flows from the blending of rational thought and feeling.
> If the two functions are torn apart, thinking deteriorates into
> schizoid intellectual activity, and feeling deteriorates into neu-
> rotic life-damaging passions. The split between thought and af-
> fect leads to sickness, to a low-grade chronic schizophrenia,
> from which the new man of the technetronic age begins to suf-
> fer. [...] Paranoid thinking is characterized by the fact that it
> can be completely logical, yet lack any guidance by concern or
> concrete inquiry into reality; in other words, logic does not ex-
> clude madness [...].

And, in an even more telling passage, he states:

> Schizophrenia, like any other psychotic state, must be defined
> not only in psychiatric terms but also in social terms. Schizo-
> phrenic experience beyond a certain threshold would be consid-
> ered as sickness in any society, since those suffering from it would
> be unable to function under any social circumstances... But
> there are low-grade chronic forms of psychoses which can be
> shared by millions of people and which—precisely because they
> do not go beyond a certain threshold—do not prevent these peo-
> ple from functioning socially. As long as they share their sickness
> with millions of others, they have the satisfactory feeling of not
> being alone; in other words, they avoid that sense of complete
> isolation so characteristic of full-fledged psychosis. On the con-
> trary, they look at themselves as normal and those who have not
> lost the link between heart and mind as being crazy.

Observing the behavior of millions of Americans, fifty years after what
Fromm predicted would happen, one cannot resist the feeling that we are
living in a society which displays all the symptoms of low-grade schizophrenic behavior. More than 240 million Americans are on some kind of
mood-regulating medication, such as Prozac (today's *soma*). This is an

overwhelming majority of American society. Though Prozac may have solved the problem of daily personal anxiety, it has not eliminated the fear that this society believes to be daily threatened by.

Fear drives much of today's legislation in the form of regulations and institutional norms. Its goal is to provide "safety" from undesirable behaviors, thoughts, and habits. Undesirable behavior is slowly turning into criminal behavior. By insisting that institutions protect us against what we fear, the majority displays considerable paranoia. Looking at a woman for several seconds in an elevator can cause one to be accused of harassment, which might lead to one's termination from employment. Examples like this are endless and trivial, but indubitably point to paranoia. Paranoia is becoming the driving force of American totalitarianism.

For example, obsession with physical health, or mental hygiene in the form of being free from prejudices and biases, using the state apparatus to go after so-called "hate" speech, and the perception of mortal danger in simple habits (like smoking and eating meat) that the majority has either abandoned or consider threatening: such neurotic behavior now takes place on a large-scale. The American Psychological Association recently added a new term to its dictionary: eco-anxiety. It concerns the anxiety over climate change. Those who suffer from eco-anxiety launch social mobilization projects—for example, "environmental justice." The term itself is devoid of logical sense, but a paranoid mind acts according to its own logic. Such projects, which mobilize millions of people and school walk-outs, are reminiscent of medieval chiliastic movements announcing the end of the world.

Erich Fromm opens *The Revolution of Hope* with a quotation from Zbigniew Brzezinski's article "The Technetronic Society," (*Encounter*, vol. 38, no. 1, January 1968) wherein the author notices that "the largely humanist-oriented, occasionally ideologically-minded intellectual dissenter [...] is rapidly being displaced either by experts and specialists [...] or by the generalists-integrators, who become in effect house-ideologues for those in power, providing overall intellectual integration for disparate actions." The idea of a class of people—intellectual, ideological, or managerial—later became a powerful explanatory hypothesis in sociology for how to understand social and political processes. Whether one thought it desirable or not that there are groups of people negotiating society's interests "behind society's back," one must admit that the managers or house-ideologues are serious people, professionals who provide social stability for its own sake. What we are observing today is something very different.

There is a new class of people and politicians with a child-like mentality.[1] They rose to prominence not by knowledge, managerial skills, or particular insight into anything. The new social activists are the professional, ideological fear-mongers, who, as is apparent from their frequent pronouncements, suffer from the newly identified psychological disorder—namely, eco-anxiety. They are afraid of eco-death more than the thought of plunging the whole world into total chaos (even within the decade) by eliminating technology and financial services. They have neither knowledge of science, nor any plan to transform the world beneficially. They are producers of slogans that create and nurture ideological minds.

2.

Mass, group, or herd behavior is not new, and was described by sociologists (Weber, Read, Ortega y Gasset), psychologists (Freud, Le Bon, Fromm, Jung), and thinkers alike (Mill, Nietzsche, and Arnold). What is new, however, is a *totalitarian twist* in the behavior of the democratic masses. Thucydides, Plato, Plutarch, and Tocqueville linked the tyrannical behavior of the masses specifically with democracy. But tyranny of the majority is not the same as totalitarianism. Tyranny can be exercised for the purpose of *ad hoc* gains without any unifying idea in mind. The examples that I used above to illustrate my point give evidence that a certain frame of mind is requisite for acting in a specific way. But more is required to create a totalitarian mind. An ideology is needed.

In discussing the operations of democratic totalitarianism in relation to *techne*, Jacques Ellul makes a number of insightful observations. First, he distinguishes between the old-style totalitarianism, which was brutal,

---

1   A new member of Congress, 28-year-old Alexandria Ocasio-Cortez, has been dominating the news in America ever since she was elected to Congress. She proposed what is called the "Green New Deal." No one, interestingly enough, decried her as insane. On September 18, a 15-year old Swedish girl testified before the Congress of the United States, regarding the very matter of climate change. So did a Canadian teenager. What U.S. Congress expected to learn from listening to teenagers is unclear, but the fact that it invited them reveals the real driving force in a democracy and the danger of it.

immoderate, deformed, and broke everything in its path, and which was no more than "a battleground of armed bullies and factions." These characteristics "represented transient traits, not real characteristics of the totalitarian state. It might even be said that they were the human aspects of the state in its inhumanity. Torture and excesses are the acts of persons who use them as a means of releasing a suppressed need for power." Those aspects, however unpleasant, are not representative of "the true face of the completely technical, totalitarian state." Ellul can afford dismissing acts of brutality, even if they are responsible for the deaths of millions of people, because he is interested in getting to the very core of rational totalitarianism. From a purely rational perspective, "torture is a wasteful expenditure of psychic energy which destroys salvageable resources without producing useful results." Thus, "the arbitrary represents the very opposite of technique, in which everything 'has a reason' (not a final but a mechanical reason)."

Although Ellul does not say this, his reasoning implies that rational totalitarianism is a form in which the irrational cannot be tolerated, and thus irrationality must be eliminated and done away with. It is a totalitarianism without emotions, and since emotions belong to individuals—be it Stalin, Hitler, Mussolini or Mao—new, technological totalitarianism has no need for individual leaders. It is impersonal, and operates on the basis of accepted rational assumptions, of which technical efficiency in organizing a society is the only goal.

Ellul's second point is this:

> The totalitarian state does not need necessarily to have totalitarian theories, nor does it necessarily even desire them. On the contrary, what we call totalitarian doctrines litter up the clear line of the technical state with aberrant elements such as 'race,' 'blood,' 'proletariat.' The technical state is the technical state only because it exploits certain technical means. There is, however, a great difference between the democracies and the so-called totalitarian states. All are following the same road, but dictatorial states have become conscious of the possibilities of exploiting technique. They know and consciously desire whatever advantage can be drawn from it. The rule, for them, is to use means without limitation of any sort. The democratic states,

on the other hand, have not attained to this consciousness and are consequently inhibited [...].

And, in conclusion of his reasoning, Ellul writes: "In order to force the democratic state to come to any decision there must always be a 'present danger,' some direct competition with the dictatorial state, in which action becomes a matter of life or death. Democracy has no choice in the matter: either it utilizes technique in the same way as the enemy, or it will perish."

It would be difficult today to accept Ellul's thesis that totalitarian tendencies in democracy are a byproduct of its confrontation with an external enemy. The opposite is the case. The disappearance of the enemy—the Soviet Empire—in 1989 did not weaken democracy's totalitarian drive; on the contrary, it made it stronger. However, Ellul's misreading of the nature of democracy can be explained. When he published his book in 1954, communism was considered to be an *ideological* force and a socialist state was the embodiment of the idea conceived in Marx's mind. Liberal democracies, on the other hand, were seen as normal, benign, value-neutral and, above all, non-ideological societies. Democracy did not have the founding fathers, sacred scrolls on which democratic philosophy was written; neither was the democratic state considered to be the guardian of an ideological order.

However, as the example of today's America shows, an ideology can grow and spread without the presence of an external enemy. All that was needed was, as Dostoevsky predicted, the conviction that we discovered a way of life that is universally valid and advantageous not just for me but for everyone else. Rationalism met this criterion. By the middle of the 19th century, Rationalism was no longer a philosophical current, or a scientific methodology, but was becoming a way of life. To be rational meant to act according to scientific precepts that are binding on all rational human beings. However, when one person's way of thinking and acting is replicated in millions of individuals, who each see the same thing as advantageous or harmful, we can expect that these millions will demand that the state act as a rational agent, the organizer of the life of millions of people, and fight those who do not. They are enemies—the enemies of those who act rationally!

Adherence to something that we consider advantageous may be as strong as (or stronger than) an ideology imposed directly from above, by the party or the state. Once this happens, there is no need for the Two Minutes

Hate and artificially concocted enemies against whom everyone's emotions are directed, as featured in Orwell's novels. An idea that millions of individuals believe by their own volition, which is the last act of free will, works like a social glue. The enemy is no longer a person or another state; it is an undesirable habit that is perceived as a threat to the collective. Only in a situation in which fear makes an individual run away from freedom in the direction of the collective, which serves as a gravitational center, can an enslaved individual see himself as free.

A way of thinking can be turned into a way of acting, as in the formation of a habit. Learning that eating certain foods is advantageous to me turns into a habit of eating such foods, and scientific support for my choice, assures me that I act to my advantage, and everyone else who does not acts contrary to *rational* precepts and his own advantage. However, since my choice is not my natural predilection, but rational, there is a high degree of probability that others who are rational will also develop the same habits and consume the same food, too. Following recommendations, an individual is convinced that he is free, since he chose what he ought to eat. Thus, what is rational is ethical, and what is ethical is good for me and everyone else. This kind of social ethics can replace religion, moral codes, metaphysical speculations on the nature of right and wrong, and philosophy as the reason-based way of justifying our moral choices. This is exactly what we find in Huxley's future world: Now, you swallow two or three half-gram tablets and you can be virtuous. Socio-political slogans are "at least half your morality about in a bottle."

The same reasoning is, of course, repeated by millions of others, whose choices coincide with mine. But the process does not end with my choosing what is "good for me." I no longer merely eat what I believe to be good for me, but I fight others' decisions to eat unhealthy foods. What started as an individual decision becomes a collective mission to abolish all that is perceived as a threat to the collective. It is not easy to find a single explanation for why this is, but given the fact that it is no longer a fight over my doing or not doing something, but an ideological battle, one can say that my "unhealthy habits" pose an ideological challenge to the collective's way of life.

Once an idea gains acceptance and followers, it starts operating on its own, growing like a cell, becoming bigger and bigger. If it grows big enough, that is, when it gains critical mass in the form of millions of followers, the collective decides what "socially acceptable behavior" is, and it starts using all available methods of growth—law, regulations, education, propaganda, media and public intimidation—to grow larger. In doing so, the collective feeds its awareness by creating its own sense of right and wrong. It is this sense of its own ethical or moral code that creates its own awareness. It is an ideological self-awareness. The process of self-feeding gives the collective a perception of strength which it previously did not have. Freedom of voicing different views is allowed only so long as the majority is undecided, but once the decision has been reached, as Tocqueville noticed, "everybody is silent."

One should not be at all surprised at the state of mass media, which evolved from traditionally being the third party—and in this role defending freedom of speech, and imposing brakes on the government by calling it out. However, since the election of Mr. Donald Trump to the presidency, we see the opposite. The government, in the person of Mr. Trump, is calling out the media's lies. The fury this causes is due partly, in my opinion, to the fact that Trump's policies slowed down or derailed progressive policies that were feeding the liberal-democratic Leviathan for decades. Mr. Trump became an affront to the progressive majority's sense of peace and self-awareness, a seemingly monstrous animal that devours everything in sight.

The panicky reaction of the *New York Times, Washington Post, CNN, MSNBC,* and *NPR* show that not a single piece of news can be presented without an admixture of ideology. Reading and watching these outlets, one gets the impression that the old-fashioned, cynical method of manipulating the public (for political reasons or monetary gains) gave way to ideological thinking, which says that the news consists only of what serves the Cause, not the Truth. This is the very essence of the ideological mind. In convincing oneself of the truth of one's own position, one naturally deems and declares every other position invalid. In this way, a conflict of competing visions (each of which contains some truth) disappears. At this point, media consists of feeding the public with outright lies and accusations against the opponents.

The collective's growth is spontaneous, and does not happen from the top, but from the bottom at the grass-roots level. It is not a high-brow speculative philosophical system, like Marxism, but a common man's philosophy whose concerns, as Tocqueville noted, are mundane. It does so either through *ad hoc* propaganda, in the form of commercial or semi-commercial advertisement, through which it gains new followers. The result, over time, is uniformity of physical and mental habits. Among the most popular in recent decades, which border on obsessiveness, are eating (so-called) "healthy food" and "working out." In the mental realm, this creates the habit of not using "offensive language," and "being open," "being tolerant of others," and not being anything that might merit the label of "deplorable."

The above habits are characteristic of today's America. Once the critical mass of people supporting certain habits is present, the habits of the collective become unofficial law, and are enforced by the augmented political power of the collective in the form of regulations. One reason Americans do not see that such laws are totalitarian in nature is, as Alexis de Tocqueville noted, because such laws are self-imposed and believed to be subject to change. Also, since the state is not perceived as the source of imposition of the new norms it is not felt to be as oppressive as communist states were. The imposition of new norms is brought about by private corporations and institutions, which, again, according to the logic of cell-growth, spread to every corner of social existence. Instead of the state being totalitarian, society in all its manifestations exerts pressure: corporations, businesses, universities, etc.

In this process, the nature of the state must be understood differently as well. The state is no longer a guardian of order that leaves individuals alone to cooperate freely and which administers justice, but becomes a parent who protects its children from the harms of undesirable habits. Since habits, either old or new, are private, preserved and generated on the grassroots level, the state must become intrusive and claim the right to rectify private behavior. A similar process to that which transformed the state also affects, not surprisingly, education—making this the most efficient arm in molding people to think alike. This is why schools take over sexual education, impose rules for how for use unoffensive language and teach versions of history that conform to current ideological assumptions.

Education is not considered to be a realm wherein children and young adults are taught to develop their intellectual skills and the critical capacity that would make them think independently. Education is an ideological boot camp, in which they are conditioned by repeating and absorbing slogans that cripple their mental capacities.[2] The new studies include subjects such as "environmental justice," "social justice," "heritage of hatred," "decolonizing gender stereotypes," "patriarchy and gender," and similar pseudotopics. The inability to think critically makes one even more dependent on the collective. (Ironically, as the level of indoctrination increases, universities offer more and more courses given the literal title of "critical thinking." Any teacher who seriously considers using such courses as a platform to teach students how to be genuinely critical would be fired for offending someone's sensitivity or for speaking about topics we assume should not be talked about.) This process should not at all be seen as abnormal. It is perfectly consistent with the spirit of democracy. If the opposite were the case, education would become a fountainhead of social disturbance because it would

2   It is worth quoting here Leszek Kołakowski, a great scholar of Marxism who was expelled from University of Warsaw by communist authorities for "shaping the minds of the young generation contrary to the dominant tendency of the country." In his article "What Are Universities For?" (written in 1993 and not today, when the situation is far worse), Kołakowski says: "The greatest danger, most clearly observable in the United States, is the invasion of an intellectual fashion which wants to abolish cognitive criteria of knowledge and truth itself, as a value established in our culture. The humanities and social sciences have always succumbed to various fashions, and this seems inevitable. But this is probably the first time that we are dealing with a fashion, or rather fashions, according to which there are no generally valid intellectual criteria and all meanings are freely generated. At the same time these fashions want to impose on others their own, purely ideological criteria, for instance feminist or racial (in accordance with black racism, but not vice versa). Should the 'ideologization' of universities in that spirit prevail, we might find ourselves longing for the old good days of universities ruled by the obligatory Marxist ideology, with its formal rules of historical correctness and truth. Even though these rules were systematically violated, it was at least possible to force the ideologues to explain things in accordance with them, and this resulted in a weakening of ideological pressure." In *My Correct Views on Everything*, ed. Zbigniew Janowski (South Bend, IN: St. Augustine's Press, 2004), 241. Kołakowski's own peregrinations (see a biographical note in *My Correct Views*) are a good illustration of the pressure to which university life under communism was subject. Despite this, many scholars, Kołakowski included among them, were willing to go "against the current" to defend the intellectual life of the nation against communist barbarism.

flood society with a variety of contrary, and possibly threatening, opinions to the ruling orthodoxy.[3] When a society reaches such a high level of social cohesion, universities can play only one role: They are ideological factories, where independent thought must be stopped before it develops.

3.

Huxley's achievement in *Brave New World* is that he understood that man's enemy is neither science nor technology, but *scientific thinking*. That is why predictions about the year 2000, made by scientists and scientifically minded authors discussed by Ellul, did not come true, or did only to a small extent, whereas those we find in Dostoevsky's *Notes from the Underground* indeed exist at the core of totalitarian thinking in America. The relationship of an individual man to society can be defined as, and measured in terms of, the degree of freedom the collective leaves to the individual which he can exercise unsupervised by the former. In a totalitarian society, all or nearly all individual goals and aspirations are subservient to the goal of the collective. Departure from it is either impossible and punished (communism and fascism), or undesirable and discouraged (as in Huxley's world).

The method used to discourage an individual from behaving in a certain way, either through punishment or award, is irrelevant and should not blind us to the fact that one can, as did Huxley, build a totalitarian society without using brutal force. Both forms of totalitarianism—brutal and soft—require that an individual man behaves, acts, but also *thinks* like the rest, and in so far as he is at all permitted to act or think differently, he must do it only to the degree that his behavior in no way departs from the implicitly accepted social norms, and certainly not in the way that would

---

3   In Huxley, science, too, is not free and must be stopped from developing. The reason is that if science is to progress, the science of tomorrow might question the science of today, and thus question the decisions of today's rulers. Symptoms of this are already visible in today's America, where the problem of different levels of testosterone in men and women, which is responsible also for leadership qualities, questions the very idea of equal political skills. News like that, as one of the scientists who was interviewed by *NPR* has said, must be carefully communicated to the public.

encourage others—intentionally or not—to follow in his footsteps. Departure is inadmissible because it could result in shaping formal or informal groups, whose way of viewing the rest—the collective—might be alien to the collective's own vision of itself, and would thereby threaten it.

The degree to which departure, however, is allowed or possible is defined by the desirable degree of social cohesion, which stems from the collective's perception and understanding of itself. This, in turn, dictates what is permissible and what is not. Undesirable behavior is "outlawed," not necessarily by punitive laws, but by *ad hoc* regulations. Law is no longer law, but a codex of positive regulations instituted for the *ad hoc* needs of stopping undesirable behavior wherever it surfaces. The collective's understanding of itself does not need to be explicit or consciously articulated (in most cases it is not, but is presumed and fluid), and so ideology does not need to be articulated either—whether in the form of a written formula, founding documents, or contained (like in Marxism) in the sacred scrolls written by the founding fathers.

In a society in which an ideology has been imposed from above, it is likely that one or many will rebel against it, rejecting the ideology, which explains why communist ideology created opposition and dissidents, and why measures even more oppressive in some respects in today's America find no resistance. An opposition is crushed within hours or days by voices of disapproval, and the would-be rebels apologize without even being threatened.

Huxley's future world is a fictionalized account of the Russian author's insights turned into predictions. His novel is based on Dostoevsky's single premise: Man will abandon belief in free will, beauty, and truth, for the sake of happiness. A reader familiar with both authors will easily recognize that many fragments in the conversation between Mustapha Mond, the Controller, and John Savage are renditions of the passages in *Notes from the Underground* and *The Brothers Karamazov*. In his Grand-Inquisitor-like moment, the Controller explains to Savage: "Universal happiness keeps the wheels steadily turning; truth and beauty can't. And, of course, whenever the masses seized political power, then it was happiness rather than truth and beauty that mattered." The future grand inquisitors will reign over millions in the name of scientific thinking. In fact, the greatest question of politics is the question of social organization: How to make people obey. For Hobbes it was fear of laws, but for Dostoevsky and Huxley, it was to find one weak point in human nature that would make man willingly lay down his freedom. In *The Brothers Karamazov* it was a "noble life" with regard to the future. Man would lay down his freedom and obey for the sake of a future reward.

But what about man in a society in which people are not religious? This is what Dostoevsky seems to ask in *Notes from the Underground*. Man renounced God and religion in the name of reason, and if there is a way of making him obey, we will enslave him by making him capitulate to his new god. Immortality, which religion had promised, will be exchanged for the promise of a long and happy life. The price, of course, is emotions: Deprive him of emotions, give him *soma* to stop his occasionally paranoid-schizophrenic behavior, and the man will not suffer nor see what was taken from him.

Stopping a disruptive behavior can be done in two ways—namely, through punishment or by encouragement. While the first method, excessive punishment, would result in creating a hard-totalitarian regime, like Soviet communism or Orwell's Oceania, the second method, more suited for a democracy, which shies from corporeal punishment, is painless but more pernicious: It enslaves man's mind. This is what Huxley understood very well and explored in his novel. As he wrote in *Brave New World Revisited*:

> In the light of what we have recently learned about animal behavior in general, and human behavior in particular, it has become clear that control through the punishment of undesirable behavior is less effective, in the long run, than control through the reinforcement of desirable behavior by rewards, and that government through terror works on the whole less well than government through the non-violent manipulation of the environment and of the thoughts and feelings of individual men, women and children. Punishment temporarily puts a stop to undesirable behavior, but does not permanently reduce the victim's tendency to indulge in it.

Since only science can create wealth, and wealth creates political and social stability, it does away with the need for old virtues and values. The new grand inquisitor is a "statistician" who can calculate man's advantages that will make him happy. As Mustapha Mond says, "Now, you swallow two or three half-gramme tablets, and there you are. Anybody can be virtuous now. You carry at least half your morality about in a bottle. Christianity without tears—that is what *soma* is." Americans' dependence on Prozac is a testimony to the rightness of Dostoevsky and Huxley's predictions. Without it, without "shrinks," counselors, therapists, the majority of the U.S. population would not be able to function. The traditional mores, social norms, and emotions disappeared, and as they disappeared, the society becomes more and more paranoid in the sense Erich Fromm described. Although no one has seen this slogan yet, everyone knows it: Prozac and deliverance from unwanted behavior and habits will set you free.

We now come to the real question: Can one drug ensnare the whole society such that *no one* will ever see that it is unfree and that life has evaporated from it? Huxley was aware that this is bound to happen, but because brutal force can only produce a mass rebellion, rebellion would only be on an individual scale. The disruptors will be sent to remote islands. "It's lucky that there are such a lot of islands in the world," Mond explains to one such dissenter, Helmholtz; "I don't know what we should do without them."

Huxley's archipelago is not a prototype of Solzhenitsyn's gulag, where hundreds of thousands of people who defied the ideological state were sent. Judged by the size of the gulag archipelago, dissent under communism was a norm, and keeping the dissidents apart, lest they poison with their unhappiness the rest of the population, was essential for maintaining the illusion surrounding the health of the socialist paradise. In Huxley, dissent is irrelevant, and limited to Helmholtz and Bernard. We see it in today's America: There are dissenting voices, but for all intents and purposes they are irrelevant and, above all, unconvincing to the rest. It is unlikely to change the country in which people have lost the taste and desire for freedom. Freedom means tolerating different views, habits, and thoughts, and above all negotiating diverse interests. We seem to have lost the capacity to be inconvenienced by others. In fact, by life itself.

When Huxley makes John Savage contradict the Controller's claim that *soma* is Christianity without tears, one reads:

"But the tears are necessary. Don't you remember what Othello said? 'If after every tempest came such calms, may the winds blow that have weakened death.' There's a story one of the old Indians used to tell us, about the Girl of Mataski. The young men who wanted to marry her had to do a morning's hoeing in her garden. It seemed easy; but there were flies and mosquitoes, magic ones. Most of the young men simply couldn't stand the biting and stinging. But the one that could—he got the girl."

To which he gets the following answer:

"Charming! But in civilized countries, you can have girls without hoeing for them; and there aren't any flies or mosquitoes to sting you. We got rid of them all centuries ago."

[...]
"Art, science—you seem to have paid a fairly high price for your happiness," said Savage.
"Yes, that's another item in the cost of stability," said Mustapha Mond.

Reflecting on the above, one should not wonder why today's artistic, and film production in particular, is so hopelessly anti-artistic and so technologically driven. They seem to be able to better handle the technological dimension of things rather than the emotional dimension of man. The imagination of today's artists exhausts itself in making movies about car-crashes and falling helicopters which have no feelings.

Once again, unhealthy, even morbid, mental symptoms of technological society were noticed by Fromm:

And who would not eventually prefer this exciting gamble to the boring un-aliveness of the organization man? One symptom of the attraction of the merely mechanical is the growing popularity, among some scientists and the public, of the idea that it will be possible to construct computers which are no different from man in thinking, feeling, or any other aspect of functioning. The main problem, it seems to me, is not whether such a computer-man can be constructed; it is rather why the idea is becoming so popular in a historical period when nothing seems to be more important than transforming the existing man into a more rational, harmonious, and peace-loving being. One cannot help being suspicious that often the attraction of the computer-man idea is the expression of a flight from life and from human experience into the mechanical and purely cerebral.

The possibility that we can build robots who are like men belongs, if anywhere, to the future. But the present already shows us men who act like robots. When the majority of men are like robots, then indeed there will be no problem in building robots who are like men. The idea of the manlike computer is a good example of the alternative between the human and the inhuman use of machines. The computer can serve the enhancement of life in many respects. But the idea that it replaces man and life is the manifestation of the pathology of today.

If it was true in 1968, how much truer Fromm's observation is today. If we do not see, it is only for the reason that Dostoevsky, Huxley, and Fromm understood. A machine is unlikely to understand what it is to be human. It can have machine-like cravings—healthy food, clean environment, etc.—but it's unlikely to see tears as necessary for man. If *soma* can cure sadness and despair, why not take it?—it is a perfectly logical question. Why wouldn't you want to be happy? Science means happiness, and if you can buy happiness in exchange for freedom, you should. There is nothing new to this story. The legend of Faustus, translated by Dostoevsky into a conversation with the Devil, is a great part of it.

4.

If we take Huxley's *Brave New World* to be a story about a *future* totalitarian world, much more technologically advanced than the world in which he lived in 1933, and see technology as the source of enslavement, then we have misunderstood Huxley's warning. The time separating the publication of Dostoevsky and Huxley's works is roughly sixty years; Huxley and Ellul's *The Technological Society* about twenty; Huxley's *Brave New World* and *Brave New World Revisited* around thirty, and Dostoevsky and Ellul, who discloses the conditions of technological totalitarianism, is ninety years. Finally, between *Notes* and Erich Fromm's *A Revolution of Hope: Toward a More Humanized Society* is a space of one hundred and four years. The chronology is important here. Huxley's state uses advanced technology, much more advanced than what was available in 1931 when he wrote his novel, but his state is not totalitarian on account of this alone. It is certainly true that a society in which telephones or cameras (let alone computers) exist allows for more efficient methods of spying, eavesdropping, and control, but the existence of technology by itself does not make a society totalitarian. The world in which Dostoevsky lived, and in whose *Notes* Huxley found the idea for his novel, did not know about cars, airplanes, radios, televisions, telephones, refrigerators, and many other scientific wonders; by the standards of today, even the world in which Huxley lived in 1933 knew only primitive prototypes of these.

The case in point is Orwellian society in *1984*. In it only very rudimentary technology, like telescreens and cameras, exists. Similarly, Nazi Germany, fascist Italy, and the Soviet Union were totalitarian through and through, with little application of technology, and what they had was of a very primitive nature. What made them totalitarian was not technology, but ideology, and ideological thinking is what constitutes the essence of the mind of the brave-new-worlders, and to a much larger degree than any of the 20th century regimes have thus far achieved.

Dostoevsky, who could not have dreamt the technology used by Huxley, nevertheless predicted what Huxley made use of in his novel: He replaced humanistic thought with rational-scientific thought, and therefore was able to render his characters robots. In doing so, Huxley made it impossible for the denizens of his world to assess or perceive their own enslavement. Their minds and behavior are thoroughly shaped by a rational-scientific worldview. It never occurs to anyone in Huxley's world to act differently than the others. The only way they can act is according to rational precepts. The "old ways" frighten them, and the language of poetry (the most intimate and personal form of expression) is beyond their powers of understanding. Feelings to which poetic words and sounds appeal disappeared and were replaced by scientific or chemical formulas (like the Bokanovsky Process). The only form of thinking of which they are capable is scientific thinking.

Dostoevsky's genius and prophetic ability is rooted in his refusal to bow to the progressivism characteristic of his epoch. It made many of his contemporaries popular for a time, but today they sound delusional, and for this very reason they are mostly forgotten. There is not much in Buckle, Mill and even Marx's writings on the progressive character of history that would draw our attention today and provide solutions to our problems. It is not 18th and 19th-century optimism that makes us return to the reading of the best authors from that period. It is the pessimistic ones that we cherish and admire the most. Pessimism is what makes Dostoevsky, along with Nietzsche, Tocqueville, and Mathew Arnold, some of the most profound thinkers ever. It is the Cleopatra-like capacity to "stick pins" to inflict pain that created 20th-century horrors, and which, one would hope, might have been prevented, at least some of it, had the pessimists dominated the intellectual scene.

The reader of Huxley's *Brave New World* can only be surprised that his entire book is contained in two chapters (VII and VIII) of Dostoevsky's *Notes from the Underground*. With a stroke of devilish ingenuity, mixed with English irony, Huxley turns Russian pessimism into a vision of a euphoric utopia wherein everyone is happy. The only person who has eyes to see the delusion is the phenomenally ungrateful John Savage, who is Dostoevsky's ungrateful biped, born outside the utopian world on the reservation. He refuses to join the rest. Dostoevsky knew and predicted that taking the world back, rebuilding the past of the future, depends on having followers. For his part he did not find them. Here Huxley may have betrayed his pessimism. Drug-injected euphoria for the present cannot cure the addicts.

No one in *Brave New World* seems to be aware of the trade-off. Freedom is a non-issue for the denizens of the world. They are happy because they are simply unaware of the extent to which the opposite of happiness—sadness, melancholy, illness, death, heartbreak, or even downright misery—is how freedom manifests itself. The saying, "only idiots are happy" seems to be the key to understand why the totalitarian nature of Brave New World is unperceived by its citizens.

One big question arises: What is the need for *soma*? The immediate answer is that *soma* changes one's perception of the world. It makes people think that things are perfect when they are not. This does not, however, seem to be the case. In *Brave New World* the old political, social, economic, and natural ills have been eliminated. So there is no need to take a drug that changes one's perception of the world. The fact that they take it daily is an indication of a deeper problem in that world. Where needs no longer exist and creativity has exhausted itself, people become idle. Idleness creates a danger of unpredictable behavior, and therefore the only need is that of averting the possibility of danger. This insight is hardly new and can be found in 17th and 18th-century works of literature—from Pascal's *Pensées* to *Princess de Cleves* and La Rochefoucauld's *Maxims*, to Le Clos' *Les Liaisons Dangereuses*, and above all in the memoirs and letters of the aristocratic ladies of that period. It is called *l'ennui*, or boredom.

Soma produces happiness—the state of intoxication that kills *l'ennui*. But this form of happiness is not contentment. Rather, it is a counterfeit of boredom, a false currency with which we pay for being diverted from realizing, as Pascal said, that we are mortal.

CHAPTER 9 | A NEW OPIUM
OF THE INTELLECTUALS:
PLATO'S TRAP AND MILL'S LIBERALISM

The Right-wing revolutions, it was obstinately maintained, kept the capitalists in power and restricted themselves to substituting the despotism of the Police State for the more subtle methods of parliamentary democracy ... The parliamentary State was in keeping, both in theory and in practice, with the demands of bourgeois society ... Bolshevism invoked all the ideology of the Left: rationalism, progress, liberty ... Does not the progress of the Left bring with it, dialectically, a worse oppression than the one it rose to conquer?

Raymond Aron, *The Opium of the Intellectuals*

To belong to the masses is the greatest longing of the "alienated" intellectual. It is such a powerful longing that, in trying to appease it, a great many of them ... now become converted to the New Faith ...The intellectual has once more become *useful*. He who may have once have done his thinking and writing in his free moments away from a paying job in a bank or post office, has now found his rightful place on earth.

Czesław Miłosz, *The Captive Mind*

1.

The title of this chapter may sound familiar to some readers. It comes from *The Opium of the Intellectuals* by one of the icons of mid-20th-century liberalism—the French thinker, Raymond Aron. Aron's book, like Czesław Miłosz's *The Captive Mind*, was, and remains, an unsurpassed analysis that allowed the previous two generations to understand the dangerous charm of socialism.[1] When Aron published his work in 1955, the ideological enemy of socialism was liberalism, or liberal-democracy. Paradoxically, today's liberalism has assumed a freedom-threatening posture, very similar to what Aron found in socialism. And unlike in its earlier periods, liberalism is not a philosophy that promotes and secures individual liberties and free-markets but, very much like socialism, is in the process of creating a collectivist gulag that forces individuals to give up the freedom to have one's own opinions. Despite its claim to promote diversity, it promotes ever-growing uniformity. Colleges and universities are no longer bastions of learning and the free exchange of ideas, but ideological institutes very much like those of Marxism and Leninism established under the socialist dictatorship present in the former countries of real socialism. There is a new class of the American and western academics and intelligentsia that promote ideological explanations, polluting the intellectual air with their egalitarian ideology. All of this, particularly the similarities between the two systems, requires a serious explanation,[2] and there is no better place to look for it than in the writings of John Stuart Mill, one of the founders of the liberal Idea.

Communism was not just a philosophy; it was a *Weltanschauung*, a world-view, that claimed to have answers to all questions. Its total pretensions accounted for its ideological self-conceit, including the simplicity of its historical explanation that rendered the study of history irrelevant—or, in so far as history mattered, it mattered only to the extent that it showed that history is a class struggle: It is the struggle between the oppressors and the oppressed. Just like

1   See Leszek Kołakowski's "Communism as a Cultural Force" and "What is Left of Socialism?" in his *My Correct Views on Everything*, ed. Zbigniew Janowski (South Bend: St. Augustine's Press, 2005).
2   Despite the growing concerns over PC liberalism, there are virtually no authors who write on the subject of similarities between it and socialism. The explanation of it lies, partly, in the fact that few Westerners possess communist experience so such similarities seem to go unnoticed. The only book that is seriously concerned with similarities between communism liberalism, and democracy (and which in many places sounds like Aron's analysis) is Ryszard Legutko's *The Demon in Democracy: Totalitarian Temptations in Free Societies*. See also his article, "What's Wrong with Liberalism," *Modern Age*, Vol. 50, No. 1, Winter 2008.

communism, Mill's liberalism offered a similar dichotomous interpretation, according to which history is a struggle between authority and liberty.

This binary scheme could not be any simpler. It allows someone who does not know a single historical event to grasp history's very essence, and like socialism, which was the promise of history's fulfillment—the earthly parousia when people are finally equal—liberal ideology points in the same direction. Both communism and liberalism have claimed that it is possible to create a society where equality and justice rule. In so doing, they sought to make us believe that inequality is not natural, but man-made, and that all it takes to change a society is an appropriate understanding of history and social relationships, which can and should be rearranged. In reality, instead of paradise on earth, socialism became the most brutal and oppressive system man has ever invented: It entailed a total ownership of citizens, including their minds.

Sixty-five years after the publication of *The Opium of the Intellectuals*, the ideological charm is still operating, but this time the charm emanates from communism's former enemy, liberalism. Liberalism is the 21st century's new faith. Like socialism, it requires total submission of one's mind to ideological slogans—sexism, misogyny, racism, homophobia, xenophobia, ageism, chauvinism—making a captive of the mind, just as Miłosz described in his book, and its enemies are pursued with a zeal akin to that with which the communists pursued theirs. Liberalism became an *ideology* that is intolerant of anyone who dares think that any of these "phobias" or "-isms" are not the greatest evils that one ought to fight.

Today's man is, as Friedrich Nietzsche predicted, obsessed with erasing all traces of inequality and merit. This ideological obsessiveness makes *us* critically-blind, and not without political and social aggression. Instead of cherishing the three classical liberal virtues of civility, politeness and gentleness, the people who call themselves liberal increasingly espouse intolerance and violence against those with whom they disagree.

Mill's great hope for changing mankind, and men's relations to one another, was to point out that a reasoned argument can be used in place of force. He was a strong believer that western man—in the first half of the 19th century, at least in most civilized countries—reached a level of moral and political development where force became superfluous in settling differences. He believed and hoped that we would listen to each other, weigh arguments and accept the strongest ones, as rational beings should. He cherished an unwavering hope in reason, as did the Enlightenment thinkers. Despotism, as he famously remarked, is a legitimate way of ruling the barbarians. One hundred and sixty years later, we can say with considerable certainty that he was over-optimistic in his belief in man, and likewise in the extent to which civilization can effect permanent changes in man's nature.[3]

What is frightening in reading Aron's book today is that, were it not for the word *communism* and the historical events to which the author refers, the book is an adequate description of the world today.

---

3   This idea was a common currency in the 19th century. It found its classic expression in Freud's *Civilization and Its Discontents*, in which the author claims that we no longer need prohibitions against taboos since these have been abandoned during the historical process. In *Notes from the Underground*, Dostoevsky ridicules progressive ideas, mentioning Mill's contemporary (who influenced him and August Comte), the influential historian Henry Thomas Buckle (1821–1862), author of *History of Civilization in England*. According to Dostoevsky's reading of Buckle, as man progresses through history he becomes "less blood thirsty," an idea reminiscent of Mill's view of man's barbaric instinct being "civilized," only to make room to lay foundations for a representative government. To contradict the progressivist claim, in his story Dostoevsky gives two ("modern") examples of blood spilling: one by Stenka Razin (1630–1671), a Cossack leader who aimed at establishing a Cossack republic along the Volga river in 1670 and mercilessly massacred all those who opposed him; and, the other, the conflict over Schleswig-Holstein (a very small, disputed territory between the Kingdom of Prussia, Denmark, and Austria) in 1864, the same year Dostoevsky published *Notes*. Dostoevsky juxtaposes these two modern examples to an ancient (barbaric) one of Cleopatra's sticking pins in her slaves' breasts, and taking pleasure at the sight of their writhing. In choosing these examples, Dostoevsky points out that man's nature remains the same, that his "barbaric" instinct has not died as a result of his progress, and indirectly, that modern (Western) social and political institutions overlook the constants in human nature, which is prone to cruelty and barbarism.

His dire warning against the optimism of Western liberalism is masterfully developed in *The Brothers Karamazov*. One should also note that the basic premise of the two famous anti-totalitarian works, Aldous Huxley's *Brave New World* and Zamyatin's *WE* (the latter most likely inspired George Orwell's *1984*), were influenced by Dostoevsky's *Notes*, in which he predicts and warns against totalitarianism based on scientific knowledge, and the consequent prediction of human behavior with absolute precision, and in so doing ignoring man's barbaric impulses ("Cleopatra's pins"). Huxley invokes Dostoevsky in the last chapter of his *Brave New World Revisited*.

2.

John Stuart Mill was a Victorian gentleman and a great mind. As long as Western civilization exists and continues to exercise its influence on its own members and elsewhere, his name will shine bright in the annals of the European political thought.[4] Mill's greatest contribution will be his oft-quoted argument for freedom of speech:

> If all mankind minus one, were of one opinion, and only one person were of the contrary opinion, mankind would be no more justified in silencing that one person, than he, if he had the power, would be justified in silencing mankind.

Given the rhetorical power and beautiful style that permeates all of his writings, it should not surprise us that Mill became an icon of European political tradition, and his argument its hallmark. For a century and a half, liberals have been pointing to Mill's argument for freedom of speech as the most precious gem in the crown of liberal thought. It was considered to be the buffer against the tyrannies of authoritarian regimes that wanted to silence their political opponents, and a litmus test against which the extent of freedom in all past and future social arrangements might be tested, which also, let's remember, made the growth of scientific inquiry possible. And since none other but a liberal society could claim to live up to Mill's criterion (at least in theory), no political arrangement could claim to be truly *just* simply because it imposed some limitations on its members in the form of *authority* as to "who has a right to talk first" (a parent before a child, an elder before a youngster, a teacher before a student, a ruler before a subject, a citizen before a foreigner, an expert before an ignoramus, and so on).

To safeguard "the equality of all voices," one had to do something that previous thinkers, Plato and Edmund Burke, for example, were concerned about: One had to abolish the traditional hierarchy, and give all people—regardless of age, experience, wisdom, and expertise—the same "right to say" what they wanted, where they wanted, and when they wanted. The implicit

---

4   See Nicholas Capaldi's excellent biography of Mill: *John Stuart Mill: A Biography* (Cambridge: Cambridge University Press, 2004).

claim that hides behind Mill's argument is that no one should be discriminated against, because discrimination implies that there is a *hierarchy* of voices.

The French Revolution (1789) provided the needed ammunition against authority. It announced the equality of all, and by supporting the expansion of equality, liberalism later became the indisputable winner in ideological and political contests. The rise and brutality of 20th century ideological-totalitarian states—communist, fascist, and Nazi—only strengthened the impression that a society, in order to be truly free and just, must organize itself according to principles created by 19th-century liberal thinkers. Almost everyone succumbed to the premise of liberalism to a degree and implicitly capitulated to liberal analysis that political authority is generated by consent of the governed.

The problem that such a view was destined to generate went unnoticed or ignored as long as liberal societies observed traditional rules of personal conduct—engrained by religion, social customs, and habits—and the problem was more or less invisible until only a few decades ago. One could say that the political realm operated on "consent," whereas the private realm (i.e., personal conduct and private relationships) was traditionally hierarchical and did not require much, if any, state intervention, save for extreme cases.[5]

However, as Plato had already noticed, equality cannot be contained to the political realm only, and, over time, the egalitarian mentality is bound to permeate all forms of relationships, leading to the dissolution of *all* forms of authority.

In a memorable fragment, in book VIII of the *Republic*, Plato describes in detail how this happens:

> Then democracy, I suppose, comes into being when the poor win, killing some of the others and casting out some, and share the regime and the ruling offices with those who are left on an equal basis; and, for the most part, the offices in it are given by lot.

5   Family relationships, responsibility for children, the relationships between parents and children, rules of intimacy, etc., were hardly ever a concern of the state. This is not so today. Almost all of the above are to some extent regulated or supervised by the state, and its intrusion into the private life of citizens through rules and regulations is unprecedented even by the standards of the former communist state, to which the private realm, unless it was a threat to the state, was of little or no concern.

"Yes," he said, "this is the establishment of democracy, whether it comes into being by arms or by others' withdrawing due to fear."

"In what way do these men live?" I said. "And what is the character of such a regime? For it's plain that man who is like it will turn out to be democratic."

"Yes, it is plain," he said.

"In the first place, then, aren't they free? And isn't the city full of freedom and free speech? And isn't there license in it to do whatever one wants?"

"That is what is said, certainly," he said.

"And where there's license, it's plain that each man would organize his life in it privately just as it pleases him."

"Yes, it is plain."

"Then I suppose that in this regime especially, all sorts of human beings come to be."

"How could they fail to?"

"It is probably the fairest of the regimes," I said. "Just like a many-colored cloak decorated in all hues, this regime, decorated with all dispositions, would also look fairest, and many perhaps," I said, "like boys and women looking at many-colored things, would judge this to be the fairest regime."

And several pages later, Plato concludes:

"Then," I said, "as I was going to say just now, does the insatiable desire of this and the neglect of the rest change this regime and prepare a need for tyranny?"

"How?" He said.

"I suppose that when a democratic city, once it's thirsted for freedom, gets bad wine bearers as its leaders and gets more drunk than it should on this unmixed draught, then, unless the rulers are very gentle and provide a great deal of freedom, it punishes them, charging them with being polluted and oligarchs."

"Yes," he said, "that's what they do."

"And it spatters with mud those who are obedient, alleging that they are willing slaves of the rulers and nothings," I said, "while it praises and honors—both in private and in public—the rulers who are like the ruled and the ruled who are like the rulers. Isn't it necessary in such a city that freedom spread to everything?"

"How could it be otherwise?"

"And, my friend," I said, "for it to filter down to the private houses and end up by anarchy's being planted in the very beasts?"

"How do we mean that?" he said.

"That a father," I said, "habituates himself to be like his child and fear his sons, and a son habituates himself to be like his father and to have no shame before or fear of his parents—that's so he may be free; and metic is on an equal level with townsman and townsman with metic, and similarly with the foreigner."

"Yes," he said, "that's what happens."

"These and other small things of the following kind come to pass," I said. "As the teacher in such a situation is frightened of the pupils and fawns of them, so the students make light of their teachers, as well as of their attendants. And, generally, the young copy their elders and compete with them in speeches and deeds while the old come down to the level of the young; imitating the young, they are overflowing with facility and charm, and that's so that they won't seem to be unpleasant or despotic."

"Most certainly," he said.

And the ultimate in the freedom of the multitude, my friend," I said, "occur in such a city when the purchased slaves, male and female, are no less free than those who have bought them. And we almost forgot to mention the extent of the law of equality and of freedom in the relations of women with men and men with women."

"Won't we," he said, "with Aeschylus, 'say whatever just came to our lips'?"

"Certainly," I said, "I shall do just that. A man who didn't have experience couldn't be persuaded of the extent to which beasts subject to human beings are freer here than in another city. The bitches follow the proverb exactly and become like their mistresses; and, of course, there come to be horses and asses who have gotten the habit of making their way quite freely and solemnly, bumping into whomever they happen to meet on the roads, if he doesn't stand aside, and all else is similarly full of freedom."

"You're telling me my own dream," he said.[6]

The remaining part of book VIII is devoted to the description of the character of a tyrant and tyranny—which follows the collapse of democracy. We must note, however, that the transition from democracy to tyranny is not sudden. It is a slow process whose intermediate stage is anarchy, caused by the expansion of equality.

In the passage quoted above, Plato does not give us a historical description of the Greek experience (although history has preserved his observation as empirical evidence), but captures the logic behind the political processes. Equality, as Plato understands it, works like an acid, which gradually dissolves authority. And since no society can function without someone exercising authority, it begins to slide into lawlessness and, eventually, tyranny follows. Tyranny is the logical outcome of democratic equality.

3.

One is tempted to ask: What does Plato have to do with Mill and liberalism? In a sense, everything. Mill's conclusions are the reversal of Plato's. While Plato saw equality as something that we should treat with great caution, Mill perceived it as an objective, and used politics as a means to an end. Mill was supportive, often enthusiastic, of the expansion of equality, but was also concerned with the dangers that it was going to present. In the words of Mill's biographer:

> What attracted Mill's attention in Tocqueville was the issue of democracy. Tocqueville's understanding of the spirit of the age was that we were living through the triumph of the democratic spirit. In Mill's eyes, Tocqueville was an aristocratic conservative who recognized democracy as the wave of the future [...]. There is a tendency for democracy to encourage the omnipotence of the majority and for the majority to become tyrannical. Mill recognized that

6   *The Republic of Plato.* Translated by Allan Bloom (New York: Basic Books, 1968).

this kind of tyranny is a threat to the notion of limited government. [...] Mill quoted with approval Tocqueville's view that 'the first duty... imposed upon those who direct our affairs is to educate the democracy; to reanimate its faith [...] to purify its morals; to regulate its energies; to substitute for its inexperience a knowledge of business, and for its blind instincts an acquaintance with its true interests.' What Tocqueville saw and what he suggested clearly reflected how Mill had come to understand his own role.[7]

Yet, despite Tocqueville's warning, Mill's sympathy for equality, which stemmed from his antipathy toward hierarchy, won his allegiance. No other modern thinker was as inimical to the idea of hierarchy or authority as was Mill. In virtually all of his writings, he relentlessly fights the idea of authority, and advocates that all relationships should be of a "consensual" nature. He even goes so far as to suggest that the authority of parents over their children is also questionable. In *The Subjection of Women* (chapter 2), Mill writes that family relationships "should be a school of sympathy in equality, of living together in love, without power on one side or obedience on the other."

Thoughts like that sound extremely naïve, but they are uttered by Mill with utmost seriousness. The context in which remarks of this nature occur indicates that they stem from Mill's personal reaction to frequent and unnecessary instances of excessive brutality in human relationships and to the harshness of life in the 19th century, but often they occur in passages concerning such mild cases (as in the passage I just quoted) that the reader feels tempted to apply psychoanalysis to understand Mill's obsessive fear of the use of power. It is true, brutality, callousness, wretchedness, and inhumanity in human relationships formed much of the fabric of 19th life, and they have been described by such distinguished writers as Balzac, Zola, Dostoevsky, Tolstoy, and Dickens. A century later, the world described by Dickens in his novels was still frightening to George Orwell, who devoted an essay to him. The pain that Mill experienced firsthand must have terrified him. However, he did not confine himself to fighting real abuses of authority by legislative channels, thinking that the social structures were essentially sound—even if they needed very serious reforms to make society gentler

---

7   Capaldi, *Ibid.*, pp. 149–151.

and authority considerably limited. He wanted, and indeed thought possible, the total elimination of authority. In fact, his entire philosophy rests on the premise that authority and power are "evil" in themselves and, as such, must be fought against and, hopefully, done away with.

In the second paragraph of his celebrated work, *On Liberty*, Mill outlines the framework of his political thought.

> The struggle between Liberty and Authority is the most conspicuous feature in the portions of history with which we are earliest familiar, particularly in that of Greece, Rome, and England. But in old times this contest was between subjects, or some classes of subjects, and the government. By liberty, was meant protection against the tyranny of the political rulers. The rulers were conceived (except in some of the popular governments of Greece) as in a necessarily antagonistic position to the people whom they ruled. They consisted of a governing One, or a governing tribe or caste, who derived their authority from inheritance or conquest, who, at all events, did not hold it at the pleasure of the governed, and whose supremacy men did not venture, perhaps did not desire, to contest, whatever precautions might be taken against its oppressive exercise. Their power was regarded as necessary, but also as highly dangerous; as a weapon which they would attempt to use against their subjects, no less than against external enemies. To prevent the weaker members of the community from being preyed upon by innumerable vultures, it was needful that there should be an animal of prey stronger than the rest, commissioned to keep them down. But as the king of the vultures would be no less bent upon preying on the flock than any of the minor harpies, it was indispensable to be in a perpetual attitude of defense against his beak and claws. The aim, therefore, of patriots, was to set limits to the power which the ruler should be suffered to exercise over the community; and this limitation was what they meant by liberty. It was attempted in two ways. First, by obtaining a recognition of certain immunities, called political liberties or rights, which it was to be regarded as a breach of duty in the ruler to infringe, and which if he did infringe, specific resistance, or general rebellion, was held to be justifiable. A second,

and generally a later expedient, was the establishment of constitutional checks; by which the consent of the community, or of a body of some sort, supposed to represent its interests, was made a necessary condition to some of the more important acts of the governing power. To the first of these modes of limitation, the ruling power, in most European countries, was compelled, more or less, to submit. It was not so with the second; and to attain this, or when already in some degree possessed, to attain it more completely, became everywhere the principal object of the lovers of liberty. And so long as mankind were content to combat one enemy by another, and to be ruled by a master, on condition of being guaranteed more or less efficaciously against his tyranny, they did not carry their aspirations beyond this point.

The historical struggle is between the Party of authority and the Party of liberty, just like in Marx, for whom it was the class of oppressors against the class of the oppressed. From such a perspective, the Party of authority is on the side of evil, whereas the Party of liberty, which strives to diminish authority, represents the good and, indirectly, social improvement. Given the narrow parameters of his historical method, all who try to decrease the use and influence of authority stand for the good of social and political affairs, and those who attempt to oppose it are evil. Politics and the public square, instead of being a forum for diverse ideas, is a place of collision—but not necessarily, as Mill suggests in his argument for freedom of speech, diverse opinions, but the collision of two kinds of opinions: the opinions that promote progress (and equality), and the opinions that oppose it. In short, his historical method—liberty versus authority—reduces his advocacy of a plurality of views to a polarization of progressive and "regressive" opinions. Instead of having many socio-political players, we have only two—the liberators and their opponents, the oppressors—who can play their power game, and the public is forced to choose between two views, rather than between a diverse spectrum of beneficial opinions.

It is rarely pointed out that the argument for freedom of speech does not stand on its own. It is based on two explicit premises, of which only one seems partly valid, and the second is highly questionable.

In the conclusion of the formulation of his argument, Mill writes,

Were an opinion a personal possession of no value except to the owner, if to be obstructed in the enjoyment of it were simply a private injury, it would make some difference whether the injury was inflicted only on a few persons or on many. But the peculiar evil of silencing the expression of an opinion is that it is robbing the human race; posterity as well as the existing generation; those who dissent from the opinion, still more than those who hold it. If the opinion is right, they are deprived of the opportunity of exchanging error for truth.

The argument takes the "utility" of opinions as a basis for allowing the individual to speak, even if the majority has the power to silence him. It is difficult to disagree with Mill that, for instance, the Inquisition's attempt to silence Galileo was not beneficial, and would have hampered the scientific progress which made Western civilization successful. However, Mill's argument is based on another premise, which he introduced just before he presented his argument—namely: "The power itself is illegitimate." If we apply this to Galileo's case, the Inquisition would be the party of authority, whose power is by definition illegitimate, whereas Galileo, the minority of one, would be on the side of liberty and progress. The example is so clear-cut that we have no problem in choosing sides. We should add, however, that if we side with Galileo, it is not just because the power of Inquisition had dubious legitimacy, or because we favor speech to institutional tyranny, but because Galileo was on the side of truth.

We need to point out, however, that in his essay, Mill is less concerned with the world of science than with social life, and his argument seems to lose its persuasiveness when we consider that not everybody's speech is as valuable as that of Galileo, Darwin, Spencer or Wycliff (the name of the religious reformer whose name Mill used to sign his early anti-religious newspaper pieces). Few among us have the intellectual powers that can increase human knowledge or accelerate human progress, and equally few have the courage to fight genuine abuses of religious authority, as did Wycliff, or political power, as did the dissidents in the former communist countries and under brutal dictatorships all over the world.

Mill's argument creates a "slippery slope" and gives a powerful weapon to all kinds of political and social activists, scientific charlatans, and destructive social reformers, whose purpose is not to benefit society or effect mankind's progress, let alone to be on the side of truth. This warrants our asking: What does a party of polygamists, or worshipers of Satan, or similar individuals and minorities, for example, have to do with progress or truth? Or, what social benefits are awaiting a society for changing the structure of marriage by allowing, for instance, polygamy? Or for declaring the days during which we celebrate Christmas to become the national holiday for the birth of Satan? The polygamists and Satanists in Mill's argument would belong to the party of liberty. Any attempt to suppress or illegitimize such cases in the name of established tradition always ends either by invoking Mill's argument for freedom of speech, or the illegitimacy of power—political, social, parental, or religious—which is the very essence of liberalism, whose beginnings, as we learn from John Henry Newman's theses on liberalism, originated with a challenge to religious authority.

In the West, the validity of monogamy and Christmas come from the common European tradition, and even though it was different two thousand years ago, many traditions and customs gained legitimacy through history, which bound individuals as a people and as nations. Cultural unity has never come from social and political activism, and when this was tried, as it was in Soviet Russia and Mao's China, it was oppressive and artificial.

To Mill, Tradition or "custom" is a hindrance to progress, and even if his personal predilection would be monogamy rather than polygamy, he would have no argument against polygamy, since his liberalism is not grounded in the natural law tradition.[8] It can illegitimize everything, and

---

8   It is worth recalling here the words of Allan Bloom, the author of the most talked about book in the late 1980's—*The Closing of the American Mind: How Higher Education Has Failed Democracy and Impoverished the Souls of Today's Students* (New York: Simon and Schuster, 1987): "Liberalism without natural rights, the kind we know from John Stuart Mill and John Dewey, taught us that the only danger confronting us is being closed to the emergent, the new, the manifestations of progress. No attention had to be paid to the fundamental principles or the moral virtues that inclined men to live according to them. [...] And this turn in liberalism is what prepared us for cultural relativism and the fact-value distinction, which seemed to carry that viewpoint further and give it greater intellectual weight" (pp. 29–30). His entire book is concerned with the problem of moral "relativism," which, one should point out, is of no concern to anyone any longer. Today's western world "imbibed" relativism to the point that it has ceased to be viewed as an intellectual problem.

thereby it legitimizes the destruction of social and political traditions, simply because they are traditions. In doing so, Mill, as Plato wisely noticed, seems to have prepared a road that inevitably leads to social anarchy and eventually to tyranny. His philosophy endows the individual with the power to precipitate changes within a well-established social fabric.

4.

One might ask how such a perceptive thinker could not notice the consequences of his own system of thought. In one of his very powerful and touching polemical pieces concerning slavery in America, Mill writes:

> Let me, in a few words, remind the reader what sort of a thing this is, which the white oligarchy of the South have banded themselves together to propagate, and establish, if they could, universally. When it is wished to describe any portion of the human race as in the lowest state of debasement, and under the most cruel oppression, in which it is possible for human beings to live, they are compared to slaves. When words are sought by which to stigmatize the most odious despotism, exercised in the most odious manner, and all other comparisons are found inadequate, the despots are said to be like slave-masters, or slave-drivers. What, by a rhetorical license, the worst oppressors of the human race, by way of stamping on them the most hateful character possible, are said to be, these men, in very truth, are. I do not mean that all of them are hateful personally, any more than all the inquisitors, or all the buccaneers. [...] There are, Heaven knows, vicious and tyrannical institutions in ample abundance on the earth. But this institution is the only one of them all which requires, to keep it going, that human beings should be burnt alive [...]. the *Edinburgh Review,* in a recent number, gave the hideous details of the burning alive of an unfortunate Northern huckster by Lynch law, on mere suspicion of having aided in the escape of a slave. What must American slavery be, if deeds like these are necessary under it? And if they are not necessary, and are yet done, is not the evidence against

slavery still more damning? The South are in rebellion not for simple slavery, they are in rebellion for the right of burning human creatures alive.

Only at the expense of human decency could one disagree with Mill. Yet, in *The Subjection of Women*, Mill writes:

> I am far from pretending that wives are in general no better treated than slaves; but no slave is a slave to the same lengths, and in so full a sense of the word, as a wife is. Hardly any slave, except one immediately attached to the master's person, is a slave at all hours and all minutes.

Mill's disclaimer that he is "far from pretending" does not seem to resolve the problem that his usage creates. By using the same word—namely, slavery—to equate the most brutal abuse of power, compulsory labor, torture, or burning a human alive, with a married, white English woman in 19th century England, he reveals his lack of proportional sense. It is *evil* to burn a human being alive and it is *evil* to exercise authority over a woman within the confines of a voluntary marital realm; it is *evil* to exercise authority over a child, since family should be "a school of equality." Such nonchalant and irresponsible use of language does not strengthen Mill's case, and all this lies on the antipodes of what we find in Plato's *Republic*. By not being able to distinguish between the legitimate and illegitimate use of power, Mill falls into the trap that Plato indicates: Freedom is not license; not all forms of authority are cruelty, abuse, or illegitimate. The legitimate use of, and respect for, authority is a necessary condition of stable social and political structures, and when they become weak the only way to prevent social and political chaos is the use of despotic-like power to ensure order.

Let me quote here a fragment from Mill's "Civilization," in which he addresses the problem of pain.

> One of the effects of civilization (not to say one of the ingredients in it) is, that the spectacle, and even the very idea, of pain, is kept more and more out of the sight of those classes who enjoy in their fullness the benefits of civilization. The state of perpetual personal

conflict, rendered necessary by the circumstances of former times, and from which it was hardly possible for any person, in whatever rank of society, to be exempt, necessarily habituated everyone to the spectacle of harshness, rudeness, and violence, to the struggle of one indomitable will against another, and to the alternate suffering and infliction of pain. These things, consequently, were not as revolting even to the best and most actively benevolent men of former days, as they are to our own; and we find the recorded conduct of those men frequently such as would be universally considered very unfeeling in a person of our own day. They, however, thoughtless of the infliction of pain, because they thought less of pain altogether. When we read of actions of the Greeks and Romans, or of our own ancestors, denoting callousness to human suffering, we must not think that those who committed these actions were as cruel as we must become before we could do the like. The pain which they inflicted, they were in the habit of voluntarily undergoing from slight causes; it did not appear to them as great an *evil*, as it appears, and as it really is, to us, nor did it in any way degrade their minds. In our own time the necessity of personal collision between one person and another is, comparatively speaking, almost at an end [...]. The heroic essentially consists in being ready, for a worthy object, to do and to suffer, but especially to do, what is painful or disagreeable; and whoever does not early learn to be capable of this, will never be a great character.[9]

This fragment is rich in reflections. One of them is that Mill assumed our civilization to be at the last stage of eliminating conflict, and all of the unnecessary pain that comes with it. He also deemed the successful evasion of pain as essentially the privilege of leisured or upper classes. However, what was the privilege of a few (aristocracy), he thinks, at this stage of civilization, when the role of aristocracy is questionable,[10] to be undeserved. This privilege

9   Emphasis mine.
10   A very different attitude toward aristocracy can be found in Mill's contemporary, Mathew Arnold, who, in his "Popular Education in France," says: "We

is therefore unjust and evil. His implicit claim is that it is *just* to extend what is, or was, the privilege of aristocracy to the democratic majority. Mill deserves credit for protecting the ordinary man from abuse through legislative measures and for promoting better living conditions for the laboring classes. However, he is a protoplast of the mentality that turned privileges (rights of the few) into rights (privileges of everyone, and therefore not privileges).

However, as Nietzsche noticed, it is in the nature of the democratic man to insist that no one deserves anything that someone else cannot obtain. Even if we could imagine a situation where the economic privileges possessed by the few were extended to the many, one cannot imagine a talent being a privilege of all. Nietzsche knew this, and with Cassandra-like shouts, he was warning us against the danger of the democratic man, who demands the same recognition that was always reserved for the most talented individuals.

It must be said that Mill was not blind to the shortcomings of democracy. On many occasions (especially in chapters 3 and 4 of *On Liberty*), he is democracy's harshest critic. Mill and Nietzsche's anti-democratic pronouncements often sound alike. However, in contrast to Mill, Nietzsche despised democracy for what it is—mediocrity. Mill, despite his very serious reservations, believed that democracy can work, provided one can "ennoble" the ordinary man through education. He learned from Tocqueville to be afraid of democracy because of its tyrannical nature. He also came to his own conclusion that democratic man lacks creativity, and that he cannot even fathom what it is:

> Originality is the one thing which unoriginal minds cannot feel the use of. They cannot see what it is to do with them. If they could see what it would do for them, it would not be originality. The first service which originality has to render them, is that of opening their eyes: which being once fully done, they would have a chance of

in England have had, in our great aristocratical and ecclesiastical institutions, a principle of cohesion and unity which the Americans had not; they gave the tone to the nation, and the nation took it from them; self-government here was quite a different thing from self-government there. Our society is probably destined to become much more democratic: who will give the tone to the nation then? That is the question."

being original […]. In sober truth, whatever homage may be professed, or even paid, to real or supposed mental superiority, the general tendency of things throughout the world is to render mediocrity the ascendant power among mankind" (*On Liberty*, Chapter 3).

And, as he says in the previous fragment, heroism cannot flourish outside the realm of suffering.[11] Yet he spent his intellectual powers trying to free us from suffering at the price of promoting mediocrity.[12]

5.

One might ask: Why did one of the greatest 19th-century thinkers fall into "Plato's trap"? The ancient philosopher drew our attention to the Sophists' use of language, and in particular, the power it has to manipulate the crowd by generating widespread delusion. In the 20th century, the methods for manipulating language achieved perfection. We owe George Orwell and Aldous Huxley[13] a great debt for their insight into the nature of totalitarianism and the power of language manipulation. The fascist Mussolini, the Nazi Hitler, and the communist Lenin were masters of linguistic and crowd manipulation. Without twisting words and impressing them on people's minds to create a false reality, none of them would have risen to their positions of political power. Totalitarianism is unlikely to succeed if words are not used to create and manipulate reality.

---

11 Capaldi, *op. cit.*, p. 150, makes the following comment: "Tocqueville had also intimated in Part I of *Democracy in America* that a democratic culture leads to a loss of the heroic aristocratic virtues. This is a point that Mill himself had made in his *Civilization*. However, in the first review, Mill distanced himself to a slight degree from Tocqueville […]. By the time he wrote the second review, Mill's position had shifted."

12 The problem, of course, is not new. John Rawls' *Theory of Justice* (1971) was considered for decades to be the most important statement about the liberal conception of justice. Allan Bloom, in his review of it, called it "the first philosophy for the last man."

13 See Aldous Huxley's less read work *Brave New World Revisited*. Each chapter is devoted to a specific type of brain-washing propaganda, its effect on the individual, and the rise of totalitarian despotism.

A careful reader of Mill cannot fail to notice his truly unusual and frequent use of the word "evil." To him, everything that opposes equality is "evil." Inequality, he intuits, is not a natural state of mankind; in accordance with human compassion for our fellow man, in Christian *caritas*, or simple decency, we should seek to diminish inequalities to make the world less cruel and more humane. For Mill, however, every form of hierarchy is "evil," and should be tolerated only in so far as it is socially or politically "expedient."[14]

Let me quote a concluding fragment from *Utilitarianism* to illustrate my point:

> As every other maxim of justice, so this is by no means applied or held applicable universally; on the contrary, as I have already remarked, it bends to every person's ideas of social expediency. But in whatever case it is deemed applicable at all, it is held to be the dictate of justice. All persons are deemed to have a right to equality of treatment, except when some recognized social expediency requires the reverse. And hence all social inequalities which have ceased to be considered *expedient*, assume the character not of simple inexpediency, but of injustice, and appear so tyrannical, that people are apt to wonder how they ever could have been tolerated; forgetful that they themselves perhaps tolerate other inequalities under an equally mistaken notion of expediency, the

14 Reading Mill, one does not always know what his position is. For example, he is vehemently against state education because it creates uniformity. At the same time, he is a strong advocate of public education in so far as it is a necessary component of universal suffrage, which, in turn, promotes political equality and expansion of democracy. He is for private banking, insurance, roads, etc., but, again, would be willing to tolerate the opposite if it promotes equality. To use a frequently used example, capitalism, which creates inequality of income, is evil, but can be tolerated only in so far as it is a mechanism which creates wealth and better conditions than the alternative economic systems do. Thus, socialism is good and just, despite its economic inefficiency, because it does not create inequality. Despotism, as Mill says, is evil, but it is expedient to govern the barbarians in a despotic manner, if it can get them to a higher level of civilization.

Such a position creates serious intellectual ambiguity. Is Mill promoting individual freedom, or equality and democracy?

correction of which would make that which they approve seem quite as monstrous as what they have at last learnt to condemn.[15]

Given that everything that hampers the expansion of equality is evil, the question arises: How far would Mill go in pushing his egalitarian agenda to eliminate inequality? The answer lies partly in his writings, and partly in the history of liberalism that he inspired. Mill was by no means the only liberal thinker, but he is the liberal *pur sang*. He is to liberalism what Marx and Engels are to socialism, and if one wishes to understand the nature of today's liberal society, no one's writings are a better source of insight.

Mill created the framework for liberal society by capturing all the issues it has faced, not only historically or during his lifetime, but *must* face. Let me enumerate some of them: universal suffrage, equality of men and women, race and ethnicity, the role and power of the state, limits of freedom, the tyranny of the majority, universal education, private and public schooling, cost of and subsidies for tuition for children from families with modest income, educational curriculum, unemployment benefits, role of charities, religion in education, religious instructions, the relationship between church and state, national tradition, the nature of the country's political institutions, conflicting social and private habits (including drinking and smoking), eating or not eating meat by religious "minorities" and the ability to sell these products in places where minorities live; selling alcohol in places inhabited by religious minorities, prison reforms, nature of punishment and the role of prisons, felons' right to vote, law of libel, oaths by public officials, foreign intervention, and many more.

The above list comes from his writings, and is by no means complete. It might make one wonder how a single individual was able to understand (and have an informed opinion on) so many topics. And yet Mill was such a man. Be that as it may, the above list contains not just the problems of mid-19th century England—they are the problems of *every* liberal society, and some of them are the very creation of liberal society itself. Some of them either never existed before or, to the extent that they did exist, they were individual or local problems, unlikely to entail redefining and rearranging entire social or political structures and institutions. For example:

15 Emphasis mine.

the oath of office by public officials (a problem that recently caused changes to legislation in several American states), the presence of religious symbols in public places; religious instruction and teaching religious history; mention of religion in education, exemptions for religious minorities at work during their respective holidays, changes to the institution of marriage (with whom, and how many). This is only a handful of problems that could potentially dismantle society and its political institutions. In societies with a strong national culture and identity—places with a dominant religion, custom, or tradition (e.g., traditional Christian holidays in western countries) in which the majority of people participate, or where there is respect for national culture as symbolic of national and historical identity—problems of this kind either do not exist, or do not exist to the degree that they threaten the very existence of political and social institutions.

The question we must ask is whether liberalism—with its hostility toward the idea of authority and social hierarchy—can solve these problems without sliding into anarchy, as Plato would have it, and avoid a totalitarian-style tyranny. All of the previously mentioned problems can be reduced, to use Mill's language, to the problem of the "majority versus minority," but not necessarily in the sense that Mill envisaged his argument for freedom of speech would work. Chapters three and four of his *On Liberty* strongly suggest that he offered his argument in defense of freedom of speech, in favor of a creative and eccentric individual, against the mob-like majority that Tocqueville found in America. In *On Liberty* and *On Representative Government* (chapters three and four), we find frequent passages that signal his deep fear that a democratic mass society, with its tendency to create a monopoly on public opinion,[16] is bound to produce cultural stagnation.

16 In his "The Soul of Man under Socialism," Oscar Wilde, in his typical eccentric style, describes the nature of public opinion: "Indeed, there is much more to be said in favour of the physical force of the public than there is in favour of the public's opinion. The former may be fine. The latter must be foolish. It is often said that force is no argument. That, however, entirely depends on what one wants to prove [...]. In old days men had the rack. Now they have the press. That is an improvement certainly. But still it is very bad, and wrong, and demoralising. Somebody—was it Burke?—called journalism the fourth estate. That was true at the time, no doubt. But at the present moment it really is the only estate. It has eaten up the other three. The Lords Temporal say no-

Let me quote a few such passages: "It is individuality that we [the present mass society] war against." And, almost as if he anticipated the words of Ortega y Gasset, in his *The Revolt of the Masses* (1928), Mill writes: "At present individuals are lost in the crowd."

Furthermore,

> The modern regime of public opinion is, in an unorganized form, what the Chinese educational and political systems are in an organized; and unless individuality shall be able successfully to assert itself against the yoke, Europe, notwithstanding its noble antecedents and its professed Christianity, will tend to become another China (Chapter 3).

One cannot be but sympathetic to Mill's effort to fight "democratic mediocrity," particularly through educational reform.[17] He was fully aware that

thing, the Lords Spiritual have nothing to say, and the House of Commons has nothing to say and says it. We are dominated by Journalism. In America the President reigns for four years, and Journalism governs for ever and ever. Fortunately, in America Journalism has carried its authority to the grossest and most brutal extreme. As a natural consequence it has begun to create a spirit of revolt. People are amused by it, or disgusted by it, according to their temperaments. But it is no longer the real force it was. It is not seriously treated. In England, Journalism, not, except in a few well-known instances, having been carried to such excesses of brutality, is still a great factor, a really remarkable power. The tyranny that it proposes to exercise over people's private lives seems to me to be quite extraordinary. The fact is, that the public have an insatiable curiosity to know everything, except what is worth knowing." In *De Profundis and Other Writings* (Penguin Classics, 1987), pp. 40–41.

17 Commenting on the intellectual atmosphere of England before and after the Great Reform Bill of 1832, D. C. Summervell writes: "Political theorists who devote their lives to books, and rub shoulders but little with ordinary people, are very apt to imagine that ordinary people are more like political theorists than is in fact the case. James Mill seems to have fallen a victim to this error, and in a greater and less degree it is characteristic of all the early Benthamites. They believed that a wide extension of the suffrage, coupled with complete freedom of political discussion, would almost automatically produce legislative wisdom," *English Thought in the Nineteenth Century*. (New York: David McKay Company, 1965), p. 48. Cf. pp. 79–80.

an "eccentric" in a democratic age is something one can only hope for, but may be likely unable to find a fertile ground on which to flourish.[18] However, his own argument against authority from the beginning of *On Liberty* can be said to create conditions in which eccentricity is unlikely to exist. As much as Mill's essay is an open war against the danger of "democratic mediocrity," it is at the same time a war against custom or tradition—i.e., social mores, religion, educational systems, etc. Custom, in his eyes, is also a form of authority, and is as despotic as political despotism. In equating the two as inimical to eccentricity or genius, Mill finds himself giving us a political theory that suffers one serious drawback.

England is the home of eccentricity: Samuel Johnson, Lord Byron, Oscar Wilde, and Winston Churchill are only a few of the most prominent names in the family of eccentrics. But eccentricity is not the same as genius, and a genius is not necessarily eccentric. Neither Leonardo, nor Newton, nor Leibniz, nor Darwin, nor Marie Curie-Skłodowska, nor Chopin were eccentrics, but they were geniuses. Einstein, Mozart, Byron, Beethoven, Picasso were both eccentrics and geniuses. When Hollywood wanted to make a movie about George Gershwin, the producers had to fictionalize his life because the reality of it was so uneventful and his personality flat.

On the other hand, if by eccentricity Mill means creativity, he seems to have fallen into another trap. A real genius cannot be born out of a thin social and educational atmosphere, one which neglects an established tradition. Creativity, among other things, is a struggle against accepted ideas, norms, and structures—be they artistic, scientific, or philosophical—something against which it must assert itself. It must be, to follow Goethe's observation, an individual's belief that it is an expression of objective truth, not self-expression, which is limited and limiting. It is a titanic struggle that requires effort, the recognition of which cannot be guaranteed unless

18 In his letter to John Adams, October 28, 1813, Thomas Jefferson, who had an almost instinctive dislike for traditional aristocracy, lays out the ways in which "natural aristocracy" can be grown and cultivated in a democracy. Jefferson's letter gives precise directions how it should be done, and how the local communities and the State should assist in creating such "aristocratic" individuals. It is interesting to note, that not a single proponent of democracy thought democracy could survive without cultivating an aristocratic spirit of excellence.

it is a scientific discovery of an objective physical fact. Van Gogh sold one painting during his life-time; Piranesi was a man of burning passion and artistic genius, who wanted to kill his master for hiding from him the secret of the acid. The impressionist school of painting was, at first, scorned by the artistic establishment, and it is difficult to imagine whether they would have created a school were it not for the authority against which they waged their war. The *a priori* acceptance without merit, or life without harshness and obstacles, was never a basis for recognition. This is not so today, and liberal democracy, as Nietzsche observed in his lifetime, became a philosophy of mass equality, where the demand for recognition with little or no merit is observed as a new social and psychological norm.

In seeing authority, rather than despotism, as a problem, and by blurring the distinction between the two, Mill limited the power of his own argument almost to the point of rendering it void of value. It can even be claimed that it works not in favor of, but against creative eccentricity.

We can reformulate the question that has already been asked: What is the value of protecting, with Mill's argument, opinions that are not beneficial (in Mill's sense of the word)? Mill, we remember, was a proponent of freedom of speech, not freedom of expression, a term which he would most likely not understand. Expression, to the extent it is a part of speech, must follow the same criteria that he delineated for speech: It must be beneficial in the sense that it helps to advance the progress of civilization, of which an individual is a member, not a destroyer.

One might also ask, challenging the logic of Mill's argument: If history unfolds itself as a battle between the party of liberty against the party of authority, is there anyone who belongs to the party of liberty who at the same time is defending the traditional order or past values; or, is the party of liberty a party of destruction, which finds nothing valuable in tradition?

Mill's liberalism, like Marx's Marxism, is a very rich, but deeply flawed philosophy, and as history unfolds itself it shows, as did Marxism, more and more inconsistencies, contradictions, and frightening signs that run counter to its promise. There was a time when communism seized the hearts and minds of half of the globe, offering a radiant future. Yet, it brought misery and death to millions of people. To be sure, Marx never intended to build a gulag, yet those who accepted the new faith did it in the name of future benefits. The alleged followers of Mill's philosophy appear to behave the same way, without realizing how similar their words and actions are to those of the old communists. They seem to suffer from the same syndrome that Aron described in his *Opium of the Intellectuals*. Only ignorance of history, or self-inflicted amnesia, should make anyone long for socialism. Although it is only a prediction, liberalism will share the lot of its old rival.[19]

Today's liberalism looks a lot like a snake devouring its tail, a scene often depicted in art. Instead of defending the individual against democratic tyranny, it insists, as George Orwell would have it, that he actually *thinks* slavery is freedom.

19 The unhealthy state of liberalism was recently acknowledged by *The Economist*. On September 15th, 2018, pp. 13–14, the Editors of the prestigious magazine published "A Manifesto," to "rekindle the spirit of [liberal] radicalism." In it, we read: "Liberalism made the modern world, but the modern world is turning against it. Europe and America are in the throes of a popular rebellion against liberal elites, who are seen as self-serving and unable, or unwilling to solve the problems of ordinary people. [...] For *The Economist* this is profoundly worrying. We were created 175 years ago to campaign for liberalism— not the leftish 'progressivism' of American university campuses or the rightish 'ultraliberalism" conjured up by the French commentariat, but a universal commitment to individual dignity, open markets, limited government and a faith in human progress brought about by debate and reform." However sober *The Economist's* statement is, it is reminiscent of similar past declarations by the communists (in 1956, 1966, 1968, 1971, and 1980). After each crisis, they made their declarations to keep the faith in the health of communist ideology by blaming the former party executive committee. Their declarations found classical expression in the slogan: "Socialism Yes, Distortions No." There are a number of works on the history of liberalism. There are none, however, which, both in scope and analysis, measures up to Leszek Kołakowski's treatment of Marxism, *Main Currents of Marxism*.

CHAPTER 10 | WHAT DRIVES DEMOCRACY? BETWEEN IDEOLOGY AND UTOPIA

> In politics it is almost a triviality to say that public opinion now rules the world. The only power deserving the name is that of the masses, and of governments while they make themselves the organ of the tendencies and instincts of masses."

John Stuart Mill, *On Liberty*

> "As long as the bourgeoisie has not been overthrown [...] petty-bourgeois traditions will spoil proletarian work both outside and inside the working class movement, not only in one field of activity, parliamentary, but inevitably in every field of public activity, in all cultural and political spheres without exception [...]. Parliamentarism is one form of activity, journalism is another. The content of both can be communist, and it should be communist if those engaged in either sphere are real communists, are real members of a proletarian mass party."

Vladimir Ilych Lenin, *"Left-Wing" Communism, An Infantile Disorder. A Popular Essay in Marxist Strategy and Tactics*

1.

In ordinary parlance, the word *ideology* means a view of the world which is not subject to empirical verification, and the person who holds such a view is thought of as blind, deaf, unwilling to consider alternatives, or suspects that his views might be wrong or unrealistic. However, in contrast to someone who is simply stubborn, inflexible, and unwilling to change his views, someone who is ideologically driven knows what the world should be like and attempts to change it according to a blueprint that he holds in his mind.

The German sociologist, Karl Mannheim, introduced the distinction between ideology and utopia. According to him, *total conception of ideology* refers to the *Weltanschauung*—worldview—of an age or historical group. Thus, each epoch has its own *Weltanschauung*, and it is the task of an intellectual historian to explain what it is, and what the assumptions are that motivated the people in a given epoch to think and act in a certain way. A *Weltanschauung* can be conscious or unconscious, which means that we can be prisoners of it without realizing as much.

In contrast to an ideology, which is supportive of the existing *status quo*, utopia, Mannheim claims, belongs to the mental realm, and only mental operations are utopian. However, "when they pass over into conduct, [they] tend to shatter, either partially or wholly, the order of things prevailing at the time." If we follow Mannheim's distinction, communism was utopian because it aimed at shattering the past *Weltanschauung*, and strove to liberate man from his delusions about the objective nature of his relationship to the world and other people.

What about democracies? Are they ideological or utopian? Can the terms "ideology" and "utopia" be applied to democracy at all? If by democracy we mean the opposite of socialism or communism, whose explicit goal was to transform the world by putting an end to the various forces of man's alienation by restoring him to his proper—objective—nature as a "social being," which previous socio-political formations prevented him from developing, then democracies appear to be neither ideological nor utopian. They do not aim—either explicitly or implicitly—at social or individual transformation according to any set of *a priori* blueprints, which would result in transforming the individual man into anything other than what he individually wishes to be. He is not required or expected to change his nature according to ideological dictates. Democracies are *pragmatic* in their basic assumptions. The only claim they make is that in so far as some individuals, or groups of individuals, want to pursue their interest at the expense of the well-being of the majority, democracies are superior because they are better equipped to curb and fight corruption than other regimes. Moreover, democracies never had a theory of democracy, and therefore could not be ideological, unless of course one considers universal suffrage to be an ideology.

That may have been the case in the past. However, the claim that democracy is non-ideological does not find much support in today's reality, or at least during the last three decades following the collapse of communism. Ever since communism's demise, Western democracies have been driven by an *impulse* that does not seem to be pragmatic in nature and displays totalitarian tendencies. They are not satisfied with their previous achievements (expansion of suffrage, greater distribution of wealth, creating open access to education, etc.). Yesterday's achievements are viewed as today's *status quo*, which needs to be shattered.

2.

If so, the question arises: What exactly do democracies want to achieve beyond what they already have? In the former countries of real socialism, the guardians of communist ideology were official chief ideologues. (Mikhail Suslov who served as the guardian of Marxist-Leninist orthodoxy for seventeen years until his death in 1982 was probably the most famous.) Their job was *not* to invent new assumptions, but to secure and implement the ideological program which was laid out in the "sacred writings" of the Founding Fathers of the socialist idea (Marx, Engels, Lenin).

Liberal democracies do not have their Marx, Engels, or Lenin, and thus it would be futile to look for *orthodox democratic* teaching. But democracies have their Suslovs. They call themselves activists. They dictate the tone and direction of the democratic discourse and the direction of future development. Their growing number in the last few years is alarming, and their constant appearance on television and in public forums legitimizes their social role.

There are a few things that these activists have in common: youth, lack of specific knowledge about anything, the conviction of being right, and the belief that they express great truths about the world. They are professionals without any profession, experts without any fields of expertise, and educators of everyone without serious degrees of knowledge about anything. They have neither the wisdom that comes with age, nor the skills that one acquires through painful and long apprenticeship under someone's direction.[1] They cannot offer any expertise that would help us solve a

---

1   My claim can be confirmed by consulting the age of *New York Times, Washington Post* journalists and CNN, MSNBC analysts. A large number of them seem to be in their twenties or thirties (the opposite seems to be the case of

particular problem, including the ones they claim to address. What, then, do they bring to the table? They see themselves as experts in raising "social consciousness." They are the new Leninists. Because the toiling masses are not always conscious of what is in their interest, Lenin created the concept of the *avant-guard* of the working-class, a group of people (who later became the leaders of the Communist Party) whose job was to give expression to problems of the working class. The solution to the problems was to implement the ideas that the founders of socialism laid out in their writings.

This is precisely what our activists do when they talk about raising consciousness. But about what one may ask. The answer is, simply, *their own fears*. And they can be fearful of anything. For example, the Swedish teenager Greta Thunberg is a "climate activist" who fears that the world is going to end soon, and thus travels around the world to share her fear with others, thereby inducing fear in those who listen to her. She does not have any solution for climate change; she is too young to have knowledge of anything, yet she appears on television, gives interviews on CNN, and screams at politicians for scaring her and other children. Seized by Greta's fear, the newly elected American congresswoman, Alexandria Ocasio-Cortez, proposed legislation in the Green New Deal, the fulfillment of which would cause economic Armageddon and bring the world to a halt within a few months.

Everyone should agree that the proposals put forth by activists lack realism. They are naïve and belong to the realm of elementary or high-school school projects. However, what is understandable and excusable in the Swedish child, should be considered schizophrenic in the case of someone exactly twice her age who is a member of the U.S. House of Representatives. But no one has questioned Ocasio-Cortez's sanity. Why not? A possible answer is that, as a society, we are becoming engulfed in pathological thinking, and therefore see nothing alarming about a congresswoman making

The Wall Street Journal, which is by far the most balanced American newspaper), and, naturally, cannot have either wisdom or enough experience to pronounce themselves with confidence on matters of politics or serious social issues. Yet in the last two decades or so, they started dominating news outlets. The general problem that coverage by the young people creates is that the foundation of public opinion is often made of emotional sentiments rather than sober and balanced thought and argument.

apocalyptic claims which she puts forth to the Congress of the United States as real proposals.

> If a man declared that in order to free our cities from pollution, factories, automobiles, airplanes, etc. would have to be destroyed, nobody would doubt that he was insane [...]. Paranoid thinking is characterized by the fact that it can be completely logical, yet lack any guidance by concern or concrete inquiry into reality; in other words, logic does not exclude madness.[2]

This was written in 1968 by an eminent social psychologist, Erich Fromm. What Fromm considered a sign of individual schizophrenia fifty years ago today seems to drive democratic politics today. Let me emphasize this point: We should take the problem of climate change very, very seriously and try to counteract it as much as possible. But if we are to be successful, we must act with realism and a knowledge of what is possible. A society driven by fears, propelled by scared psyches, is less likely to create a political climate in which we respond properly to very profound problems facing the planet. Fear harbored in the mental realm can only grow, and ultimately contribute to creating a political climate more dangerous than climate change. It is called anarchy.

Climate change rallies are only one of many events that attract fearful people. Observing American society, one cannot resist the impression that it is a place where everyone is afraid of something or someone: the gays are driven by fear of straight people; the transgendered boys and girls by fear of rejection from natural boys and girls; blacks by fear of whites, whites by fear of blacks, women by fear of men, Americans by fear of foreigners, illegal immigrants by fear of Americans and the American Justice system, liberals by fear of "white supremacists," and so on. The list seems to be endless. And their fears are presented by the activists as socio-economic and political programs.

Politics is not seen as a way of resolving conflicting interests, in which some groups win and others lose, or abandon some of their high-minded

2   *The Revolution of Hope: Toward a Humanized Technology* (New York: Bentham Books, 1968), p. 42.

aspirations and lower their sails, moving on to problems which people with expertise can solve. Rather, the political realm looks like a spider-web created by loud fearmongers in which the rest of us are expected to entangle ourselves. The fearmongers do not expect the rest of society to join them on the basis of their rational analyses of their target issues, but by inducing fear in others and proposing unrealistic solutions. They want others to buy into fears from which they themselves suffer. Such a situation is bringing us ever closer to mass hysteria, which the traditional political mechanism in the near future may not be able to handle.

3.

The political manifestation of an emotional impulse, which has its roots in the human psyche, suggests that democracy is not free from ideological assumptions broadly understood, and relative to Mannheim's distinction, it is utopian, since these assumptions operate in the mental realm. But as they aim at transforming or undermining the present-day *status quo*, paradoxically, the defenders of today's democratic *status quo* are at the same time prisoners of a *Weltanschauung*. Thus, in the eyes of the activists, the democrats who want to preserve the *status quo* are in essence not different from the defenders of, say, monarchy in the past, and those who defend the Protestant-Christian cultural roots and identity of America are seen as white supremacists.

In their drive to shatter any *Weltanschuung* of old, including the older democratic ideal, one might compare democracies to the Russian nesting doll. When the last doll inside is liberated from the constraints of the one in which it was contained, it starts growing a new child inside, which also calls for the destruction of the older layer from which it wants to be liberated. In other words, the democratic child of today will destroy its parent, just like it will be destroyed by its child.

In contrast to socialism, which was to be the final stage of historical development beyond which no higher social formation could be expected, this process in democracy may be unstoppable. socialism promised a paradise on earth by designing a specific process of social and political transformation (abolition of private property, socializing the means of production, political and economic participation of all). Democracies, on the other hand, do not have a theory, nor a program of the future. They seem to create programs of further transformation as they develop. The programs are created *ad hoc* and develop in response to the social conditions, or, rather, to the perception of the problems at a given moment.

4.

One of the major claims made by Jacques Ellul in his *Technological Society* is that, in contrast to totalitarian states (that is, totalitarianisms built on ideological foundations), democratic societies are "inhabited" in their totalitarian tendencies because they have to maintain a "façade between private and public morality" and are preoccupied with the voter's individual choices, that is, his freedom to choose. However, those fundamental conditions that restrain democracies from becoming totalitarian may yet be overridden when placed in confrontation with a rival. "In order to force the democratic state to come to any decision, there must always be a 'present danger,' some direct competition with the dictatorial state, in which action becomes a matter of life or death." In short, democracies have resources to mobilize a society to become totalitarian and turn against itself. Ellul wrote in the 1950s, and recreates the politico-ideological situation of the time *à la* communism. History revealed a different trend than what Ellul anticipated. Democracy showed its totalitarian face not when the Soviet Union ruled half of the globe, but, paradoxically, in the decades that followed communism's demise. Was Ellul fundamentally wrong? Not necessarily, so long as we reconsider the idea of both danger and enemy.

Fear of real or imagined dangers can mobilize a society to behave in an abnormal, or even schizophrenic way. George Orwell illustrated this when he presented us with the images of the changing political alliances in Two Minutes Hate. The communist propaganda under socialism operated in a similar way, when it conveyed to the masses the image of the Soviet Union as benign and non-aggressive and the United States as the imperialist empire in which the workers were exploited and oppressed. Despite the fact that the citizens of a socialist state could not leave their country, purchase basic goods such as food and clothes, and lived on a monthly salary about eighty times lower than that of their counterparts in the West, propaganda impressed itself on people's minds. This shows that what makes a political system ideological is the mobilization of the individual's mental energy, which *on a large social scale* can be used for the purposes of fighting a danger. The enemy does not have to be real; it can be imaginary, like the face of a marching army, or Goldstein on the TV screen in *1984*.

Orwell's novel is convincing not merely because of his novelistic virtuosity, but because of his psychological insights. From a psychological point of view, a great fear of something does not have to come from a great external danger. An individual or a society can gravely fear things that neither exist nor pose any threat, so long as they are believed to exist and threaten. An adult does not fear things that he feared as a child because over the years he begins to understand that he has no reason to fear and that he can minimize danger by not putting himself in dangerous situations. Fear can be eliminated by reason and understanding. An adult can and should fear torture, abuse, mistreatment, and death. But there is a difference between fear of the communist secret police, as well as its counterparts in military or authoritarian dictatorships—who have no respect for the rule of law and who act in arbitrary ways, and the American citizen's fear of police—who must have a reason to stop a citizen and who, when executing an arrest, must read to the suspect his rights (that he can contact his lawyer, or a lawyer can be appointed to him by the state at the states' expense).

Similarly, imagine an American woman who is asked out by one of her colleagues from work to go out for a drink. Should she be afraid that he is going to rape or commit a violent act against her? Not really, but she is. One reason is that she has been told in feminist philosophy classes that men are dangerous, that, according to statistics, a woman is raped every minute and she needs to be watchful for signs of certain behavior, attentive to the words a man uses, and so on. When such a woman is being asked to go out for a drink with her colleague, she is very likely to be seized by fear of him, or will turn down the invitation because her idea of men automatically surfaces associations with violence, rape, abuse, none of which necessarily come from her personal experience. Her fear is a product of ideological brainwashing supported by "statistics."

Now contrast the American woman with a woman in a "third-world country," who walks miles on a village road in the evening to get from work to home, so that she can feed her children and join her husband. She fears too, but her fear is real; it stems from being helpless on a road where there is no one to help her in case of danger. The fear of the former is abstract and induced by propaganda spread by ideology, just like in Orwell.

Fear as a psychological reality does not know the difference between the real and the imaginary. But fear of something is also objectively relative, and is shaped by many factors: circumstances, living conditions, exposure to danger, ideas, imagination, or even by metaphysical angst, like in Pascal, who noted in a memorable fragment in the *Pensées*, "the infinite spaces fill me with dread." Metaphysical fears of the infinite cosmos, death, the universe crushing us, are not statistical, and thus cannot be confirmed by experience or statistics, whereas the fear of a woman who is too afraid to go on a date because she learned that men are dangerous, can be. Fear in a child is natural because it is grounded in the undeveloped psyche, helplessness, and lack of experience; the fear in a woman who is afraid of men is induced.

Pascal or Kierkegaard's fear expresses deep reflection on the place of man in the universe, his not being able to make sense of who put him here and why, of what he ought to be doing, and what will happen to him when he dies. It is the ignorance of man's existential situation that one cannot overcome because one will never attain a certain or statistical answer to such questions.

As we develop biologically and cognitively, we master fear through our understanding of the world around us, and we balance between the world and the statistical average. Once we reach mental maturity, we reject certain fears as childish and retain other fears as valid. Becoming an adult also means that we can master our mental realm—the fears produced individually by our respective psyches. We can cure ourselves from fears of certain situations and people that we were told to fear because we make gains in experience, and eventually realize that what we were told has no firm foundation. A person who is unable to distinguish between fears that come from real dangers, who fears everything and cannot gradate between different levels of fear, thinks and acts, regardless of age, as a child.

5.

One need not worry about encountering adolescent adults. They have always existed, and their existence proves that there is little difference between sanity and mental illness. However, what is alarming is their number today, which has a direct impact on large-scale political and social life. The 19th century was a turning point in the Western man's understanding of himself in a new *democratic* world. As several thinkers—Thomas Buckle, Benjamin Constant, John Stuart Mill, Nietzsche, Sigmund Freud, and others—noted, Western man softened and changed his "blood-thirsty" nature. The perception of pain and cruelty changed as well. The improved living conditions, development of technology, lessening of brutality in the public and private realms, changed our sensitivity and thus our perception of danger. This is even more pronounced in the 20th century, particularly in the realm of medicine, which made the experience of pain much more remote. Since the end of World War II, the West and particularly America, has acquired conditions of virtually no fear and prosperity for an unprecedented period of time. Those who grew up in such conditions for three generations encounter obstacles in understanding the experience of brutality inflicted by state officials, arbitrary rule of law, hunger, shortage of basic goods, limited access to uncensored books and publications, the everyday struggle for survival, and many other things. The perception, but also the understanding, of reality of such a person has very little to do with mankind's actual history, or even the reality of the lives of their contemporaries, who may have lived under different conditions, such as autocratic regimes or totalitarian rule.

In some respects, such a person's understanding can be compared to "historical kindergarten" conditions, where adults remain children, and cry when they are inconvenienced in the slightest way. It is a society which creates "safe-spaces" for adults to protect them from reality, where the university discussion about great works of literature is preceded by disclaimers ("trigger warnings") that the pages in a book may cause traumatic experiences, that the language may be offensive, and images and ideas might be shocking,[3] and, last but not least, where students at prestigious institutions

3   For many years, in my Ethics class, I have been using a few pages from Sir Kenneth Clark's great study *The Nude*. After a student complained to the administration that she felt "uncomfortable," I was asked by the college administration to explain what caused her discomfort, had a visitation from my superior, and was asked to include in my future syllabi a disclaimer that "we will discuss controversial issues, such as nudity." As I was told by my colleague, a classicist, who taught Greek mythology, she had to include a similar warning that the stories about Greek gods abound in scenes of violence. I soon realized

of higher learning—Yale, Michigan State University and many others—are given coloring books after the election of the President of the United States in the event their candidate loses the election. All such things, as Heather MacDonald masterfully describes in her *Diversity Delusion*, must result in producing an infantile mentality, socially and intellectually, among adults. They see life as an extension of the university.

6.

If Mannheim is correct, that mental life drives utopian thinking (in so far as fear is a subjective phenomenon), then given that the present generation of adults thinks and acts like adolescent students, there is every reason to think that the democratic politics of today and tomorrow will be propelled by childish fears.

> that our experiences were not singular. It is a norm in America. Here is a fragment from an article by Greg Lukianoff and Jonathan Haidt that appeared in *Atlantic Monthly*, May, 2015: "The Coddling of the American Mind. In the name of emotional well-being, college students are increasingly demanding protection from words and ideas they don't like. Here's why that's disastrous for education—and mental health [...]. For example, by some campus guidelines, it is a microaggression to ask an Asian American or Latino American 'Where were you born?,' because this implies that he or she is not a real American. *Trigger warnings* are alerts that professors are expected to issue if something in a course might cause a strong emotional response. For example, some students have called for warnings that Chinua Achebe's *Things Fall Apart* describes racial violence and that F. Scott Fitzgerald's *The Great Gatsby* portrays misogyny and physical abuse, so that students who have been previously victimized by racism or domestic violence can choose to avoid these works, which they believe might 'trigger' a recurrence of past trauma. Some recent campus actions border on the surreal. In April, at Brandeis University, the Asian American student association sought to raise awareness of microaggressions against Asians through an installation on the steps of an academic hall. The installation gave examples of microaggressions such as 'Aren't you supposed to be good at math?' and 'I'm colorblind! I don't see race.' But a backlash arose among other Asian American students, who felt that the display itself was a microaggression. The association removed the installation, and its president wrote an e-mail to the entire student body apologizing to anyone who was 'triggered or hurt by the content of the microaggressions.'"

The example of climate change that I used above is just the most recent among many examples of fears that we believe assail us. But there are many more fears that the people in democracies experience. One can find out what they are by listening to their language. The first thing that one notices is that the current American speech pattern often sounds militaristic and, in so far as it is militaristic, those who use it are looking for an enemy.

We hear on a daily basis the expression "war on [...]," as in the "war on terror," "war on drugs," "war on cancer," "war on obesity," "war on smoking," "war on fats," and so on. Another term, belonging to the same militaristic family, is "survivor," as in "cancer survivor," "abuse survivor," "date rape survivor," "assault survivor," and so on. Signs with the word "zone," such as "Hate-speech free zone," "Smoke-free zone," "Drug-free zone," "Alcohol-free zone," "Stress-free zone," and "guns-free zone," make the world appear to be a mine-field, with places that are safe and those that are not, and in order to survive in it, one has to be truly vigilant. The problem here is that vital fears are conflated with subsidiary ones. There is a difference between knowing that one is in a place where people do not have guns, and, on the other hand, that he is in a zone which is free of hate, smoke, stress or aggression. The first case concerns survival; it is unlikely that death will occur due to smoke or hate. There are also "hotlines" which one can call "just in case." Universities offer phone apps so that potential victims can press a button and be saved from danger. Being constantly bombarded by the words "war," "zone," "safe spaces," "trigger warnings," and "survivor" must have a psychological effect, as it likely creates a sense of threat even though it is rare that these threats are real.

Another term is "Post Traumatic Stress Disorder" (PTSD, which was termed "shell shock" during World War I and applied to the experience of soldiers caught in heavy artillery bombing). PTSD is now applied to the experience of virtually any stressful situation. The African Americans, one hears, suffer from a "post-slavery syndrome" even though slavery ended over a century and a half ago.

One can add to these fearful terms and precautions the instances of so-called "offensive" language—from the use of "he" instead of "he or she," or "they," to signal a sexist, racist, homophobic, and misogynistic language— to the so-called "trigger warnings," which alarm us to the possibility of a stressful or dangerous situation. The case of Jordan Peterson, who within a few months of his refusal to adopt the Newspeak became the most famous person in the Western hemisphere, is a very good illustration of the seriousness of where we have found ourselves.

Another word which one sees or hears often is "-free." "Smoke-free building," "fat-free mayonnaise," "cholesterol-free butter," "pollution-free air," "debt-free life," "stress-free environment," "hate-speech-free college campus." In all such linguistic hybrids the use of the word "-free" does the trick. Being in a smoke, pollution, fat, cholesterol, debt or hate-free environment is presented as a form of liberation from danger, but not in a single case are we threatened with immediate death, torture, abuse, or harm.

A moment of reflection shows how manipulative such language can be. Take the sign "Smoke-free Building." In Germany, we see signs "Rauchen Verboten," in France "Defense de fumer," in Poland, "Palenie wzbronione," and in England, a country in which the same language is spoken, we read "No smoking, please." In the first three cases, we deal with interdiction ("Smoking forbidden"); in the English case, we deal with a polite request; only in America are we told about being free from something: free from a habit, free from harm, free from an attitude. In each case, by waging war on a habit or attitude, or the presence of something, we are made to believe that we expand our realm of freedom, and since it is inconceivable that someone would not like to be freer than he presently is, in so far as something is deemed dangerous, we can impose new regulations, disregarding individual people's tastes, mental habits, the traditional use of language, or even tradition as such.

Some twenty years ago, the city of New York banned smoking from restaurants, and within several years the whole country followed suit. Smokers today are like the lepers of old. However, those who do not smoke are no different from the smokers—not by *not* smoking, but because most of them acquired a mental habit of displaying an open condemnation of smoking as an unacceptable "social habit." Long before anti-smoking legislation flooded the U.S., already in 1987, Allan Bloom, in his *Closing of the American Mind*, noted: "Just as smoking and drinking overcame puritanical condemnation only to find themselves, after a brief moment of freedom, under equally moralistic attacks in the name not of God but of the more respectable and powerful names of health and safety [...]." Recent legislation in California, which removed meat from the menu on Mondays, has already been followed by New York Mayor de Blasio's decision to ban meat from schools on Mondays. "Cutting back on meat a little will improve New Yorkers' health and reduce greenhouse gas emissions. We're expanding Meatless Mondays to all public schools to keep our lunch and planet green for generations to come." "Meatless Mondays are good for our students, communities, and the environment," added School Chancellor Richard A. Carranza. "Our 1.1 million students are taking the next step towards healthier, more sustainable lives. Our students and educators are truly leaders in this movement, and I salute them." The last phrase sounds like an exact copy of the language from a communist commissars' manual. They would congratulate the workers for reaching the party's ideological objectives and for being one with the party; party leadership, which imposed its objectives, would be one with the masses. But the drive to impose new rules in one state or country is not enough. In 2018, the World Health Organization announced that it would eliminate trans-fats by 2024 all over the world. Thus, a supra-world organization thinks of itself as an organization that acts as an arm for a new liberation, delivering the individual from the choice of what to eat. All that is done, of course, in the name of *freedom from making wrong choices.*

In 1999, at a time when America embarked on the "war on smoking," Robert N. Proctor published an interesting book *The Nazi War on Cancer*, which deals with public health issues in Nazi Germany. Cancer was the number one enemy, but there were others, too. The Nazis recommended natural food, opposed fat, alcohol, sugar, and fought tobacco. One of the slogans was "The German woman does not smoke." The image that emerges from Proctor's book is that Nazis fought two wars: one against their declared enemies, the other as a "health war," creating "a sanitary utopia." The communists did not seem to attach as much importance to health as the Nazis did, which should make us think that our concerns with health follow the fascist's totalitarian path rather than the communist's. In the conclusion of his review-analysis of Proctor's book, Pierre Lemiuex makes the following observation:

> Can we say that Nazism produced good public health measures? Perhaps, but only if we are blind to the costs they imposed on individuals. No public health consequences are good in themselves,

regardless of their costs. Even if we accept that smoking contributes to lung cancer, this does not justify prohibiting adults to do what they want with their own lives [...]. Of course, there is a difference of degree between the Nazi tyranny and the quiet administrative tyrannies we now live under. But perhaps future observers will wonder how, at the end of the 20ᵗʰ century, an apparently normal life could coexist with the accelerated onslaught on our liberties.

Today, twenty years later, we can see that eating meat, fat, drinking, etc. are increasingly looked upon as undesirable, almost to the degree that smoking was in 1999. The most recent (British) addition to the list of undesirable habits is "flight-shame," that is, shaming people for traveling by airplanes. Because airplanes add to environmental pollution, travelers need to be shamed for using them.

7.

Freedom is, partly, a psychological (private) feeling of being the author of one own's actions, and it is impossible to persuade someone whose mind is imprisoned that he is unfree. The case of one person, or small groups that allow themselves to be manipulated, brainwashed, or indoctrinated, does not present itself as a danger. Identifying the behavior of an individual or a small group as abnormal might be done by comparing it to the behavior of the rest of society. Such a standard has problems of its own. However, for our present purposes it should suffice.

If the majority of Americans feel that doing exactly what everyone else does is the right thing, and think that one should only have certain opinions and other opinions are unacceptable, it would be impossible to make them feel otherwise. However, two questions arise in this context. First, is it statistically possible that so many people came to the same conclusion about so many habits and mental predilections? And, second, how did such a world come about?

No one would think it a normal outcome if, having a choice between ten different detergents, all American housewives bought the same detergent X. Only robot housewives, like in the film *The Stepford Wives* movie, could make such a singular choice, but the likelihood of human housewives buying the same product seems unlikely. One could say that their choice is the result of being bombarded daily by commercials for detergent X or because the alternatives have been suppressed, boycotted, and so on. This is certainly true, but mental life, in so far as it is the life of an individual self, different from the lives of other selves, is not subject to the same criteria as shopping choices, and if too many of us have opinions that happen to coincide, we should be highly suspicious of the originality of our opinions. If I happen to have the same dream as my wife, neighbor, or my students, I should be alarmed. For the very same reason, all of us should be alarmed when it comes to opinions.

Is such a situation possible, and if so, under what conditions? In his essay *On Liberty*, John Stuart Mill wrote that the Chinese educational system which molds everyone to think alike in public opinion exists in a democracy. Mill's insight overlaps with Tocqueville's first-hand description during his visit to America. Observing how democracy works, he noticed that once the majority has made up its mind, everyone is silent and does not dare to depart from the majority's opinions. If we give credence to Tocqueville and Mill's claim that public opinion creates uniformity, we must come to the inevitable conclusion that the expansion of democracy cannot lead to greater freedom but to a collective-democratic solipsism that will manifest itself in ever greater uniformity of mental habits, which will dictate not only the choice of detergent but of all habits and opinions, and will go unnoticed by anyone. Then a democratic society, as Ryszard Legutko argues in his essay under the same title, is likely to become a "department store." However, since the mental habits of the opinion shoppers will be the same, there is likely to be only one form of mental product available in that there will be no demand for any other, and no one to produce them either. Accordingly, the greatest promise of democracy—expansion of freedom—is bound to be, not freedom, but mental enslavement, which Mill saw to be a result of one rather than a variety of competing educational systems. What emerges from such considerations is a paradox: The way to promote diversity of opinions and views is to limit democracy from expanding.

John Stuart Mill saw uniformity both as a political and a cultural problem. In the political realm, he feared that uniformity would encourage the encroachment of the majority on the sphere of individual action. But its cultural aspect was even more alarming to him: It was bound to create an atmosphere of intolerance, and promote the ostracism of eccentric individuals who are the engines of progress. The rule of a uniformed majority would inevitably extinguish the sources of creative energy. In the long run, such a state of affairs was going to result in stagnation and lack of development. It happened in China and Egypt, two civilizations that flourished for a time and stagnated for thousands of years.

8.

The problem of uniformity, however, has psychological consequences, which philosophers and political theorists usually ignore, dismiss, or simply do not find interesting. The opposite seems to be true as well. Few psychologists attempt to apply their knowledge of the human psyche to explain political behavior, and many of them find in their craft a way of justifying socio-political pathologies rather than helping the individual to see certain forms of political and social behavior as pathological. Notable exceptions are Erich Fromm and Carl G. Jung. It is enough to say that from a psychological point of view, the numerical preponderance only occasionally says whether someone acts or behaves in a normal way. However, given the human psyche's vulnerability to external influence, of which mass propaganda is the most extreme form, numerical preponderance does not make any form of behavior in which millions of men behave like programmed robots non-pathological.

This is the point insisted on again and again by Erich Fromm in his many works. As he writes in *The Revolution of Hope: Toward a Humanized Technology,*

> In all low-grade forms of psychoses, the definition of sickness depends on the question as to whether the pathology is shared or not. Just as there is low-grade chronic schizophrenia, so there exist also low-grade chronic paranoia and depression. And there is plenty of evidence that among certain strata of the population, particularly on occasions where a war threatens, the paranoid elements increase but are not felt as pathological as long as they are common.

The extreme unity of thought and behavior among Americans in the last two decades or so would, undoubtedly, fall under what Fromm terms a chronic paranoia, and, as he suggests, only a threat could cause such a high degree of unity and conformity. However, the United States has not been engaged in a military conflict that could threaten its population at home, and even the September 11 attack, however threatening it was at first, was not a *Blitzkrieg* that could transform the psyche of the entire population. The linguistic explanation that I suggested earlier may serve, however, as a clue to explain what happened.

Being constantly bombarded by words such as "war," "survivor," "safe zone," "hotline," "safe spaces," "trigger-warnings" can create a sense of real threat. Someone who lives a day absorbing such slogans—subconsciously thinking of fighting a war, moving through dangerous zones, believing that a person sitting at the next table may be a predator, a rapist, a smoker, a white-supremacist, and so on—can feel like a survivor in a world of danger. Fighting to be "free" from danger—be it the danger of cholesterol, second-hand smoke, fat in one's lunch, or opinions that are different from ours—might very well be believed to be a fight over one's life. Life in such conditions requires constant mental effort, and in order to lessen the psychological stress at some point in the future, such a fight must by definition continue till the last person or habit that poses a threat ceases to exist. The world requires total reconstruction. This is what communism was like. It made people see everyone who did not share the same outlook as an enemy, who should be reported to local or state authorities, just like Pearson was treated by his son in Orwell's *1984*. Yet this is not communism, and since physical elimination of the enemies and habits is impossible, the danger can be eliminated only by changing people, and changing them in such a way that they do these things voluntarily.

The surest method is to induce in others the fears from which we ourselves suffer. "The new study shows," and "according to a new research," are the two most popular catch-phrases we hear daily. They induce in us the belief that eating certain things is good for us, and eating something else can cause illness or even death. The same goes for certain forms of behavior. This popular language of science, supplemented by the language of "war on," creates fear—fear of shorter life, illness (which we can avoid only if we follow recommendations presented from the newest "research" or "study"), trauma, stress, or some other kind of harm. It militarizes the American society to fight dangers and look for enemies. Because this is not a military operation, but a "war" played out on the societal front, we fight by enacting more and more rules, regulations, laws against inimical or harmful attitudes and habits (bans on fats, sugar, meat, smoking, offensive language, and so on) that have already transformed our daily existence beyond recognition. The mounting legislation limits our freedom daily, but we are willing to put up with new regulations because we believe that our safety and longevity will increase as a result, and, most importantly, because we accepted the *false* belief that all ills can be eliminated. This is the faith that inspired all egalitarian ideologies in the past, and the one we face presently is no different.

As transparent or obvious as such manipulation ought to be, it actually is not and that is why brainwashing works, producing what Mill, Nietzsche, and Ortega y Gasset called herd-mentality characteristic of mass-society. Those who adopted this fuzzy language can no longer distinguish between real danger and enemies from imaginary danger and imaginary enemies. They believe that the enemies and danger are real, that the enemies of society exist, just like the class or state enemies under socialism existed. It was believed that they wanted to sabotage the building of the perfect utopia. Once threats are identified, dangers can either be banned or eliminated, and enemies ostracized (for smoking, eating meat, or flying airplanes from London to New York instead of using a boat) or imprisoned (if he uses what has been deemed to be hate-speech, which is how those who oppose it have chosen to identify it).

We are willing to sacrifice freedom for the promised security from everything that can possibly harm us. It can be a bagel with more than three hundred and thirty calories, milk with more than four percent fat, Coke or Pepsi with more than zero percent sodium, carbohydrates, and sugars. Since ninety-nine percent of us are incapable of making sense of this kind of scientific jargon, we must rely on experts who work for local and federal governments, different advocacy and consumer groups, and various supranational organizations (like the UN, World Health Organization, European Union, and so on), which issue directives and orders that affect ordinary men in Kentucky, Cordoba, Dover, Krakow, Vilnius, and Berlin. This new Health International, like the old Socialist International, has no respect for the local customs, habits, traditions, and tastes of the ordinary Americans, Spaniards, English, Lithuanians, Poles, and Germans (who happen to like schmaltz/laird). It appeals only to the New Man, the new global population, which by no means forms the majority. However, it claims it has the legitimate power over everyone, everywhere. Its political legitimacy is based on the alleged scientific study of man and his optimal development as an abstract human being.

The problem is that we are not at all certain about being freer by following the dictates of science. "The ten foods you should always eat" in a few weeks can change into "the ten foods you should never eat." "You should take one baby aspirin a day to minimize the risk of heart attack," after over a decade of research, turned out not to be "good" because, as "the new research" showed, it thins your blood cells. Not disciplining your children was to lead to their greater creativity and self-expression; it led to quite the opposite. The list of such examples is endless. Given the current ideological atmosphere in the educational sector, one would be right to talk about "content free education," which validates Orwell's slogan—ignorance is strength. Allowing students to speak and write ungrammatically and not correcting them because that can lower their self-esteem, is one reason why everyone gets As. Nevermind that an intervention with a red pen to correct their errors can cause "trauma," for which a teacher is likely to be fired because he used oppressive methods of education.

Despite the fact that one's freedom decreases every day, we no longer see it. It is almost as if the will to live freely and spontaneously—with as little intervention from the state as possible—has evaporated from us. The Orwellian slogan—slavery is freedom—left the world of fiction and assumed flesh in the form of powerful slogans, screaming at us from the telescreen and internet, telling us what to think, what to eat, what to do, and how to behave and interact. The size of the American Leviathan grows as the imaginary fear does. The only way to counteract it is to stop the fear.

9.

It is probably correct to say that democracy is non-ideological in its assumptions. It is simply an electoral mechanism of the majority that in itself does not hide a blueprint for any specific organization of a society, and for a long time it allowed individuals in the West to conduct their business without encroaching on their respective cultural and historical traditions, making them seem different, whereas the countries of real socialism, precisely because they were ideological, required all to look the same. Moscow and Pekin, Warsaw and Havana, looked like the Holiday Inn. However, in recent decades, one could observe that the cultural distance that previously existed among different democratic countries—the U.S. and France, for example—is closing. In the cultural realm, France was always the most distant country from the U.S., and the French did not hide their disdain for Americans. It was a vulgar MacDo-Land which the sophisticated French population looked upon with open distaste, and no two democratic populations could look more dissimilar in their mental outlook. This is not so today.

The narrowing of this ideological gap is not a result of the same legislative mechanisms—like the EU, by means of which Germany and France look alike—but because of an *ideology* that they adopted. Demonstrations in Paris and Washington are carried out under the same banner of rights or justice. The language of rights and different forms of justice are becoming more and more absurd, and for someone who learned to read the language of serious political theory, it sounds "ungrammatical."[4] Yet, it is the only *lingua franca* that is universally understood, and any attempt to speak differently makes a person sound poorly educated. This new language is like a language in a fairy-tale of old, except that it is designed for today's adolescent

---

4   Here is an example of an absurd use of the word justice. "Food and Water Watch" (reminiscent of "Human Rights Watch") published a piece by Jackie Filson, in which we read: "Baltimore Is a Water Justice Leader: Charm City Is About to Ban Water Privatization [...] and There Are a Few Reasons That's So Cool. This piece has been updated to more accurately reflect Mayor Pugh's commitment to public water. On August 6th, the Baltimore City Council unanimously passed a resolution setting the city on course to become the first major city in the country to ban the most extreme forms of water privatization. With voter approval this November, Baltimore will be the first city in the country to amend its charter to declare its water and sewer systems are 'inalienable,' outlawing the sale and lease of these essential public services." However, given that many universities offer courses called "Environmental Justice," one should not be surprised.

adults who believe that the world can be transformed by the touch of a magic wand, upon which the sources of evil will vanish. Nothing in the political and social realm is closer to infantile mentality than such a belief.

The democratic demonstrations in the name of rights and justice are reminiscent of the May 1st Day parades in former socialist countries. In their outer appearances, they were a display of the belief in utopia, but in reality, they were organized by cynical members of the Polit-Bureau, who were far from believing that utopia had a real chance of being brought about. In democracies, the dream is utopian, too, but it is firmly believed. The demonstrations are not organized by cynics, but mostly by scared and young fear-mongers, or adults with an adolescent outlook on life. To young people and adolescent adults, democracy appears to be a toy that one uses to get what one wants, not as a mechanism which, as John Stuart Mill thought, can replace violence in the cynical and dirty struggle for power. Adults understand that loss is a part of life; children do not, and unless we grow up, we can expect more and more violence.

There can be little doubt that democracy can become totalitarian. The question is, what turned the electoral and majoritarian mechanism into a totalitarian leviathan? If, as I suggested, the propeller that drives things in the direction of totalitarianism is fear, one might say that the ultimate propeller is the human psyche. And when it becomes sick it can act in a pathological way.

CHAPTER 11 | ONLY PSYCHOLOGY CAN SAVE US: FROMM AND JUNG IN DEFENSE OF A SANE SOCIETY

> Modern man *has* everything: a car, a house, a job, 'kids,' a marriage, problems, troubles, satisfactions—and if all that is not enough, he has his psychoanalyst. He *is* nothing.
>
> Erich Fromm, *The Revolution of Hope*

> It is, unfortunately, only too clear that if the individual is not truly regenerated in spirit, society cannot be either, for society is the sum total of individuals in need of redemption.
>
> Carl G. Jung, *The Undiscovered Self*

1.

In America, psychology assumed the form of crutches without which most of the population who visits shrinks on a weekly basis would not know how to walk. It is a new form of Christian religion that promises salvation from the misery of life. However, unlike religion, which relies on the redemptive power of the Savior, psychology claims salvation can come through self-understanding.

Yet the great promise of gaining understanding of the *self* seems to be as remote today as it was when psychology originated in the second half of the 19th century. It would not be an exaggeration to say that contemporary man, visiting a counselor once a week, is even sicker than his forefather who knocked on the office door of the first psychologist.[1] Given the

---

1   The depression rate in the U.S. is the highest in the world; the suicide rate among people ages 10–19 went up by 50% between 2007 and 2016 alone.

current mental state of over two hundred million people in the U.S. who take medications daily, it would be easy to criticize psychology as a discipline that failed to deliver on its promise. At its very best, it is an inefficient (and often deceptive) way of helping people with their problems; at its worst, it is a form of social charlatanry that prevents us from facing problems man coped with for millennia. Shrinks play a role of a shield or a bumper between me—*my* life—and the problems I am too scared or too weak to face on my own. Although the shrink knows nothing of them, his very presence in my life is to help me to find the courage to articulate what I fear, and thereby understand that I can face the dangers. This protective environment does not seem to make us stronger, though. We continue the conversation each week, which often lasts for years. And the question remains: Why?

There are many reasons why psychology has a limited power for healing the afflicted. One of them is that, in contrast to religion, it does not have a normative concept of good and evil, right and wrong, which we must have in order to direct ourselves in daily life. Without them life is like a set of roads without traffic signs showing us where to go, and the passing traffic appears dangerous. It is the sense of being lost in the world that is a source of existential anxiety. But there is another reason why psychology is inefficient. Ever since Freud, psychology has taught us to be suspicious of the philosophical and religious claims that stand behind the idea that the good and true are forms of transcendent reality. In doing so, psychology undermined the norms that would ensure man of the rightness of his decisions and conduct. Such norms cannot be conjured up by men through social consensus, or enacted in the form of laws and regulations, and even if we agreed to follow norms concocted in such a way, psychology would transform itself into an ideology in the service of communal standards or the state's dictates, in which case its goal would not be the well-being of man

---

One could go on with the list of mental related problems in the U.S. One thing, however, shows that the mental health of the nation is deteriorating rapidly. It is worth comparing today's statistics with the old ones. A detailed chart of suicide, alcoholism, and other destructive acts for 1951 one can find in Erich Fromm's *The Sane Society* (Greenwich, Conn.: A Fawcett Premier Books, 1955), pp. 17–18. In its suicide rate, the U.S. was 5th in the world.

but the well-being of some social organization.[2] To ensure the human psyche of its mental health, such moral norms must be trusted as universally valid, but they must also refer to a normative standard of what human nature actually is, and, consequently, what is good for us. In other words, we must assume that human nature is not an infinitely malleable piece of clay or a blank slate, nor that it is (completely) relative to the current standards of social or political institutions, or cultures.

This is only a handful of arguments against psychology that a skeptic could and should raise, but arguments against psychology were assembled by psychologists themselves. Some of the most devastating were formulated by the finest of its practitioners, such as Carl G. Jung and Erich Fromm. According to the former,

> there is and can be no self-knowledge based on theoretical assumptions, for the object of self-knowledge is an individual—a relative exception and an irregular phenomenon [...]. And if the psychologist happens to be a doctor who wants not only to classify his patient scientifically but also to understand him as a human being, he is threatened with a conflict of duties between the two diametrically opposed and mutually exclusive attitudes of knowledge, on the one hand, and understanding, on the other.[3]

The latter, on the other hand, famously attacked psychology and psychologists for being complicit in making a healthy man's protest against the causes that create all kinds of mental problems to be a manifestation of *his psychological maladjustment,* rather than an unhealthy (unhealthy from psychological point of view, that is) organization of society that increased his alienation, and thereby created conditions in which the human psyche is bound to deteriorate and express itself in all kinds of pathological ways.[4]

---

2   Such a view was forcefully expressed by Carl G. Jung in the second chapter ("Religion as a Counterbalance to Mass-Mindedness") of *The Undiscovered Self.*

3   *The Undiscovered Self,* pp. 17, 18.

4   For example: "The identity crisis of our time is based essentially on the increasing alienation of reification of man, and it can be solved only to the extent

The last point is the leitmotif of Fromm's *oeuvres*,[5] and it is what I would consider one of the greatest defenses of psychology and the paramount role it could play *if* it understood its function.[6] Without it, we are helpless in defending

to which man comes to life again, becomes active again. There are no psychological shortcuts to the solution to the identity crisis except the fundamental transformation of alienated man into living man." *The Revolution of Hope: Toward a Humanized Technology* (New York: The Bentham Books, 1968), p. 87. This is one of very many places in his works that Fromm makes use of Marx's concept of alienation to explain psychological problems of modern or 20th century man. In fact, Marx's economic analysis of society is the cornerstone of Fromm's social psychology. His explanation of what pushed the alienated individual into the arms of totalitarian leaders that constitutes much of Fromm's *Escape from Freedom*, gives considerable credibility to Marx's concept of alienation as a source of totalitarianism.

5 "Today," wrote Erich Fromm in *The Sane Society* (New York: Fawcett Publications, 1967), in 1955, "the function of psychiatry, psychology and psychoanalysis threatens to become the tool in the manipulation of men. The specialists in this field tell you what the 'normal' person is, and, correspondingly, what is wrong with you; they devise the methods to help you adjust, be happy, be normal." In the *Brave New World* this conditioning is done from the first moth of fertilization (by chemical means), until after puberty. With us, it begins a little later. Constant repetition by newspaper, radio, and television does most of the conditioning. But the crowning achievement of manipulation is modern psychology. "What Taylor did for industrial work, the psychologists do for the whole personality. There are many exceptions to this among psychiatrists, psychologists and psychoanalysts, but it becomes increasingly clear that these professions are in the process of becoming a serious danger to the development of man, that their practitioners are evolving into the priests of the new religion of fun, consumption, and selflessness, into the specialists of manipulation, into the spokesmen for the alienated personality" (pp. 151–152).

6 The two authors of the famous Blindspot, to whose work I referred in one of the previous chapters, fit very well the description of psychologists who turned their discipline into pure ideology. What better ideological service could psychology play than explaining to the entire American population that its minds are full of unhealthy biases and prejudices, and they are in urgent need to subject themselves to all kinds of training, which is nothing other than a form of lobotomy. One could subject their approach to Jung's claim contained in the quote I used above in the main body of the text and Fromm's criticism of psychologists who try to adjust maladjusted people to the norms of a sick society.

ourselves against poisonous effects of all kinds of ideological pollution that accompanies building social and state institutions, including the disastrous effect of the socio-economic organization of a society whose primary drive is, for example, economic efficiency. But economic efficiency is only one of many factors in this psychological equation. Any form of human organization—political, economic, and social—that puts an idol above man's optimal development is bound to create psychological problems. To avoid the spread of psychological abnormalities, social organization must therefore meet the conditions in which the human psyche remains normal and healthy—that is, non-pathological, on the one hand, and, on the other, it can be spontaneous and creative, in contrast to being passive and nothing other than a "punched card." Society in which either of these two conditions is routinely or permanently violated is likely to stifle man's "innate striving for sanity," and, to use Fromm's words, will produce "moral and mental idiots."

The defense of man's autonomy—the realm in which he should be left without any supervision by others, including the state—has been offered many times by philosophers, and one can ask whether psychology adds anything to his defense against the threatening forces of social or political institutions. At the very least, the philosophical language in defense of man does not always appear sufficiently convincing because it is too abstract, just like the man whom it defends is an abstraction. This is especially true of modern and Enlightenment conceptions. A man that emerges from these is endowed with an abstract set of rights that do not meet the requirements that a fully human life calls for. One would look in vain in these philosophies for such words as love, friendship, affection, intimacy, tenderness, sense of belonging to a community, religious faith, sense of transcendence, and so on. Organizing a society on the basis of such abstract philosophical assumptions may be part of man's psychological problems.

For one, an abstract man does not understand himself as a *historically and psychologically* given individual, whose character and needs stem from this double sense of identity, and therefore his demands must be of an abstract nature as well. Ever since modern times, particularly the Enlightenment, the anthropology of this man makes him look thin in his philosophical appearance. Such a man is neither American, nor Polish, nor Brazilian, nor Nigerian—in cultural terms—except that he happens to carry the passport of one of these countries. This Thin Man does not defend his cultural identity; in fact, he defends himself against being inculcated into national culture. As a result, he is culturally impoverished, and his knowledge of other cultures is limited to occasional visits to ethnic restaurants.[7] Any attempt to make him rooted in national tradition—through education, habits, and social mores—is seen as an onslaught on his thin identity. He even invented his own language of defense against becoming educated, that is, against the acquisition of a thick cultural identity. It is the language of "safe-spaces" and "trigger warnings." It alarms him that there are others who claim strong cultural identity, that there are works of literature, philosophy, and art which were written from a specific perspective. Because he is not outer-directed, or is too afraid of facing the challenge of being in a world that he did not create, he builds his identity on the only thing he has— namely, his biology or sexuality, with which he experiments and which he believes can sustain him psychologically and culturally.[8] His so-called culture is not part of long history of human experience that stretches to the ancient Greeks, Romans, Hebrews, Medievals, and others; it is a fragmented and arbitrary concoction of names and attitudes taken from different time periods and cultures. But even here, we encounter a new problem. His history is often simply made up—fictitious and of mythological rather than historical nature. It is easy to see that such a concept of identity has no continuous cultural history, and as such it must be hostile to any and every culture rich in records.

For all intents and purposes, it is a man who is ill-adjusted to the conditions of real human existence, existence which is only sometimes dangerous, only sometimes threatening, but ultimately normal, as it always has

---

7   This problem, before identity politics became part of our language, was noticed by Leszek Kołakowski. See his "Where are the Children in Liberal Philosophy," in *My Correct Views on Everything*.

8   It should not be surprising that there is no specific educational content in gender studies, and other "studies" departments. In such studies programs critical and objective analysis is non-existent for the simple reason it is limited to "sharing" one's inner experiences, and in so far as my experience is unique (and it is, because it is different from yours), it never deserves anything but an A. An F grade would mean giving a student a failing grade for his life. The old hierarchical language of grades was replaced by a horizontal vision of "sharing" experiences, each of which is both unique and deserves respect.

been. The more "safe-spaces" the Thin-Man is granted—always at the expense of traditional duties, obligations, respect for authority, national institutions, and holidays (which in the language of Freud was the authority of the super-ego, which kept him tied to others), his alienation grows and his psychological well-being deteriorates. As a matter of fact, it is bound to deteriorate because contrary to its intention, instead of creating a safe-environment it produces a lonely environment, a cultural desert, with no connection to the past and tradition. The world around appears alien, and therefore threatening. It is a state in which an already weak psyche augments the fears of the outer world.

Secondly, abstract philosophical systems often miss the point of providing a real man with rich existential sustenance, which can be a fertile ground for psychology, provided that it sees man in the garment of this double historical and psychological identity. Historical reality is rich; it attaches man to the historical time, symbols, language (including the language of love and emotions) literature, and many other aspects of human existence. It is an antidote to mental loneliness. What philosophy leaves out, and why it may be ineffective as a defense of man, is the horrifying picture of the ruined human psyche that only psychology can paint in a truly vivid way. What more vivid presentation might there be than the description of man and a society sliding from a normal psychologically healthy state into the abyss of mental illness?[9] To lessen his suffering man has only two options: suicide or joining mass movements composed of others like

9   "There is, however, an important difference between individual and social mental illness," writes Erich From, "which suggests a differentiation between two concepts: that of defect, and that of *neurosis*. If a person fails to attain freedom, spontaneity, a genuine expression of self, he may be considered to have a genuine *defect*, provided we assume that freedom and spontaneity are the objective goals to be attained by every human being. If such a goal is not attained by the majority of members of any given society, we deal with the phenomenon of *socially patterned defect*." Erich Fromm's *The Sane Society*, p. 23." Later (p. 123) Fromm introduces the concept of alienation and alienated personality that experiences the sense of inferiority for not being "in line" or not conforming. To overcome the sense of inferiority, he conforms to anonymous authority (cf. p. 139). In other words, the greater the sense of alienation produced by "socially patterned defect" the greater conformity will a society display, and, consequently, will more likely fall into the totalitarian trap.

himself that always provided the *ersatz* for the lost ties to real and human community.[10]

2.

Just as philosophy's weakness is its abstract language, psychology has its weakness, too. Psychologists do not appear comfortable invoking the idea of conscience. It is as if there were no room for it in their discipline. Reading books by psychologists, one gets the impression that they are afraid of invoking it for fear of invoking religion and being accused of mixing science with the irrational, or of tarnishing their science of man with superstition. Of course, it is also possible that psychologists, like many of those who see them, have no religious feelings, and therefore are likewise unconcerned with conscience. Telling their patients about religion could be seen as imposing religious views on them. They prefer the objective language of scientific explanation, which tells them that for one reason or another the patient suffers because of "chemical imbalance" which we can fix with a pill. The pill, which science invented, like in Huxley, replaced religion.

Yet when faced with pathological behavior (either on a large scale—Nazi or communist genocide—or serial premeditated killings), we fall back on the idea of conscience and ask: *Don't these people have a conscience? How*

10 Such a psychological state explains the rise of totalitarian movements in the past and the high suicide rate—higher than ever before—today. Albert Camus once wrote that there is only one philosophical problem—suicide. This statement is paradoxical, but paradoxical not because of what it claims, but because it was uttered in the mid of 20th century, after twenty-five hundred years of philosophical tradition, implying that all previous philosophers missed the point of philosophy. If one is to take Camus' idea seriously—and one should, particularly today when the suicide rate in the United States is going up at an unprecedented rate and mindless mass killings have become a new reality—it is because man in the mid-20th century found himself in an alienated world created in large part by abstract philosophical systems. One could say that the abnormality of his existential situation made him abdicate all other—philosophical—considerations in favor of one: his non-existence. It is as if with each suicide or killing one hears Queen sing, "what are we living for [...] another mindless crime [...]."

could they commit such crimes? It is inhuman! Such reactions do not necessarily imply that those who have them are religious. They simply imply that a popular scientific-psychological explanation in terms of "chemical imbalance" is hardly satisfactory in accounting for pathological behavior on a large scale. We can understand that one person's abnormal behavior can be caused by chemical imbalance in his body, but this explanation does not apply to a nation committing atrocities. It is further implied that pathological behavior is inhuman, which leads us to think that without reference to conscience and the normative concept of humanity, against which we can measure an empirical man's inhuman behavior, we would never be able to pass *moral judgment* without which the concept of humanity would vanish.

No one would think of Beria, the head of Stalin's secret police, members of the state agencies in authoritarian regimes, or an S.S. officer who killed tens of people in one day at close range, aiming at his victims precisely so as not to waste more than one bullet for each victim, as someone who was "chemically imbalanced." Nor would we be willing to excuse the whole nation for being complicit (not just for reason of fear) because *it* was "chemically imbalanced." If we pass moral judgment on anyone, it is because our judgment is based on the supposition that we have the *will* not to do something that the conscience tells us is wrong. In other words, doing or not doing something cannot be a result of chemical imbalance or mechanical malfunction. It must be the function of something in us that science cannot locate in the human body. To go for a scientific explanation is to say that human beings are robots. If chemical imbalance is found, it should be considered a result, not the cause, of something else that makes people behave in a way that does not conform to the normative concept of humanity, which presupposes the existence of conscience. This "something else" points not to chemical or mechanical failure, but to the loss of moral balance, that is, conscience.

Social conditions and certain forms of political regimes may never allow for individuals to develop moral sense. This is what happened under totalitarian fascism and communism. If there were people who acted in pathological ways on a massive scale, it was not because those who acquiesced in playing the role of sadistic executioners, informers, or traitors were more "chemically predisposed" to do it than their victims were to suffer. In so far as large-scale pathological behavior is characteristic of totalitarian regimes, it is because totalitarianism not only allows pathologies to develop and flourish to an extent that would be considered pathological in what we call free societies, but because totalitarianism is itself pathological.

It is an unfortunate fact that only a few psychologists or schools of psychology paid attention to socio-political organization as a cause of conditions in which pathology becomes normal, and in some cases (as I will explain below referring to Skinner's behaviorism and Blind spot theory) they even lend a direct hand to the totalitarian organization of society.

In his *Brave New World Revisited,* Aldous Huxley points to a paradox that emerges between freedom and 'unfreedom.' He draws the distinction between *habeas corpus* and *habeas mentem.* The first term is a well-known legal term in the common law tradition. *Habeas corpus* ("you have a body") means that one has to be physically present before the judge. No one else can give *false* testimony in your absence to imprison you. This legal demand implies that freedom means the faculty to move freely—not be (physically) imprisoned by someone, or on account of someone's false statement. In other words, *no one* can, *no one* has the power to, deprive you of your freedom. This is not so in the mental realm, Huxley remarks. We will never have *habeas mentem*—a guarantee that we are *not* mentally imprisoned. We cannot be sure whether we are manipulated either through brainwashing or propaganda, and therefore in a mental prison. We can be physically free and yet mentally enslaved without knowing it.

Ever since the 17th century, when René Descartes offered an alternative, mechanical explanation for the movements of the human body independent of the will, the idea of freedom had to be understood as a subjective—psychological—feeling of being the author of my own actions.[11] In the Cartesian picture of the world, I can only claim that I am free when I move

---

11 In Meditation 6, Descartes writes the following: "And as a clock, composed of wheels and counter weights, observes not the less accurately all the laws of nature when it is ill made, and points out the hours incorrectly, than when it satisfies the desire of the maker in every respect; so likewise if the body of man be considered as a kind of machine, so made up and composed of bones, nerves, muscles, veins, blood, and skin, that although there were in it no mind, it would still exhibit the same motions which it at present manifests involuntarily, and therefore without the aid of the mind."

to the left or right because only I know that, through the command of my will, I made the decision to move it. However, I cannot make the same assertion concerning anyone else's movements. If there is another source of movement than the will because it is part of one's mind, to which only the individual that possesses it has access, I cannot know whether a person is being manipulated to move or not. A simple experiment with electrodes used to stimulate parts of the brain in such a way that makes someone move proves this point. The external observer would not know whether I move because I have a will or because someone uses electric impulses to affect my movements.

However, in Huxley's picture, the distinction between mechanical explanation, on the one hand, and the psychological feeling of being free, on the other, is insufficient to make the claim that "I am free." I might be convinced that X is what I want but I could be manipulated to want it. In other words, if my subjective feeling of being free could also be manipulated—either directly, through external stimuli (drugs, for instance), or internal (through different forms of propaganda that I absorb because my mind cannot resist it), I would never know. I could even vehemently fight against any suggestion that what I do or want is *not* my doing.

The above example implies that one could change a normal psyche into a sick psyche, and the sick psyche would, as such, most likely not know that it is sick: It would consider itself quite normal. "Stockholm Syndrome," or the example of "Manchurian Candidate," tell us that given "proper conditions" the human mind can be manipulated into believing anything. George Orwell's slogan "slavery is freedom" is the utmost expression of this kind of psychic manipulation. It is the exact opposite of what we take freedom to be, and yet, it is perfectly logical to believe that slavery is freedom. It also gives validity to Huxley's claim that we will never have *habeas mentem*. There is nothing that could convince me that I behave in a pathological way as long as I am convinced that my behavior is normal, or that reality around me is abnormal. Without an external, independent concept of truth, anything goes, as Dostoevsky told us, which explains why people can commit inhuman crimes without knowing it is wrong.[12]

12 I remember seeing an interview with an SS officer who was in Auschwitz when the first transport of people arrived. After they separated the younger people

Dostoevsky's saying—"If you want to swindle, why do you need the sanction of Truth?"—gets right to the heart of the matter. However, it should not be taken to mean that a person who is on the opposite side of truth or the good seeks a justification for his evil actions in order to *cover* them. The claim is based on the supposition that a sick mind's demand to sanction its evil actions with the good or truth implies that an insane mind does not perceive (its) insanity as insanity. Rather, it accepts insane or abnormal perception to be a *true* perception of the world.

Accordingly, evil that stems from insanity *appears* good because a sick mind does not see it as evil. The fact that this idea occurs in the chapter "Delirium," in Ivan Karamazov's conversation with the Devil who makes him doubt his own sanity, confirms my claim.

3.

I started this chapter with the claim that one of the promises of psychology is salvation from the misery of life through self-understanding. However, understanding of the self presupposes that what we discover in it is intelligible, and can be grasped by reason. Accordingly, what we seek is the increase of our rationality through the mastery of irrational forces in us. The triumph of rationality is man's triumph over himself. Consequently, the rational organization of life is what can and will help mankind in its quest for a better world. What is also implied in such an assertion is that freedom, too, will be part of this future; in fact, freedom will increase as we become more rational and act to our advantage. The advantage, of course, would have to be accounted for in a rational way *as well*, and thus what is rational is what is advantageous.

from the older ones from who were destined for immediate extermination, they were led to a place where a ditch was prepared to bury them. Several SS guards stood on one side of the ditch, while the prisoners at which they shot would slowly walk on the other side only to fall into their grave. The execution lasted several hours. When asked what he felt shooting about 200 people, he responded: "Nothing." As far as we know, SS men were subject to intense ideological indoctrination. But, as this example points out, indoctrination of whatever kind must aim at the seat of human emotions—or, the "heart"—which Erich Fromm, whose discussion I relate below, saw as the problem of totalitarianism that renders man a robot.

A moment of reflection shows, however, that this assertion is not only far from obvious but poses the totalitarian danger, and the reason for this is forcefully explained by Dostoevsky in his *Notes from the Underground* and, in a different context, by Jacques Ellul in his *The Technological Society*. Dostoevsky predicts that science, in so far as it aims at ever more precise explanations of human actions, endangers man's ability to act in any other way than a technologically constructed robot devoid of soul, or will, would act. No one would say that a robot, like the Cartesian man, without will is human. But Descartes' philosophical argument that reduces freedom to the idea of subjective sense of being the author of my own actions is a weak defense of humanity in a mechanically constructed human body. Once again, psychology seems to offer a powerful explanation of how to defend this human machine against its total reduction to being merely a rational robot.

Dostoevsky was not a psychologist, but his observation anticipated Carl G. Jung's idea of the "shadow" or "inner man"—the instinct that goes back to primitive times, when the unconscious or instinctual part of nature, the shadow that exists in animals, was more pronounced in us than it is presently. Ever since man developed his capacity for learning, this capacity transformed his instinctive behavior.

> It, more than anything else, is responsible for the altered conditions of our existence and the need for new adaptations which civilization brings. It is also the source of numerous psychic disturbances and difficulties occasioned by man's progressive alienation from his instinctual foundation, i.e., by his *uprootedness* and his identification with his conscious knowledge of himself, by his concern with consciousness at the expense of the unconscious.[13]

13 *The Undiscovered Self* (New York: A Mentor Book, 1957), p. 92. In his *The Revolution of Hope*, Fromm wrote: "Man, lacking the instinctual equipment of the animal, is not always well equipped from flight or for attack as animals are [...]. His decisions are *not made for him by instinct. He* has to make *them.* He is faced with alternatives and there is a risk of failure in every decision he makes. The price that man pays for consciousness is insecurity. [...] Man is born as a freak of nature, being within nature and yet transcending it," p. 62. Emphasis in the original.

In other words, as rational behavior increases, the instinctual behavior, which is the principle of man's emotional life, is pushed farther and farther into the background. The increase in rationality in the human animal is part of his historical development, but it accelerated as a result of other factors as well. One of these factors is the abstract forms of social organization.

Jacques Ellul is primarily concerned with Western civilization, in which this process of *rationalization* progressed the fastest as a result of the ideas that developed in it. The period of fastest acceleration occurred in modern times, during the 17th century onward. Science brought about not only technological progress, which was in keeping with the intentions of the founders of modernity—Bacon and Descartes—and made man's life easier, but it increased the scientific mentality, which slowly replaced all other forms of reasoning. It also resulted in thinking of society as a function of reason. Rational organization of society gained legitimacy, thereby illegitimizing virtually all traditional forms of organizations. It is not clear what the purpose of rational organization is except greater efficiency.

Yet a moment of reflection suffices to lead to a simple question: Efficiency in what? The answer might be economic efficiency. But economy is only one aspect of human existence, and even if having more easily accessible goods is desirable for good living, should all other aspects of man's social existence be dominated or subsumed by economy? And should the only function of a rational state be to be facilitator of economic exchange? The answer, of course, is no. Its most perceptive criticism came from the pen of Karl Marx who saw the increasing economic efficiency as the very source of man's alienated nature. Although Marx did not think of his alienation theory in psychological terms, Erich Fromm made it the axis of his social psychology in *Man for Himself*, *The Sane Society*, and *Escape From Freedom*. In simple terms, Fromm's thesis can be reduced to the following: Under capitalism, in which economic efficiency is the primary goal of social life, man's life is dominated by economic factors that reduce him to a cog in economic structures. The side-effects of this one-sided existence leads to all kinds of pathologies from which man under capitalism suffers. Although Fromm's interests are psychological effects, his general line of reasoning overlaps with Ellul's observation about the nature of rational efficiency in modern capitalist societies in the West that lead to an ever-greater totalitarian nature of rational societies.

In ordinary language, the rational method applied to society came to be known as social engineering—the term that shows clear scientific provenance and presents man as a cog in a great piece of social machinery. However, what is not always realized, and often ignored, when we talk about social engineering is that it takes into account only the rational side of man's nature and leaves the irrational out of the picture. In this view, the irrational part is irrelevant, a hindrance, and has no role to play in man's life. In so far as engineering is rational, it must *ex definitione* ignore the irrational force in human nature because the irrational cannot be accounted for in its rational calculations. At best, irrationality is a result of ignorance, a phase in the historical process where man would seek recourse to non-scientific explanations, but not something that is part of human nature.

Such a view is a grave omission on the part of social engineering itself and one that hides a double danger. First, it leaves room for the psychological Black Swan, that is, an unpredictable event that can be occasioned by an impulse of one person or a small group to destroy a rational society.[14] Second, in so far as it views man as rational, it claims that human nature *today* has been forever and fundamentally transformed from what it was known to be historically, and therefore it does not take into consideration the possibility of historical relapse, that is, a return to barbarism.[15] Furthermore, it considers the taming of the irrational in man as something fundamentally positive and desirable, both for society and for the individual man.

14 "[T]he future," Jung writes, "will be decided neither by catastrophes nor by danger of world-wide changes in man. It needs only an almost imperceptible disturbance of equilibrium in a few of our rulers' heads to plunge the world into blood, fire and radioactivity" (*Ibid.*, p. 97). One finds similar explanation of the rise of fascism and Nazism in Erich Fromm's *Escape from Freedom* and *The Anatomy of Human Destructiveness*. Once again, the premise of the idea goes back to Dostoevsky's *Notes from the Underground*, where the author invokes Cleopatra who used to stick pins in her female slaves' breasts and derived pleasure from watching them in pain. As the Russian author remarks, boredom that rationality must bring will make even the most rational man blow things up, just to prove to himself that he is free, that is, that he is not a rational robot.

15 This view was propagated by 19th century philosophers of history, Thomas Buckle and John Stuart Mill, and, later, by Freud in his *Civilization and Its Discontents*.

But is it? There are many schools of psychology, but only two that are supportive of the idea of social engineering. Both, let me emphasize, are American. The first one is the behaviorism of Skinner. In its simplest formulation, it maintains that one can stimulate human behavior by positive and negative reinforcements. Human beings can be trained, like animals, to behave in a desirable way, provided their desirable behavior can be properly targeted by some form of reinforcement. If a human being responds positively to a given incentive, it means that reinforcement works well, and incentives ought to be used to permanently ingrain desirable behavior.

Accordingly, Skinnerism is a science of psychological engineering that is not concerned with values and man's well-being. It assumes that people are almost totally malleable and can be conditioned to behave in almost any desirable way. Skinner's behaviorism does not allow for the distinction between value judgments and facts. Thus, for example, equality is not seen as a value judgment but as a fact, and since facts can be conditioned by reinforcement, lack of conformity of my mind's perception is only a matter of imperfect facts, not conflicting values. Reforming our minds cannot, therefore, be seen as a violation of human nature, or as an onslaught of the individual, but of making us better humans.[16]

The second school, very similar in its ideological aspirations, is the most recent blind spot theory, which claims that it is desirable to remove undesirable biases or prejudices from us, or regulate their pernicious nature—pernicious from political or social point of view. The massive-scale sensitivity training in

16 Devastating criticism of Skinner's psychology can be found in Erich Fromm's *The Anatomy of Human Destructiveness* (New York: Facett Crest, 1973). The ideological scope of Skinnerism, Fromm described in the following way: "[His] system attracts those psychologists who are liberals and who find Skinner's system an argument to defend their political optimism. He appeals to those who believe that desirable social goals like peace and equality are not just rootless ideals, but can be established in reality. The whole idea that one can 'design' a better society on a scientific basis appeals to many who earlier might have been socialists. Did not Marx, too, want to design a better society. Did he not call his brand of socialism 'scientific' in contrast to 'Utopian' socialism? [...] Moreover, Skinner's theory rings true, because it is (almost) true for the alienated man of the cybernetic society. In summary, Skinnerism is the psychology of opportunism dressed up as a new scientific humanism." *Ibid.*, 63–64.

America is an expression of this. To use old psychoanalytic terminology, what the blind spot theory amounts to is the suppression of the unconscious by social norms. Before I return to this point, let me briefly signal the danger of such a procedure. Any attempt to suppress the subconscious feelings—good or bad—can be done only through an appropriate technique. Such procedural technique might assume the form of brainwashing, either by propaganda or fear.[17] It is important to bear in mind that what the above theory says is that what is desirable is determined by socio-political goals, not by norms that constitute a healthy human psyche. This positions the human psyche into open conflict with political objectives of the State. Only a demolished psyche could cooperate fully and willingly with ideological dictates because it would not recognize its own objectives as incommensurable with those of the State. This is how science was used in Nazi Germany. The training of S.S. officers, for example, was nothing other than a version of American "sensitivity training" adjusted to the demands of the ideology of the Third Reich. To be sure, America is not the Third Reich, but in so far as the goal of any training is to condition millions of people to think and act in exactly the same way, the difference lies in the goals we want to achieve, not the method by which we achieve them.

Given the two theories' shared objective—soliciting a desired behavior—the question of which of the two is a truer description of what is good for man does not come to mind since the well-being of man is not a consideration. But one thing is obvious: Both theories are well suited to be used as manipulative devices to reach the goal and can be easily employed in the service of state-designed social engineering.

The danger is neither merely theoretical nor imaginary. Scientific evidence in support of Nazi science of racial superiority was hogwash, and probably only few scientists sincerely believe that it is true science, but the conviction of the German superiority made scientific data appear real. Its reality was the effect of the ideological manipulation of the psyche of the German people, which compelled them to accept the results of what appeared to be scientific research.

17 One should note, that not a single classical psychoanalyst would agree that the elimination of the subconscious can have a positive effect on one's mental health. In fact, it would have disastrous effects for emotional life. However, the authors of blind spot theory hardly seem to be familiar with psychoanalysis. Freud is mentioned only twice; Jung never.

How different is the blind spot theory from the Nazi theory? Very little, except, as I said above, in the nature of the objective it seeks to achieve. A moment of reflection should suffice to conclude that as long as an ideological criterion—be it superiority of some *or* equality of all—determine what the human mind should perceive as positive, the health of the individual man and his nation are both at stake. Equality of all may, at least at first glance, seem much more benign than the superiority of some, but insofar as it is an ideological objective that society seeks to achieve, it can be reached only by the destruction of a healthy human psyche.

4.

The question naturally arises: Can one establish what a normal human psyche is? Can one even make a claim that there is a way of providing a definition of what a normative, healthy psyche is—the psyche that could serve as a yardstick against which we can measure psychic abnormality? After all, human beings behave differently, they do not experience reality the same way, nor are they emotionally identical. They react differently to pleasure and pain, and therefore empirical behavior cannot be a guide to establish what a proper non-empirical norm of healthy psyche is. Anyone who claims such a norm might be accused of falling into a trap of naturalist fallacy, according to which normative claims cannot be derived from empirical facts.

This is true, but one could offer a line of defense to the above, reasoning that we are not looking for an *ideal* of human psychic health; such norms, without necessarily being exact, exist. For example, in the business world, we use the idea of "profit margin," which informs us whether a business is healthy or not, and as long as the "profit margin" is relatively healthy, that is, as long as it brings revenues that sustain business, the business stays afloat and it is considered to be sound. The same could be said of human behavior. As long as we act according to socially acceptable norms, we are said to be healthy.

This explanation, however, is not entirely satisfactory, at least in a psychological sense. Carl G. Jung, for example, pointed out on numerous occasions that there are many individuals who are fully functional in daily life, who never display any signs of abnormal behavior to the outside world, and yet who, at the same time, are far from meeting proper standards of psychological health. Erich Fromm once wrote that "Mental health is achieved if man develops into full maturity according to the characteristics and laws of human nature. Mental illness consists in the failure of such development."[18] Fromm defended his position by creating what he called a normative or humanistic concept of psychology. It stands in opposition to what he termed a *pathology of normalcy*, that is, the "consensus" among the psychologists that sickness manifests itself as maladjustment to the social environment. The task of such a psychology thus conceived is to reduce the discipline to a *method* whose aim is to help a "malcontent" accept the social environment in which he lives. In other words, the task of psychology is to make man overcome the feeling of alienation by adjusting his psyche to abnormal circumstances.

Overcoming alienation is tantamount to overcoming sickness, so as to make sickness become a normal state of mind. The character Winston Smith in Orwell is based on Fromm's premise of the individual's mal-adjustment, and the final scene of Winston's reconciliation to the abnormality of the totalitarian environment supports Fromm's claim of the dangerous and destructive power that psychology can wield over us. Fromm's critical stance seems to be strong, but the problem it encounters might be said to be this: How can we distinguish between a psychologically healthy psyche, which has legitimate claims against an abnormal environment, and a psychologically sick psyche that is ill-adjusted. In support of his position, Fromm introduced several crucial distinctions which I need to enumerate here. The healthy person, he writes, is someone

> who relates himself to the world lovingly, and who uses his *reason to grasp reality objectively*; who experiences himself as a unique individual entity; and at the same time feels one with his fellow man; who is not subject to irrational authority [of the leader], and who accepts willingly the rational authority of conscience and reason.[19]

And:

18   *The Sane Society*, p. 23.
19   *Ibid.*, p. 241.

We must differentiate between intelligence and reason. By intelligence I mean the ability to manipulate concepts for the purpose of achieving some practical end. [...] The chimpanzee—who puts the two sticks together in order to get a banana because no one of the two is long enough do the job—uses intelligence. So do we all when we go about our business, 'figuring out' how to do things. Intelligence, in this sense, is taking things for granted as they are, making combinations which have the purpose of facilitating their manipulation; intelligence is thought in the service of biological survival. *Reason*, on the other hand, aims at understanding; it tries to find out what is behind the surface, to recognize the kernel, the essence of the reality which surrounds us. Reason is not without function, but *its function is not to further physical as much as mental and spiritual existence.*[20]

Intelligence is sufficient to manipulate properly one sector of a larger unit, whether it is machine or a state. But reason can develop only if it is geared to the whole.[21]

Use of reason presupposes the presence of self; so does ethical judgment and action [...]. Ethical behavior is based on the faculty of making value judgments on the basis of reason; it means deciding between good and evil, and to act upon the decision.[22]

This string of quotations contain all the major elements of Fromm's psychic jigsaw puzzle. However, the distinction between intelligence and reason is most crucial. While the former is an intelligent creature's weapon that ensures its biological survival, the latter is a lens through which the animal gains insight into the world as a whole *as something to be understood* and the animal's own place in it as a separate entity from other animals. What emerges from this understanding or recognition turns into conscience. To

20   *Ibid.*, p. 152.
21   *Ibid.*, p. 153.
22   *Ibid.*, p. 155.

humans, unlike the rest of the animal kingdom, the world no longer appears as a place in which one wants to survive in a biological sense, where instinct, not ethics, reigns supreme, but also as a place in which one *relates* to other beings in a non-biological and non-instinctual way. This form of reflection, which goes beyond the need to survive, creates the conditions or the foundations of ethical behavior.

Ethical behavior presupposes the existence of the self—which is different from other selves. This is the moment or stage of the human animal's development when the idea of conscience appears. "Conscience," Fromm continues, "exists only when man experiences himself as man, not as a thing, as a commodity."[23] As one could expect, the context of considerations naturally led Fromm to invoke Descartes, the philosopher who originated this form of inquiry which provided the insight into conditions which are necessary to yield the human self. The idea of self is invariably connected to, and in fact stems from the idea of reason. But Fromm's invocation of Descartes goes beyond what the French philosopher discovered: It has a psychological twist. "Descartes deduced the existence of myself as an individual from the fact that I think [...]. The reverse is true, too. Only if I am I, if I have not lost my individuality in the It, can I think, that is, can I make use of my reason."[24]

Descartes' considerations were of an epistemological nature and were not intended to create insights into the human psyche, but Fromm is right to see Descartes as a forerunner of the way of thinking based on the distinction between mind or soul (self) and body, without which psychology would never develop in the form in which conscious and unconscious relate to each other in classical psychoanalysis. Their relationship remains as mysterious as the connection between mind and body in Descartes. I know that I move my body by the command of the mysterious will that I cannot locate in my body, just like the unconscious directs our actions but we have no access to it, either.[25]

23   *Ibid.*, p. 153.
24   *Ibid.*, p. 153.
25   "There is an unconscious psychic reality which demonstrably influences consciousness and its contents. All this is known, but no practical conclusions have been drawn from it. We still go on thinking and acting as before, as if

In his later work, *The Revolution of Hope: Toward a Humanized Technology*, Fromm invokes Descartes' younger contemporary, Blaise Pascal (a mathematician, scientist, theologian and a great 17th-century humanist), who gave Fromm the tool to distinguish between sane and insane psyche. In one of his *Pensées*, Pascal famously distinguishes between what Fromm calls intelligence and reason. For clarity's sake, we should say that reason in Pascal corresponds to Fromm's intelligence, and the heart corresponds to Fromm's reason, the ability to grasp the whole, rather than the ability to find a specific way of solving a limited problem. Pascal's heart is reason's emotional or ethical intuition, whereas reason is intelligence or logical thought. The latter, Fromm writes,

is not rational if it is merely logical and not guided by the concern for life, and by the inquiry into the *total process of living* in all its concreteness and with all its contradictions. On the other hand, not only thinking but also emotions can be rational. 'Le coeur a ses raisons que la raison ne connait point,' as Pascal put

we were simplex and not duplex. Accordingly, we imagine ourselves to be innocuous, reasonable and humane. We do not think of distrusting our motives or of asking ourselves how the inner man feels about the things we do in the outside world. But actually, it is frivolous, superficial and unreasonable of us, as well as psychically unhygienic, to overlook the reaction and standpoint of the unconscious." C. G. Jung, *Ibid.*, p. 96. Once again, what we find in Jung, can be found in a literary form in Dostoevsky's *Notes from the Underground*: "I have a friend for instance [...] Ech! gentlemen, but of course he is your friend, too; and indeed, there is no one, no one to whom he is not a friend! When he prepares for any undertaking this gentleman immediately explains to you, elegantly and clearly, exactly how he must act in accordance with the laws of reason and truth. What is more, he will talk to you with excitement and passion of the true normal interests of man; with irony he will upbraid the short-sighted fools who do not understand their own interests, nor the true significance of virtue; and, within a quarter of an hour, without any sudden outside provocation, but simply through something inside him which is stronger than all his interests, he will go off on quite a different tack—that is, act in direct opposition to what he has just been saying about himself, in opposition to the laws of reason, in opposition to his own advantage, in fact in opposition to everything."

it. (*The heart has its reason which reason knows nothing of.*) Rationality in emotional life means that the emotions affirm and help the person's psychic structure to maintain a harmonious balance and at the same time to assist its growth. Thus, for instance, irrational love is love which enhances the person's dependency, and therefore also anxiety and hostility. Rational love is love that relates a person intimately to another, at the same time preserving his independence and integrity.[26]

And, for the grand finale, Fromm concludes: "Paranoid thinking is characterized by the fact that it can be completely logical, yet lack any guidance by concern or concrete inquiry into reality; in other words, logic does not exclude madness."[27]

One might say that a highly rational, non-spontaneous society—a society that Dostoevsky, Zamyatin, Huxley, Ellul, and Fromm warned us about—is bound to display signs of a high degree of paranoia among its members, and, as Huxley realized, it is likely to be a highly medicated society at the same time. Paranoid thinking is likely to express itself in fear of something or someone, be it habits, speech, or behavioral patterns. Not all objects that cause fear should be feared equally, *but* to a paranoid mind everything appears threatening. When the number of paranoid people in any given society reaches a high level, we can be pretty sure that we are sliding into large-scale social paranoia, which can, and likely will, seek refuge under an umbrella of totalitarianism. Totalitarian slavery in such circumstances does not appear to be a menace to freedom, but, once again as in Orwell, as the highest manifestation of freedom, or, again in Huxley, the use of drugs changes the perception of lack of freedom to an ecstatic belief of being rational.

5.

Fromm's distinction between intelligence and reason looks very much like the distinction between the conscious and unconscious in psychology. This

26　*The Revolution of Hope*, 42.
27　*Ibid.*

is indeed the case, and it is an area where the fate of humanity plays itself out. The idea of a rational society, a society where the unconscious has been suppressed, is what Huxley's novel is based on. Sex is no longer, like in Freud, a fundamental and hidden drive under the supervision or authority of the super-ego, without which society and morality would disappear, but an individual-centered physiological pleasure instinct without a social function—procreation. Nor is it a peak of human life in which emotions find a physiological point of culmination. What appears thrilling in fictional accounts is a nightmare in real life. Let me stress that all the characters in Huxley must be medicated to withstand the unbearable weight of rational existence. Even a constant supply of sex is not enough because it is not linked to the feeling of intimacy and tenderness. In Fromm's account, they are fundamental features of a truly human life.

6.

The origin of the problem was described by Jung in the following way:

> Separation from his instinctual nature inevitably plunges civilized man into the conflict between conscious and unconscious, spirit and nature, knowledge and faith, a split that becomes pathological the moment his consciousness is no longer able to neglect or suppress his instinctual side. The accumulation of individuals who got into this critical state starts off a mass movement purporting to be the champion of the suppressed. In accordance with the prevailing tendency of consciousness to seek the source of all ills in outside world, the cry goes up for political and social changes which, it is supposed, would automatically solve the much deeper problem of split personality.

And:

> *Western man is in danger of losing his shadow [i.e., instinctual nature] altogether, of identifying himself with his fictive personality and of identifying the world with the abstract picture painted by*

215

scientific rationalism. His spiritual and moral opponent, who is just as real as he, no longer dwells in his own breast [...] violation or neglect of instinct has painful consequences of a physiological and psychological nature for whose removal medical help, above all, is required.[28]

Once again, it is difficult not to recognize Dostoevsky as the source of insight for Jung's psychology. For example, *The Brothers Karamazov* presents the panorama of the conflict between the Western European mentality in the grip of Enlightenment rationalism and the traditional, religious Russia. As Czesław Miłosz often emphasized,[29] what Dostoevsky's novels reflect is the panicky reaction of a backward, religious, and traditional country against Western rationalism which flooded Russia within the span of a single generation. One might look at the Jungian shadow man as if he were the old Russian man in the process of being transformed into the atheist Ivan Karamazov, whose inevitable destiny is delirium, described in the chapter under the same title. Ivan's rationalistic predilections grounded in the idea of Euclidian geometry make him reject God (or, as he says, "return the ticket"). The consequence of Ivan's position is to see what Dostoevsky made explicit: "If there is no God, everything is permitted."

However, it must be stressed that Ivan's rejection of God is based on his acceptance of reason, or the idea of Euclidean geometry that precedes "The Legend of the Grand Inquisitor." Now, if the rejection of man's irrational part, on which one's faith in God is based, results in the attitude of "anything goes," the acceptance of rationality ushers in madness, and

28 *Ibid.*, pp. 92–95. Emphasis mine. Once again, let me quote Fromm, whose idea overlaps with that of Jung: "The split between thought and affect leads to a sickness, to a low-grade chronic schizophrenia, from which the new man of the technetronic age begins to suffer. In the social sciences it has become fashionable to think about human problems with no reference to the feelings related to these problems. It is assumed that scientific objectivity demands that thoughts and theories concerning man be emptied of all emotional concern for man." *The Revolution of Hope, op. cit.*, p. 42

29 See his "Swedenborg and Dostoevsky," *The Slavic Review*, No. 2, 1975, and "Dostoevsky," in *To Begin Where I Am: Selected Essays* (Farrar, Strauss and Giroux, 2001).

indirectly, as Edmund Burke saw it, the inhuman organization of society. It is inhuman because it is totally rational.

Let us note that most of the books predicting the future, published after World War II, were written from a purely rational or scientific perspective. Yet none seem to have gotten things right, or have even come close to describing the present day as it is. Cameras at airports, streets, and shopping malls, the NSA eavesdropping, and so on, have more to do with September 11 than events as the rationalists of the 50s and 60s predicted. What happened is not control by technology but the rise of a new democratic-rational ideology that dictates how we are supposed to think and act, and the application of the devices—such as distribution of phone applications among students to call an anti-sex squad—serve the purpose of enforcing ideological rules.

How was such a discrepancy between predictions and reality possible? One such explanation is offered by Ellul, who in the conclusion to *The Technological Society* writes:

> We are forced to conclude that our scientists are incapable of any but the emptiest platitudes when they stray from their specialties. It makes one think back on the collection of mediocrities accumulated by Einstein when he spoke of God, the state, peace, and the meaning of life. It is clear that Einstein, extraordinary mathematical genius that he was, was no Pascal; he knew nothing of political or human reality, or, in fact, anything outside his mathematical reach.[30]

This is the second time the authors I referred to in this chapter bow to Pascal's wisdom. Pascal was an outstanding mathematician and scientist; yet in his essay on *The Spirit of Geometry*, he showed a limited scope of reason, which he rejects on behalf of the heart. This is one reason why so many distinguished minds missed what the year 2000 was going to look like. Their lack of the humanistic orientation made them think of technological devices as the source of control, without ever asking themselves

---

30 Jacques Ellul, *The Technological Society* (New York: Vintage Books, 1964), p. 435.

about the purpose of such control. It appears they never thought of what stands behind social engineering or rational control. They did not even think of the difference between communism and liberal democracies and the use of technology in their respective societies. While the use of technology in a communist society could, as it is in China today, be used to increase surveillance over the citizens, the use of technology in a democratic society does not seem to be immediately obvious, and can be derived only from democracy's practice at any given point in history, which may also change in the future. So far one thing seems certain: Although there exists a wide application of technology to gather information about our habits, its main scope in a democratic society is to enforce man's belief in his own rationality: Rationality of shopping choices, proper parental technique, cleaning, learning, eating, dating, or even sexual habits. None of these seem to stem from the nature of the *techne* itself. However, the belief in *techne* gives us a great assurance that we do things *right*; to do things right is to follow the rational path.

All this leads to an ever-greater uniformity of thought and actions among Americans who give the impression of acting like human robots. Once again, their robotic behavior is not, as some suggested in their science-fiction *coup de grace*, a result of them having a chip inserted into their *brains,* but of emptying their *minds* of the humanistic spirit.[31]

The danger of it was perceived by Carl G. Jung. Only three years after Ellul castigated Einstein and other scientifically minded rationalists, Jung wrote the following:

> What happened not so long ago to a civilized European nation? We accuse the Germans of having forgotten it all again already, but the truth is that we don't know for certain whether

---

31 "The possibility that we can build robots who are like men belongs," Fromm writes in *The Revolution of Hope*, p. 47, "if anywhere, to the future. But the present already shows us men who act like robots. When the majority of men are like robots, then indeed there will be no problem in building robots who are like men." Kurt Vonnegut, the American novelist, connected the dots in his 1961 short novel *Bergeron* when he made Americans act like robots because their minds were constitutionally mandated to follow the new Amendment to the Constitution that made everyone equal.

something similar might not happen elsewhere. It would not be surprising if it did and if another civilized nation succumbed to the infection of a uniform and one-sided idea. America, which—*O quae mutatio rerum!*—forms the real political backbone of Western Europe, seems to be immune because of the outspoken counter-position she had adopted, but in point of fact she is perhaps even more vulnerable than Europe, since her educational system is the most influenced by the scientific *Weltanschauung* with its statistical truths, and her mixed population finds it difficult to strike roots in a soil that is practically without history.[32]

We should not forget that America is a child of modernity and the ideology of the Age of Reason or Enlightenment. And it is not an accident that Jung pointed to America as the possible future battleground over humanity. But insofar as the belief in reason is strongest here, America is becoming a battleground for humanity itself. To win such a battle, psychology, as Fromm suggested, would have to take a stance against what it has preached for the last several decades. It must stop turning man into a robot—this new *Homo Americanus*—whose goal in life is to meet the demands of a purely rational social organization, devoid of eccentricity, individuality, spontaneity, and thereby life.

One can also pinpoint the moment in history when the problem of the rational man overpowering Jung's shadow man started. It goes back to the Enlightenment, the same place where the roots of America lie. The Jungian shadow man is Dostoevsky's irrational man, who, as the Russian author noted in *Notes from the Underground*, is in conflict with the man of the Enlightenment who wants to dominate him. If one may use a metaphor, Jung's (old) shadow man can defend himself against his nemesis, *Homo Americanus*, only if he rebels against the epoch that created him. Edmund Burke was the first to rebel against him in his *Reflections on the Revolution in France*. Burke was not a psychologist, but we find in him a similar intuition concerning man's predicament as read in Jung and Dostoevsky. He understood the danger of the "cold heart," as he calls reason. All it can create is the inhuman environment that poses a threat to our psychological sanity.

32 *Ibid.*, p. 51.

It appears that our fight to regain sanity—social, political and personal—must begin with a fight against the Enlightenment, whose assumptions must be revisited and many rejected. There is no shortage of scholars whose books of criticism of the so-called Enlightenment project can fill libraries, but they seem to have little effect on the general population. The reason for this is that they discuss the intellectual shortcomings of the project, but none touches on the disastrous psychological consequences that the Enlightenment had on us. To be sure, many material benefits that we enjoy are the gift of the Enlightenment. Yet the Enlightenment is responsible for a great sense of alienation and uprootedness, which in turn is responsible for the rise of totalitarianism in the 20th-century, and which, once again, is paving the road toward a new democratic totalitarianism of the present century.

It would be pointless to pour tears over the loss of the part of the *shadow* that transformed us over the period of millions of years, and whose partial loss made us what we are as human beings endowed with reason. However, the transformative *cultural* mutations that occur over historical epochs, like the Enlightenment, and which have their share in our transformation as well, are not inevitable in the same way we say evolution is inevitable. They have a basis in ideas, they were produced by us in a conscious way, and insofar as they are the product of human reason (and not evolution that strives for preservation), cultural mutations can be bad. But they can be also be resisted and rejected. This has already happened. One can hardly imagine a more powerful force than 20th century communism. It was heralded as the most advanced social formation. Yet communism is gone, and it would have been gone earlier had we only lost faith in the assumptions that gave rise to it sooner. It was only when the critics started to question these assumptions that communism started to crumble.

The same goes for the present-day Enlightenment ideology of reason that sees man as a creature who has neither a historical nor psychological dimension. All kinds of ideological training that have intensified lately might be easily abolished by an act of disobedience, provided that we realize that despite their sweet-sounding names of these training sessions, they are no less dangerous than the communist and Nazi propaganda was.

Given all we know from Jung and Fromm, the intervention into human relationships is catastrophic for the human psyche. If what we call "public health" is of concern to state institutions, people in charge therein should demonstrate deep understanding that forcing people to undergo any training not directly related to professional duties is psychically detrimental for everyone who participates in them.

Life, as Jung and Fromm understood it, is spontaneous by its very nature, and cannot be thwarted. For example, schools may be more *efficient* when students are medicated to focus, but they seem to be losing the humanity that comes from mastering their own behavioral problems by means of understanding that only rarely is their bad behavior a result of their being chemically imbalanced. More often than not, their bad behavior is a function of a lack of discipline at home and bad parenting. The causes of most of our social problems have the same roots.

Psychology has a paramount role to play in getting our society straight, provided it renounces the claims that make it sound like an ideological call to social action, and instead concerns itself with individual human beings, as did Jung, the great lover of humanity. The popularity of Jordan Peterson, whose *12 Rules* is full of references to Jung, may be an indication that the *shadow man* may be once more rising. The question is: Will he survive in the hostile egalitarian-democratic environment?

CONCLUSION | CAN DEMOCRACY SURVIVE?
WHAT CAN BE DONE

The Soviet Union collapsed because nobody was man enough to stand up and resist [its downfall] [...]. Constitutional monarchy, imperial restoration, parliamentarism, a multiparty system and presidential system—we considered them, tried them, but none worked.

Xi Jing Ping, President of China, address to European dignitaries in Belgium, 2014

A society that puts equality before freedom will get neither. A society that puts freedom before equality will get a high degree of both.

Milton Friedman

1.

As Tocqueville predicted in the passage I quoted in the introductory chapter, democracy is bound to be *more tyrannical than any system* man invented in the past. While this process is still unfolding, the growing tyranny of "public opinion" and the homogenization of Western societies today are a testimony that democracy evolved in the direction that Tocqueville (and Mill) predicted. Freedom, particularly freedom of speech, is no longer part of our lives, and those who claim otherwise are very much like the citizens of Huxley's *Brave New World*—that is, they have no minds of their own.

Tocqueville's warning, one would think, should make us accept the inevitable conclusion that democracy must be rejected before its grip on the individual becomes total—that is, before democracy becomes totalitarian. If we are reluctant to accept this logic it is because, as Tocqueville noted in the conclusion of his work, in the contest between equality and liberty, equality is likely to win.

We need to remember that there is nothing inevitable in this contest, and certain social processes, provided that we reflect on the dangers of equality, can always be channeled. Equality does not need to be the only, nor the dominant, tendency in democratic societies. True, the world of the last two centuries witnessed a political awakening of the mass-man, who wants to be equal and have a guarantee that he shall have equal access to everything that the world offers. The spread of egalitarian ideology contaminated his mind to the point where he is almost incapable of understanding the simple truth that only merit gives legitimacy to one's claim about being entitled to something. But he rejects merit and hierarchy, thinking that it is unjust, and, therefore, to accommodate his anti-hierarchical and egalitarian nature, he demands changes to political and social structures. Politics is no longer an art of government that makes citizens good and virtuous, but an art of tailoring suits to satisfy the mass-man's desires. He likes talking about democracy, but is unaware that his egalitarian nature and hatred for hierarchy is the very source of democracy's problems.

Several years ago, the respected British magazine *The Economist*, worrying about the fate of democracy, published an article under a telling title: "What's Gone Wrong with Democracy." "By 1941," we read in it,

> there were only 11 democracies left, and Franklin Roosevelt worried that it might not be possible to shield 'the great flame of democracy from the blackout of barbarism.'[...] Outside the West, democracy often advances only to collapse. [...] In the first half of the 20th century nascent democracies collapsed in Germany, Spain and Italy [...]. But democracy's problems run deeper than mere numbers suggest. Many democracies have slid towards autocracy [...].

This should be neither shocking nor surprising to anyone who has ever read Plato's *Republic*. In fact, it is a confirmation of the Greek philosopher's analysis of democracy. As Plato noted, the reason for democracy's tendency to collapse is the expansion of equality. When respect for the hierarchical nature of relationships weakens, social and political instability increases, and when it reaches a critical point, democracy begins to slide into *anarchia*.[1]

1   *The Economist*, 1 March 2014.

This process of transition from democracy to tyranny (or *autocracy*, in the language of *The Economist*) unfolds according to inevitable logic. And tyranny, contrary to what we tend to think nowadays, is not a simple, arbitrary rule, but an attempt to restore order caused by egalitarian lawlessness.

However insightful Plato's analysis may be, it does not appear to overlap with what Tocqueville thought the future of democracy might be. For Plato, democracy leads to the breakdown of the entire social and political structure, which must be rebuilt by autocratic means. In the 20th century experiences of Spain, Greece, Argentina, Brazil, and Chile (and later, of African countries) offer a number of instructive cases in support of Plato's interpretation. The regimes that followed democracies in those countries were autocratic or authoritarian, but not totalitarian. Totalitarian regimes replaced democracy only twice in the 20th century: in fascist Italy and Nazi Germany. Whatever roots, or ideological provenance we trace them to, neither Italian fascism nor German Nazism are part of the same ideological strain that Tocqueville had in mind. For him, democracy initiated a *process* that turns it into a totalitarian regime. He also understood democracy to operate in a non-violent way; its objective is not external conformity, but the deprivation in man of his individuality or soul.

Didn't ancient democracy demand the same? We need to bear in mind that ancient Greek societies did not know the concept of individual rights. The citizen's life, as Benjamin Constant remarks in his "On the Liberty of the Moderns Compared with that of the Ancients" (1816), exhausted itself in communal activities, and as Fustel de Coulanges demonstrates in his seminal *La cité antique* (*The Ancient City*, 1864), religion dominated individual life. None of that left room for individual independence. Accordingly, freedom could not, as modern political theory teaches us, be defined in terms of individual rights that delineate the realm of defense of the individual against the state. It is, therefore, very difficult, not to say futile, to determine what the ancient democratic mind was.[2]

2   Unfortunately, we do not have sufficiently extensive records of Greek society to form a definitive opinion concerning the mental constitution of democratic man and antiquarian society, or whether it also reached an equally high level of homogeneity characteristic of modern democratic societies. However, Plato's description of the behavior of the democratic man bears striking resemblance to the behavior of today's man, and there is every reason to believe

The ingenuity of Tocqueville's analysis of modern democracy consists of his grasp of the intrusive nature of democracy, which can annihilate *individuality* without the use of force, and leave the individual convinced that he is in full possession of individual rights. Since this cannot be done openly by simply taking those rights away from the individual, democracy instead must make the individual voluntarily abdicate his claim to individuality. This problem occupied Tocqueville's friend, John Stuart Mill, who devoted an entire chapter of his *On Liberty* (1859) to individuality.

The illustration of this point is the situation of freedom of speech in America. Freedom of speech matters to those who have opinions different from those of others, but when the majority have lost the ability to form independent opinions, they perceive independence of thought on the part of the minority as a danger which must be fought against and eliminated. One might introduce artificial devices in the form of the American First Amendment Right to defend an individual against imprisonment, but it does not prevent him from what Tocqueville perceived to be democracy's *modus operandi*—namely, social annihilation through public ostracism. Today's "confessions" look like religious exorcisms that purge the soul of the devil. This homogenizing nature of democracy's operational drive must, over time, as Mill and Tocqueville warned us, extinguish individuality and the corresponding craving for individual freedom. The democratic man may believe he is free to do or say anything he wants, but he wants to do and say only what everyone else wants to do and say.

that this man's external behavior, like that of his modern counterpart, was prompted by similar mental processes. Another problem which additionally complicates any comparison between ancient and modern democracies is that the Ancients did not know the concept of individual rights. The most penetrating historical analyses of the problem of the freedom of the individual in the Ancient world are the works of Sir Moses Finely, an eminent historian of Greece and Rome. See particularly, "The Ancient City: From Fustel de Coulanges to Max Weber and Beyond," and "The Freedom of the Citizen in the Greek World," published in his *Economy and Society in Ancient Greece.* See also, *Democracy Ancient and Modern, Aspects of Antiquity,* and *Politics in the Ancient World.*

The similarities and differences between ancient and modern democracies notwithstanding, an important conclusion emerges: While Plato saw equality to be an acid that dissolves authority and leads to the breakdown of social order, Tocqueville understood equality as a force inimical to individual liberty. The result of equality's expansion by means of the democratic mechanism is the total extinction of individuality.[3] The finale of this process is the absorption of the individual into the collective.[4] One can observe this process by reflecting on the homogeneity of democratic peoples everywhere. It manifests itself in the ever-growing uniformity of their physical and mental habits. This was the conclusion Dostoevsky reached in his *Notes from the Underground*, Zamyatin in *WE*, Huxley in *Brave New World*, Koestler in *Darkness at Noon*, and Orwell in *1984*.[5]

2.

All of the above authors present us with a grim picture of the future. However, one could argue that the experience of fascism and communism is proof

3   This sentiment was shared by John Stuart Mill, a friend of Tocqueville's. See *On Liberty*, chapter 3.
4   Following Mill (*On Liberty*, chapter 3), one might ask oneself in this context why democracies, which pride themselves on allowing people to have more individual freedoms than other societies, do not produce eccentrics; that is, individuals who are unlike others, whereas the socially hierarchical Britain, or England, became the home of eccentricity? One possible explanation is that eccentricity, which is a form of defying and ridiculing social norms, can exist only in societies where such norms are strongly rooted. A list of British eccentrics is endless (Dr. Johnson, Lord Byron, Oscar Wilde, Bernard Shaw and Winston Churchill), but, interestingly enough, around the end of WWII, that is, the time of democratization of England, we find fewer and fewer eccentrics. In other words, as the hierarchies disintegrate and class norms decline, there is less to rebel against. Unlike in Britain, Continental Europe, which earlier destroyed hierarchical structures, did not produce eccentrics, but rather small groups of individuals who came to be known as "bohemian." However, the term was reserved for artists, that is, people who were never fully integrated into a society.
5   One should add here the authors of non-fictional accounts of totalitarian reality: Czesław Milosz's *The Captive Mind* and Aleksander Wat's *My Century*.

that oppressive systems are unlikely to last, and democracy when it becomes too oppressive will share the fate of its totalitarian predecessors. Such a response, however, is not entirely convincing. It is true that communism was rejected and ultimately collapsed, but the experience of Eastern European democracies in the decades following the collapse of communism, particularly in the last twenty years, shows a dissatisfaction with the democratic alternative. The generation that remembers communism has the feeling of *déjà-vu*, and this feeling intensifies with each year. The former anti-communists, who cheered the advent of liberal democracy in the early 90s, after about a decade became the most vocal critics of the present-day democracy. What they realized is that the new system bears astonishing resemblance to the old one, and the degree of freedom is decreasing rapidly.

The question is not whether they misread the situation—since everyone did—but *why?* One might propose the following explanation: The anticommunist opposition, just like Western political scientists, did not understand that 1989 was not a moment of liberation, but the moment when one *collectivist* ideology (communism) was replaced by *another collectivist* ideology (democracy).[6]

---

6   One should note here that virtually no political scientist in 1989 and in the years following the collapse of communism predicted how democratic-liberal ideology would unfold itself in the next decade. Francis Fukuyama's "The End of History" gave expression to the optimistic sentiment that liberal-democracy is man's highest aspiration. There is one exception, however. In 1994, I interviewed, at the University of Chicago, an eminent English historian, Jonathan C.D. Clark. In this interview, published in English in *The University Bookman* (Polish version appeared in *ARKA*), Clark made the following remark: "I think it is extremely unfortunate if Eastern Europeans or Russians imagine that the only alternative to the communist state is a liberal state. They will immediately go from one unhappy state form to another equally unhappy state form." His words seemed outrageous in 1994; today, they sound almost prophetic. Liberal democracy, contrary to Fukuyama's predictions, did not liberate mankind; it became its oppressive tool. Why was Clark right? The response can be found in his three books: *Revolution and Rebellion*, *English Society*, and *The Language of Liberty*. According to him, the American Revolution was not, as most American historians claim, a war of liberation from the oppressive British order in America, but the last war against religion, against Anglican order and theology. What may appear to be Clark's eccentric interpretation is in keeping with Mat-

If we bear in mind that both communism and democracy are the children of the Enlightenment and the egalitarian ideology that lies at the root of the American and French Revolutions, then we are less likely to be surprised at how we got where we are today.[7] The two revolutions proclaimed equality of all, and all subsequent regimes were built on the assumption that equality should be the platform on which all modern societies are to be organized. In other words, what we misunderstood for the last two hundred years was that the enemy of liberty is not hierarchy, but collectivism.

Accordingly, the enemy was not fascism, Nazism, communism, or democracy *per se*, since they are different faces or expressions of the same idea, but egalitarianism. What post-1776 and post-1789 political thinkers missed is that equality is bound to produce collectivist ideologies. Insofar as they place an emphasis on the collective rather than the freedom of the individual, it is inevitable that they end as totalitarian.[8]

Why this is so can be explained in the following way. All societies need a degree of social cohesion to bind individuals together. This social glue

thew Arnold's analysis of democracy in his essay "On Popular Education in France." Arnold understood that the rejection of ecclesiastical (Anglican) and aristocratical order will give, as it did according to him in America, the state more power than the British monarchs could ever dream of. Consequently, the American war of independence from the British Crown was bound to turn against itself. Instead of making people free, it made them subjects to an even more oppressive power—the State. The mounting legislation in America proves this point. See also Leszek Kołakowski's remarks on this topic in his "Where are the Children in Liberal Philosophy?" in *My Correct Views on Everything*. Kołakowski's point is that liberalism, being value neutral, is unable to inculcate values into "children." Their absence, which makes societal relationships impossible, must result in the state becoming an oppressive "parent" who forces us to act in a social way under the duress of legal punishment.

7   The reader should consult two classic works: Jacob Talmon's *The Origins of Totalitarian Democracy* and Hannah Arendt's *Origins of Totalitarianism*, as well as the works by American politicians and political scientists Jeanne Kirkpatrick and Zbigniew Brzezinski.

8   The ultimate expression of totalitarianism was, of course, communism, which, unlike fascism, was its most perfect embodiment. See Leszek Kołakowski's *Main Currents of Marxism*, and numerous essays on communism included in two collections of his essays: *Modernity on Endless Trial* and *My Correct Views on Everything*.

under the *old regime*, in pre-Enlightenment societies, consisted of tradition and religion. Enlightenment, with its belief in reason, destroyed both. But the new foundation was not reason, but rather ideological mythology masked as reason. In America there emerged the creed, "All men are *created* equal"; in France it was, "All men are *born* equal." This claim was accepted not because it was true (one cannot provide empirical evidence to validate it), but because modern man wanted to *believe* it was so. The fact that it was unverifiable was shrugged off by saying that inequality, as Jean-Jacques Rousseau taught us, is due to unjust social arrangements. Over two hundred years later, Rousseau's language is still alive. The call to reform existing "power structures" and "creating equal opportunities for all" are the two engines that drive democratic policies today.

20th-century regimes were mythological and collectivist, which helps to explain why they were brutal. They considered everyone who refused to subscribe to the collectivist mythology to be an enemy of the new order, and, consequently, these were chosen to be eliminated. Today's democracies are no exception. The only difference, as Tocqueville noted, is that democracies stop short of physical elimination of the enemy. Physical harm was replaced in today's America by collective "training" in schools and workplaces. Their purpose is the readjustment of individual behaviors and mental processes to fit the ideological norms of the new egalitarian Leviathan.

This collectivist thinking has manifested itself in many ways, but the main object of its attack has always been the same: hierarchy. After World War II, the countries in which neither communism nor democracy took root were considered to be either backward or third-world. communism, on the other hand, was considered modern because it abolished classes; liberal-democracies were considered modern because they abolished social hierarchies and privileges. Classes, hierarchies, and privileges were perceived as manifestations of the oppressive past; egalitarianism, on the other hand, was by definition modern, but also benign. The absurdity of this idea becomes obvious when we observe the economic realm. The fact that communist regimes were economically inefficient, and lacked the ability to modernize their industries, or that shelves carrying basic products, easily available in capitalist countries (including those under dictatorships) were empty, did not matter. South American countries, with economies much more advanced than anything known in Eastern European countries, belonged to the "developing" (third) world, while the German Democratic Republic or socialist Romania were modern. Democracies retained hierarchy in the economic realm, and in this they manifested its practical superiority. Private property and wealth create their own forms of hierarchy or classes, but it is the only form of hierarchy that is tolerated, probably because it is based on the myth that everybody can become rich in America.

The abolishing of the old regimes created a problem of social organization. The glue that held individuals together under the old regime was *reverence* in the form of chivalry, honor, and virtue. (All three, it must be noted, are indicators and manifestations and recognitions of inequality.) Submission to authority was voluntary and, therefore, as Burke and Constant wrote, made it seem that "power was gentle."[9] Democracy could claim to be less arbitrary than old monarchies, but could not claim to be less oppressive merely because the elected officials could no longer exercise power in an arbitrary way. As Tocqueville pointed out, when the elected officials in America know that they have the support of the majority, they tend to exercise power to an extent unknown to European officials, whose power is often arbitrary. As a consequence, in any democracy, the minority is deprived of recourse to justice.[10]

9   This idea can also be found in Plato. In the passage previously referenced, he draws the distinction between rulers and the ruled, parents and children, men and women, citizens and foreigners, elders and youngsters, teachers and students. Plato's list can be reduced to a simple formula: those who are in the position of authority and those who are not. Once this recognition of authority breaks down, social structures start breaking down too.

10   In the section "Tyranny of the Majority," Tocqueville addresses this issue by refusing to bow to the decisions of the majority only because it is a majority. "I regard it as an impious and detestable maxim that in matters of government the majority of a people has the right to do everything, and nevertheless I place the origin of all powers in the will of the majority. Am I in contradiction with myself? There is one law which has been made, or at least adopted, not by the majority of this or that people, but by the majority of all men. That law is justice.

Justice therefore forms the boundary to each people's right. A nation is like a jury entrusted to represent universal society and to apply the justice which is its law. Should the jury representing society have greater power than

What happened as societies transitioned from old to new regimes? In the absence of reverence, honor, chivalry, and virtue—all expressions of a hierarchical vision of human relationships—submission must be imposed on the individuals who assert their freedom from natural obligations and their right to do so. The only way to keep them together was compulsion. However, unlike in hard totalitarian regimes, which use brutal force, fear, and intimidation, in democracies, compulsion manifests itself in mounting legislation to regulate each aspect of human existence. Therefore, it is not surprising to see that the core of democratic politics is to pass new legislation in mass quantities. Legislation fills the vacuum that piety and reverence traditionally played. And as legislation increases, so does the state and its power to enforce it. This point forms the centerpiece of Mathew Arnold's analysis of the danger of democracy. In attacking hierarchy, democracy, he predicted, must endow the state with an excess of power that no monarch could ever attain.

3.

Given that the force that threatens freedom is the expansion of equality, the question that stands before us can be formulated in the following way: Can one limit democracy's expansion—which is equality's engine—in a way that is consistent with the idea of democracy at the same time? To put it differently, can one limit equality to preserve democracy?

> that very society whose laws it applies? Consequently, when I refuse to obey an unjust law, I by no means deny the majority's right to give orders; I only appeal from the sovereignty of the people to the sovereignty of human race."
>
> An echo of this argument can be found in John Stuart Mill's famous argument for freedom of speech. However, in contrast to Tocqueville, who denies the majority's right to impose its opinions on the individual by invoking inviolable right of universal man, Mill's argument is based on the premise that "the power itself is illegitimate."
>
> Needless to say, neither argument seems to solve the practical problem that the democratic rule of the majority creates. A number of decisions made by the American Supreme Court (such as gay marriage), and the British Judge's decision (referred to above) that the Biblical assertion of two human sex groups is inconsistent with human dignity (i.e. the dignity of a man who claims to be a woman), shows the difficulties in protecting an objective notion of justice against the pressure of the idea of equality of all lifestyles.

Some of the earliest criticism of democracy comes from Plato, who, in his dialogue *Protagoras*, asserts through Socrates that when it comes to ship-building, masonry, etc., the Athenians look for experts, but when it comes to politics, everybody claims to be an expert. Socrates' insight strikes at the very heart of the democratic rule, that is, the ability of average man, who lacks sufficient knowledge, to participate in political decision making.

Modern thought provides justification for the average man's participation in politics. As Montaigne and Descartes claimed, commonsense is equally distributed in all men and, therefore, everybody is the best judge in matters that concern him. Their claim was not intended to become a political tool, but insofar as it marked the distinction between the ancients and the moderns, it prepared the foundation for democratic politics of later centuries. The second claim can be found in John Stuart Mill, who famously claimed that power is illegitimate, and, therefore, no single person—provided that he is in possession of full rational powers—should have more power over another.

Even if we accept both of claims, the problem of government "by the people" does not entirely disappear. The claim regarding "common sense" refers to the private, not public realm—that is, the *res publica*. Accordingly, I can legitimately claim that no one should interfere with how I organize my private life, or how I run my business; it is another thing to infer from it that my "common sense" is good enough to make political decisions concerning the organization of the public realm.

Is such an organization of public life, by people who lack sufficient knowledge and cultivation, even possible? Mathew Arnold, for example, feared that in the absence of any permanent aristocratic and ecclesiastical[11] element, which dictates "the tone to the nation," democracy will lead to the loss of "social cohesion," the inevitable result of which will be the growth of state power—the substitute for voluntary submission based on virtue.

---

11 One should notice the problematic nature of the Catholic Church in America, which is perceived by many as an authoritarian institution. While Protestant churches, whose centralization is much weaker than that of the Catholic Church, found the accommodation to the demands of democratic world easier. At the same time, the relative ease with which Protestant churches accepted democratic demands is the reason why their theology became an extension of secular social messages and limited to popular claims about "social justice."

The lack of a mechanism in a democracy that could elevate ordinary men, so that virtue, rather than coercion, would hold people together, was of concern to Jefferson, Tocqueville, Arnold, and Mill. Mill thought American democracy was based on a "false model" because it excluded the most cultivated members of American society from running for office, and those who did, as Tocqueville noted, could succeed only if they became a "mouthpiece" of the majority. To counteract this tendency in democracy, Thomas Jefferson and John Adams thought of devising a way of finding a natural, as opposed to hereditary, aristocracy. In his letter to Adams (October 28, 1813), Jefferson wrote:

> For I agree with you that there is a natural aristocracy among men. The grounds of this are virtue and talents. And indeed it would have been inconsistent in creation to have formed man for the social state, and not to have provided virtue and wisdom enough to manage the concerns of the society. May we not even say that that form of government is the best which provides the most effectually for a pure selection of these natural *aristoi* into the offices of government.

The Jeffersonian idea remains unrealized, but what is worse is that in the minds of democratic people today, democracy means absolute rejection of the belief that there is anyone who is by nature better qualified to make decisions for others. Accordingly, democracy is not just a system of non-exclusion through voting, but also a system which disregards personal virtues, or mental qualities, which in the past were believed to be essential for those who wanted to exercise political power. Such reasoning implies, first, that democracy is a mechanism that can function independently of the established habits, norms, religion, culture, wisdom, knowledge, and personal qualities of people who are elected, and that the only thing necessary for democracy to function is the acceptance of the non-arbitrary procedures.

The absurdity of this reasoning can be easily demonstrated. If the elected officials do not have to display any superior qualities, everyone, as Socrates noticed, is indeed qualified to rule. Electing Mrs. Jones rather than Mrs. Smith means that we judge Mrs. Jones to be more qualified than Mr. Smith. Otherwise, the electoral process would be pointless and we could choose random individuals by lot.[12] This reasoning should appear absurd, and if we accept its absurdity, we should accept the conclusion that universal suffrage, which gives everyone the power to elect officials, is *not* the same thing as the possibility of anyone becoming an elected official. What is needed is virtue and knowledge. This analogy can be extended to other disciplines and realms of human endeavors, such as literary criticism, music, or architecture. I do not have to be a pianist, a writer, a painter, or an architect to appreciate a work of literature, a piece of musical composition, a painting, or the beauty of a building. No one excluded me from becoming a pianist, a writer, a painter, or an architect, except lack of natural talent or my own negligence in developing necessary skills.

We can apply this reasoning to democratic politics. Even if we accept the assumption that universal suffrage precludes the idea that there are no individuals or groups in a society who are excluded from casting a vote, there is nothing undemocratic about the suggestion that those who run for public offices should meet certain criteria. John Stuart Mill, one of the greatest champions of universal suffrage, expressed this sentiment in his *On Representative Government* (Chapter VIII; 1861). In it, Mill formulated an argument for universal suffrage, though he imposed limits.

> I regard it as wholly inadmissible that any person should participate in universal suffrage, without being able to read, write, and, I would add, perform the common operations in arithmetic [...]. It would be eminently desirable that other things besides reading, writing, and arithmetic, could be made necessary to the suffrage; that some knowledge of the conformation of the earth, its natural and political divisions, the elements of general history, and of the history and institutions of their own country, could be required of the electors' world.

12 Ancient democracy was based on such reasoning, and the election to many offices were by lot. The best book on Greek democracy is still the classic by A.H.M. Jones: *Athenian Democracy*. See also Jacqueline de Romily, *Actualité de la démocratie athénienne*; John Thorley, *Athenian Democracy*; Robin Barrow, *Athenian Democracy*, Kurt Laaufraub, Josiah Ober and Kurt Wallace, *Origins of Ancient Democracy*. Peter Jones' *An Intelligent Person's Guide to Classics* contains a very good chapter on democracy and references to its Ancient critics.

Allowing people who do not meet these requirements is, Mill continues, like giving suffrage to "a child who could not speak; and it would not be society that would exclude him, but his own laziness [...]. Universal teaching must precede universal enfranchisement." Today's democrats, who think of universal suffrage as a God-given right, would probably decry Mill's suggestions as discriminatory, undemocratic, or as an open attempt to undermine democracy itself.

Mill's suggestion contains two important insights that may have provided older democracies with a mechanism against its self-destructive drive. It also points to the inability of democracy to manage the affairs of massive societies. First, it is said that democracy is unlikely to function in societies that have not achieved a certain level of civilized development and that intellectual skills, developed through education, are a condition of democratic government. This in itself sounds commonsensical, but it carries a further implication that Mill may not have anticipated.

On Representative Government was published in 1861. This was a world in which no one had seen a car, airplane, radio, television, telephone, electrical devices, refrigerators, computers, internet, atomic bombs—to name a few wonders we take for granted. Mill's world was not only unlike ours, but much simpler than ours. The knowledge needed to master the wonders of the world in 1861 was nothing compared to what was needed in 1961, nevermind in 2021. One can say without exaggeration that we have accumulated more knowledge between 1861 and 2021 than we did from the time of ancient Greece to 1861. Mill's "education for democracy" consists of basic literacy, geography, and world and national history. By today's standards, this does not sound like much, and most high-school graduates would meet Mill's requirements. But Mill's education was designed for the world in the second half of 19th century. Given the complexity of the world today, one wonders how much more demanding education should be today to sustain democracy. In fact, there is not a single person who can master the innumerable wonders of today. This increase in knowledge poses consequences for the very life of democracy as a political system in 21st century.

Observing the discrepancy between the average man's knowledge of the world and what is required to govern this present world reveals that the average man is ill-equipped to direct the political process safely. The fact is that there are fewer and fewer people who can make "informed decisions," and since the world is becoming more and more complex each day, there may be no one person in the near future who will be able to make qualifiably "informed decisions." They will be no more than educated guesses, as unreliable as the average man's best wager. This leads to the conclusion that democracy may collapse because we can no longer master the knowledge required to ensure that the exercise of political and social control actually provides social stability.

4.

The question I raised at the beginning of this chapter concerns the relationship between the freedom of the individual and the equality of all. Is there something anti-democratic in suggesting that democracy should be limited, say, to the electoral and judicial realms, and excluded from, for example, education, employment, etc.? One could say that, so long as in other realms there is a non-democratic alternative—in the sense of being better or more efficient as a mechanism—it should be employed. Can one sensibly argue that we need democratic-egalitarian procedures in selecting the best students, teachers, and candidates for employment, the best scientists and scholars for awards, beyond recognizing those who plainly meet the criteria contained in the nature of the profession or discipline?

"Multiculturalism," or the representation of so-called minorities, has become a universal litmus test of democracy. But a moment of reflection suffices to show that it only replaces the criterion of excellence. All such a criterion can do is lead to a lowering of standards, which is detrimental to a discipline or profession; but above all, it is morally wrong and harmful. How can one award, select, or employ someone inferior to another candidate, and claim that it is the morally right thing to do? Given that this is how things are (and that in good faith, not cynicism), we may conclude that we have been brainwashed by egalitarian propaganda, which has made us believe that future benefits will outweigh today's evils. This is exactly what the former communists believed.[13]

13 Here is an explanation given by a former Marxist philosopher: "My strong impression is that in the early postwar years, committed communists [...] in

In 1963, Aldous Huxley published *Brave New World Revisited*. The book consists of several chapters concerned with different forms of mind manipulation, from crude forms of Nazi propaganda, to democratic-consumerist propaganda (advertisements, subliminal cuts, etc.), and the influence of drugs on human cognitive processes. The book is easily accessible, and there is no point in repeating the author's warnings. There is one exception. Huxley introduces the distinction between *habeas corpus* and *habeas mentem,* to which I referred earlier. The first one is a well-known English legal term, whereas the latter is the author's invention for the purpose of highlighting the contrast between lack of physical freedom and lack of freedom in the mental realm. *Habeas corpus* is "a writ requiring a person under arrest to be brought before a judge or into court, especially to secure the person's release unless lawful grounds are shown for their detention." While the first defines freedom from physical imprisonment, the latter defines *freedom from mental imprisonment*. As Huxley remarks, so long as we succumb to propaganda, we cannot be said to be free. To put it differently, we are victims of mental manipulation or brainwashing.

We might apply Huxley's distinction, on which, let's note, the premise of his *Brave New World* is based, to the situation in today's America. Although the realm of freedom has diminished, in some respects surpassing the restrictions seen in former communist countries, only a few Americans see it, let alone rebel against it. The overwhelming majority are like denizens of the Brave New World; they do not appear to see that they no longer enjoy the freedoms that they used to. Freedom of speech is hardly existent, and the majority of colleges are now bastions of the politically correct orthodoxy, having achieved a sovereignty in this regard unknown under communism. Yet we see no signs of preparation of mass rebellion against the enemy of freedom. The propaganda about living in the freest country in world's history is as loud today as it was fifty or a hundred years ago. The

Poland were intellectually less corrupt but more cynical than was the case in other countries. By 'cynical' [...] [I mean] they knew that what the Party wanted to convey to the 'masses' was a pure lie, but they accepted and sanctioned it for the sake of the future blessings of the socialist community." Leszek Kołakowski, "Totalitarianism and the Virtue of the Lie," in *My Correct Views on Everything.*

same propaganda never tires of highlighting the contrast between freedom in America and, for example, lack of freedom in China. This was certainly true one hundred and sixty years ago.

As John Stuart Mill observed in 1861, "The modern regime of public opinion is, in unorganized form, what the Chinese educational systems are in an organized; and unless individuality shall be able successfully to assert itself against this yoke, Europe [...] will tend to become another China." However, what was true of China is, according to John Gray, England's most perceptive political philosopher, true of America today:

> When students from China study in Western countries, one of the lessons they learn is that the enforcement of intellectual orthodoxy does not require an authoritarian government. In institutions that proclaim their commitment to critical inquiry, censorship is most effective when it is self-imposed. A defining feature of tyranny, the policing of opinion is now established practice in societies that believe themselves to be freer than they have ever been.[14]

It is not China that caught up with America; it was America that caught up with China, and if the Americans do not see the difference,[15] it is because propaganda really does work, just as it did in Huxley's world.

5.

Is there something that can be done, and if so, what? Different authors to whom I referred in earlier chapters identified different sources of the totalitarian dictatorship. For Jacques Ellul, it was the nature of technology. There is no doubt that technology deprived us of privacy. The presence of cameras, computers, financial and phone records, Alexa's recording of everything we say, let alone facial recognition devices—all of these threaten privacy, without which there is no free society. However, social consensus and understanding

14 "The Problem of Hyper-Liberalism," in *TLS*, March 2018.
15 Of course, the difference is the physical brutality of Chinese Communist regime, which, happily, we here in the West do not experience.

of the danger that technology poses can easily provoke legislation that would limit the intrusive nature of technology.

For Aldous Huxley, it was propagandistic mind manipulation that posed a threat. However, Huxley, in my opinion, made an error in his assessment of democracy. He thought of democracy by analogy to previous totalitarian regimes that divided a society into a small group of cynical rulers and the rest, who were manipulated by the propagandistic masters *à la* the Grand Inquisitor, whom he invokes at the very end of his *Brave New World Revisited*. For all we have learned about democracy since he published his book in 1963, Huxley was wrong to think that in a democracy there is a permanent class of cynical rulers who are either exempt from democratic propaganda or whose minds are strong enough to resist it. Even the most powerful classes do not exercise their power in any way that would guarantee them a permanent seat from which to control and manipulate the mindless masses.

It is not Dostoevsky's Grand Inquisitor in whom we must look for a solution to our problems, but Plato's Socrates. When asked about the name of the greatest sophist, Socrates did not name any great man of his time. Instead, he said that it was democracy itself—the system that makes truth relative, and in doing so, renders the opinion of the majority the supreme ruler. Thucydides and Plutarch's writings abound in examples of how this worked. This is the insight that Tocqueville explored in his work. However, what Tocqueville understood, and what in Plato, at least on the surface, seems to play a secondary role, is the paramount importance of the idea of equality as the mechanism of mass-enslavement.

If there is a way of stopping democracy from further expansion, it is through the limitation of the egalitarian propaganda that permeates democratic societies. How different is it from the Nazi or communist propaganda? It is not different at all. The idea of equality lies at the root of what in ordinary language we call "discrimination." Sexism, racism, xenophobia, homophobia, misogyny, etc., which are different names for discrimination, are no more than ideological clichés. They are not helpful in describing our reality, let alone in solving those problems to which such terms allegedly refer. They misidentify the enemy, and this misidentification makes addressing the problem—to the extent to which it can be solved—impossible. Not every manifestation of, say, "under-representation" of a group in certain disciplines and walks of life is due to discrimination, and using this term only encourages the problem to persist.

The first thing that the people formerly enslaved by communism did was shake off the ideological Newspeak. An example is the phrase "economic exploitation under capitalism"—a phrase that the communist propagandists used daily to discourage the population from thinking about private property. Under socialism, on the other hand, we were told that exploitation did not exist, since private property was abolished. The fact was that economic efficiency was abolished as well, and the new economic alternative created permanent shortages of basic goods. People were willing to suffer shortages of goods because the alternative—namely, exploitation—appeared even worse. When the system collapsed, private property was restored, and the former denizens of the socialist countries could buy goods that surpassed their wildest dreams. Under socialism, it was not the economy that was distorted, rather the language distorted economy. The same can be said of today's America. What is an unsatisfactory reality in the eyes of some parts of the population has more to do with the deceptive language than observable facts. The social problems in America persist not because there is no solution to them, but because the language we use makes us look for empty-handed solutions.

The next thing to be done is to "deregulate" human relationships. The state, legal system, schools, and employers must refrain from telling people how to act. Their internal rules should be limited to basic rules of civility and *politesse*. For this, however, we must revive the notion of civility, which can be done only by condemning certain forms of behavior that we glorify now by calling "multiculturalism." Police and legal forces should be involved only in matters that concern someone's physical safety, not in purely ethical regulations concerning how men and women act under peaceful conditions. Therefore, Title IX concerning human sexuality and similar regulations should be removed. College dormitories should be no more than places where a student rents a room. Otherwise, universities seem to be more concerned with telling students how to have sex rather than what to study. The counselors who establish those rules and regulations act like ideological commissars of the worst kind, organizing meetings for boys and girls explaining to them how to engage in sexual activities. It would be naïve to believe that this is just about "safety." They impose an egalitarian view of sexuality, divorced from emotions, and in doing so, they damage the younger generation—it is now unlikely that they will think of sexuality as an expression of intimacy and love. This will probably transform their future life and the way they see marital relationships.

Another problem that we must temper is environmental activism, which is a species of our misunderstanding of cruelty. Listening to the news, and to presentations by social activists, one is under the impression that we inhabit an inhuman world, permeated with cruelty and unprecedented abuse. A moment of historical reflection suffices to realize that the opposite is the case. It would be inappropriate in this context to invoke the examples of concentration camps, the gulags, and genocide; or the lynching and mutilation of people, in some cases burning them alive.

But even if we leave aside such atrocities, we cannot match the instances of wrong-doing in civilized 19th-century societies. Today's societies in the Western world are more gentle than any past society, and to some it may sound outrageous that we cannot force ourselves to exact the death penalty on those who have committed the most hideous crimes. The word "punishment" is hardly heard, and various forms of punishment—from school discipline of old, spanking, parental authority, etc.—disappeared from our lives, which is partly the reason why Western societies lack discipline. While the idea of human rights in the 1970s was a weapon that Western governments used to defend dissidents from totalitarian brutality, abuse, or death, today, as Hilary Clinton announced, a woman's right to abortion, for example, has ascended to the same level. Thus an American woman who does not have access to an abortion clinic has joined people like Alexander Solzhenitsyn, Vladimir Bukovsky, or Joseph Brodsky, all of whom spent decades in the Soviet gulags.

Activists never tire in their fight for more rights. Animal rights have been on the agenda for some time. But what in some instances was a commonsensical fight, preventing animals from unnecessary cruelty, turned into an ideological battle against fox hunting in the United Kingdom, or against cockfighting in America. Last year, the American Congress enacted a law making cockfighting illegal in the U.S., including the territory of Puerto Rico, where it is a 400-year-old tradition. In order to stop the cruelty of cockfighting, the order required that over a million cocks be slaughtered. Given the social attitude surrounding "the carbon footprint," one can expect something similar to happen to cows and pigs in the near future. They will be uselessly slaughtered to prevent their being eaten by humans. However, considering that man is an omnivorous animal, and has been so for ages, we can expect such policies to lead to serious health and mental problems in a generation or two. We must realize that living in harmony with nature, or saving the environment, is not the same as making animals equal to us.

Furthermore, the influence of popular psychology in the life of the *Homo Americanus* is unprecedented. It manifests itself in the dependence of Americans on counselors, psychologists, social workers, and other experts. Most of the problems they try to address were not considered problems in the past, rather normal parts of life that one had to deal with and respond to. Facing them always made people stronger. Today's *Homo Americanus* is weak, and the new generation rightly gained the name "flakes." And the flakier they are, the less prepared they are to cope with problems.

The counselors are like crutches, and since their advice is helpful only to a limited degree, they often act as an army of social engineers, giving large-scale advice on how to transform institutions. This is true in the educational sector in particular, in which methods of teaching replaced teaching, and the methods are being taught by specialists as part of the so-called "professional development." Yet these pedants are unfamiliar with the subjects taught by teachers. Much of it is a form of psychological and educational charlatanry that has detrimental effects on the level of education and on our behaviors.

The ubiquitous belief in science is a problem as well. *Homo Americanus* is a strong believer in scientific recommendations. Often, the recommendations are based on the most recent "research" or "study."[16] They assume

---

16 We are flooded with publications that pretend to have scientific validity, but are nothing other than commonsense with a semblance of science. For example, *Psychology Today* (November/December, 2019) published an article "Awakening a Sluggish Sex Drive"; *New Scientist* (25 January, 2020) published "The Great Nutritional Collapse." Others use "science" to enforce ideology. *USA Today*, a leading publication for nonsense, in the article "The Nap Ministry Gives Busy Adults a Timeout," writes: "The Nap Ministry also strives to create a safe space for people who are struggling to process traumatic events such as mass shootings and racism. Naps, Hersey said, help people to heal and can empower them to find ways to fight social justice."

a form of authoritative recommendations. However, as history shows, what the "new study" says today will be replaced or disproved by a newer study tomorrow. All one can say is that science should be presumed to have limited authority over our decisions, and common-sense and tradition should take precedence. The scientific orientation of America and the weak attachment to tradition poses a problem here, and it is one thing that may prove the most difficult to fight.

It is essential to rescue education from the hands of the multicultural ideologues, and reinstate old intellectual criteria into education for the sole purpose of teaching students objectivity. Colleges and universities must return to what they were created for—as Julian Bend insists in *The Great Betrayal of Intellectuals*—the pursuit of truth. This recommendation is nothing other than what we find in Plato. Polluting students' minds has direct effects on public and political life. It is a truism to say that what we learn in college has lasting influence on everything else we do later in life. If education suffers, so will the country, which is our home.[17]

Finally, the greatest danger to freedom is egalitarian collectivism, and it is collectivism that one must fight against. Unless we abandon the idea of equality that holds collectivist ideology together, we will be replacing one collectivist ideology for another. This recommendation is consistent with what Tocqueville understood to be the source of the democratic danger, and what he recommended as a bastion against the majority's power. It is imperative that we rebuild small private associations, not unlike the medieval guilds or later associations of different kinds, as well as private clubs[18] with their own rules and regulations.

---

17 A very interesting, practical idea for how to rescue education is Nicholas Capaldi's "A Modest Proposal to Rescue Higher Education," in *The Postil Magazine*, March 1, 2020.

18 In the late 80s the U.S. endured criticism of private clubs, like Gentlemen's clubs, which, under pressure, opened their doors to women, ceasing *de facto* to be Gentlemen's clubs. Instead of following the example of the British clubs, which made exceptions for members of the opposite sex (as they did, for example, for British Prime Minister Margaret Thatcher) or creating similar clubs for Ladies, they embarked on a campaign against discrimination. One might wonder why? Given the relative social insignificance of such institutions, the explanation cannot lie in any social harm that the existence of such places

The membership in such associations is neither inconsistent with, nor contrary to the larger notion of the idea of equality, only because membership is based on certain criteria, such as sex, age, income, level of education, merit, etc. Insofar as it is a private association, it is not different from the idea "my home is my castle," to which I can invite any guests I so choose. The idea of total non-discrimination is inconsistent with freedom, and it gives the state power to decide what is right and wrong. The state, unlike religion, it must be remembered, is not a moral institution, and insofar as it can impose rules, those rules must be consistent with national tradition and history, but never with abstract rules that conceive of man as a creation of abstract reasoning.

The reader will likely come up with other problems and other solutions, but the ones I listed appear to me to be most pertinent. They revolve around privacy and mental independence, without which one cannot guard oneself against the intrusion of the state in the name of the collective ideology.

***

Knowledge and the complexity of the world will undoubtedly grow in the future, and democracy may not be able to keep up with the demands of social organization for the reasons I indicated above. There may be nothing we can do anything about it. In this case, democratic societies not only *may*, but *will* become unmanageable, and we will slide into a worldwide anarchy. It is also possible that the totalitarian tendency in democracy,

poses, but in the anti-class, anti-hierarchical obsession of the democratic collectivist. Once again, one must remember the practice of communism, where all private associations were virtually abolished. The only places which were left "unattended" were stamp, coin, and rod-fishing clubs, probably because the communist ideologues could not push ideology on stamp and coin collecting, nor fishing. However, writers' associations were under strict ideological supervision. One can observe a similar tendency in American "creative writing programs," and different writers' "public library" meetings, where the prospective writers present their potential works, counting on their peers' advice, something unheard of in previous epochs. It appears that official communist censorship has been replaced by the idea of public acceptance, being the latest hallmark of what passes for good literature.

which makes people mindless and docile, will save mankind from chaos. But it will be a very different mankind from the one we recognize in the history of the West—a mankind that enjoys freedom of thought and speech, the engines of creativity.

It is conceivable to think of the future of the planet populated by 9 billion robots, each of which does what it was programmed to do and thinks what everyone else thinks. But then, as John Stuart Mill feared, the world will look like China.[19]

19 The theft of intellectual property from the West by China is a well-known fact, just like it is a commonplace for hundreds of thousands of students from China to study in Western countries. Why is that so? Chinese themselves openly admit that the educational system thwarts creativity because it does not allow for independent thought.

AFTERWORD | WHENCE *HOMO AMERICANUS?*
RYSZARD LEGUTKO

Zbigniew Janowski's fascinating, if bitter depiction of today's *Homo Americanus* is not a manifestation of the author's eccentricity. On the contrary, what he says in his book is an updated version of a recurrent theme one encounters in various inquiries into the nature of American society throughout its history. America, "the land of the free," was from the very beginning haunted by the specter of despotism that would come from within, straight from the deep-seated democratic disposition of American society. It is remarkable that often the warnings were articulated by those for whom America was a beloved fatherland and land of hope. It is not the enemies, but the friends, the sons of the American nation that feared the worst.

It all began as early as the founding. The Founding Fathers, as every student of American history knows, were at least as committed to constructing a viable political order with a strong democratic element as they were concerned about the dangers inherent in democratic mechanisms. They warned against the uncontrolled rule of the majority, which, they thought, could bring about a new type of democratic authoritarianism. Instead of democracy, they, therefore, preferred to talk about the republic, which they carefully structured, and into which they introduced an ingenious, though somewhat complicated mechanism of various institutions of power checking, that each may balance one another.

Several decades later, a French aristocrat, Alexis de Tocqueville, made a long journey to the United States, and, after initial enthusiasm for a new democratic society free from Europe's feudal heritage and animated by impressive self-governing energy, he began to see a serious danger looming behind the democratic mores, threatening not only America, but all societies that embarked on the democratic road.

His book ended with a vision of a future society that he thought was likely to materialize if the democratic tendencies continued, and the vision was not optimistic. What he predicted was a soft, yet extremely intrusive despotism, to which the denizens of the democratic country would willingly accommodate, having their unambitious desires gratified by the efficient bureaucratic government. "I think," wrote Tocqueville,

> that the species of oppression by which democratic nations are menaced is unlike anything which ever before existed in the world.... The first thing that strikes the observation is an innumerable multitude of men all equal and alike, incessantly endeavoring to procure the petty and paltry pleasures with which they glut their lives.... Above this race of men stands an immense and tutelary power, which takes upon itself alone to secure their gratifications and to watch over their fate. That power is absolute, minute, regular, provident, and mild. It would be like the authority of a parent, if, like that authority, its object was to prepare men for manhood; but it seeks, on the contrary, to keep them in perpetual childhood; it is well content that the people should rejoice, provided they think of nothing but rejoicing.

There were more warnings to this effect voiced over the course of American history, but surprisingly (or perhaps, not surprisingly), they were never treated with sufficient seriousness. To this day, the Founding Fathers have been reverentially acknowledged as the framers of the democratic system, rather than as critics of unconditional democracy who had more sympathy for the mixed regime than for the rule of the majority. Nowadays, Tocqueville is remembered more for his eulogy of the American civic spirit than for his critical opinions about the New World's nascent democracy. Some of his statements would certainly be met with disbelief today and are rarely quoted. "I do not know any country," one reads in his *Democracy in America,* "where, in general, less independence of mind and genuine freedom of discussion reign than in America."

The reasons why Americans tended to ignore all these warnings are many, but undoubtedly one of them seems particularly important. The critics located the danger in the idea of equality and its growing influence, whereas it was precisely this idea that the American people particularly cherished, and considered the nucleus of their creed. All men are equal, and all have equal rights—this truth, enshrined in the Declaration of Independence, was declared binding for all subsequent generations. To the question of what it meant to be free, the obvious answer was: to have rights. To be free was to bear rights.

In reality, of course, there were many external factors which enabled Americans to be free—a federalist system, the size of the country, social mobility, opportunities that resulted from free economic development, checks and balances, and many others. Also, various aspects of democracy contributed to a sense of freedom. But doctrinally, it was the concept of rights that founded the American notion of liberty. Those rights, however, were not sustainable by themselves, but depended on the principle of equality. What was considered, or rather "declared" self-evident, was the equality of human beings, all of them being endowed with inalienable rights. The rights were rights precisely because everyone could claim them. The rights for the few could not be rights: they were privileges. In other words, equality, rather than liberty, was the key to the American soul.

When Americans proudly distanced themselves from Europe and her feudal traditions, from inherited privileges and hereditary aristocracy, from the hierarchies of the Catholic Church and of established religions, they automatically assimilated a specific, narrow, and highly ideological concept of despotism. Despotism meant monarchy, hierarchy, elitism, and suchlike European diseases. It could not mean—at least not *prima facie*—democracy and democratic equality. Still less was it associated with liberalism, the concept which etymologically is derived from *libertas*, Latin for "freedom." The mere suggestion that the etymology might be misleading seemed ludicrous. How can a political theory that grants every human being inalienable rights be inimical to freedom?

For this reason, the American mind was most reluctant to react to the ills of its society that resulted from excessive egalitarianism, the ideology of rights, and the incessant invasion of democracy into every area of life. The American people seem to have accepted a basic assumption that whatever the ills, the only efficient remedy would be more egalitarianism, more rights, and more democracy. The retort that the remedy would exacerbate the problem was never considered seriously, and sounded suspiciously un-American. The thinkers who had reservations about the remedy were few and, in spite of their analytic brilliance and prophetic power, never really managed to make a difference.

Zbigniew Janowski came to America from communist Poland, in which he spent the first twenty-five years of his life, a period sufficiently long to give him an insight into the nature of the totalitarian system. In the next twenty-five years, he resided in the United States, first studying, then teaching at various American universities. Not only did he have enough time to acquire first-hand experience of contemporary America, but he could compare it with his previous life under the communist dictatorship. That there are great differences is obvious, and they are clear to every thinking person. What is far from obvious is that there are also similarities.

On this point, Janowski's view differs from Tocqueville's: for Janowski, the despotic aspect of American life is not an entirely new phenomenon, having no precedent in the past, but can be partly grasped in the language used to describe the communist society. Stated in more down-to-earth terms, living in the States and teaching at American universities, Janowski was often—too often—experiencing déjà vu. The conclusion might not convince everyone, but it is justified, at least as regards the last decades of American history, during which the concept of rights and an anti-despotic animus have formed an extremely dangerous combination.

I said above that in their opposition to Europe's pre-democratic heritage, Americans imported the European view of despotism, construed within the framework of egalitarianism. Despotism was simply extreme inequality. This interpretation, let us note, differed from the ancient philosophers' view, according to which the main trait of despotism, or rather, to use a Greek word, of tyranny, was lawlessness. Tyranny was, of course, a one-man rule, but this rule was of a particular kind, namely, as we read in Plato's *Republic*, it violated all laws, human and divine. For the ancients and for medieval philosophers, inequality as such was not morally opprobrious.

The communists accepted this modern view of despotism, and provided it with Karl Marx's theory that the basic structure of every system is in a way despotic, no matter which historical epoch, and that the formal structure remains essentially unchanged: there is always one social class that dominates other classes, exploits them, and imposes its own norms and beliefs on the entire society. Marx's theory not only explained the structure of the society, but also discovered the process of change: in particular, how and why one structure of social and economic inequality changes into another. The mechanism of change—and his answer made a spectacular career worldwide—was a war between the antagonistic classes. In other words, the history of humanity is, according to Karl Marx and his followers, a history of a class struggle that has been waged from time immemorial, and will continue until the final revolution occurs and the last of the exploited classes, the proletariat, will crush the last exploiters, the capitalist bourgeoisie, and by defeating them, they will emancipate humankind. After the victory, there will be no classes because the mechanism of inequality will vanish, and all human beings will be equal.

This glorious moment was not only to be a political and economic victory, but also an emancipation of the human mind. The argument was the following: The ruling class controls the people by instilling into their minds "false consciousness," a set of views that legitimize the existing inequalities, and prevent human beings from understanding the repressive nature of the system in which they live. The enslavement has its deepest roots in the way we think and speak, in the associations that we have, and in the stereotypes through which we interpret the world. All this—the Marxists said—is not of our own making. The opinions we express have been imparted to us from outside, and therefore, it requires an effort on the part of the enlightened revolutionary elites to raise our consciousness and to cleanse it from the wrong ideas through intensive ideological training.

Americans rejected this theory of the class struggle, the political gospel of universal emancipation, and the nebulous Marxian ruminations about false consciousness, being repelled by both the content and the political methods those ideas implied. They did not accept the class struggle because they did not accept the concept of class. American society exhibited a high degree of social mobility—not only horizontal but also vertical; career-making was believed to be open to every person. Besides, the concept of class clashed with the American creed, which was built on individualism, that is, on the notion that the society consists primarily of individuals, not of groups or classes.

Americans did not like the idea of universal emancipation, either. For one thing, they were patriotic, and had no intention of joining some universal movement they could not control and did not quite understand. Torn between two opposing forces, isolationism and the spirit of crusade, Americans preferred either to keep away from world affairs (particularly, from European affairs), or to engage in them, but on their own: that is, on American terms.

And, finally, Americans could not really look favorably at the theory of false consciousness. They assumed—and it seemed like one of those non-negotiable assumptions—that every individual is a master of his mind and will, and that America's history evidenced such a spectacular triumph of creativity and productivity precisely because no institution or group was allowed to interfere with what people thought and said. The rights, that sacred principle of the American nation, protected the freedom of speech and thought, regardless of whether the speaker's consciousness was false or not false.

For many years, one of the often-discussed topics was "why there is no socialism in the United States," and it was clear to those who participated in the debate that American society was the last place on earth in which the communist ideology could take root. Obviously, there were exceptions to this. Some groups, particularly intellectuals and artists, flirted with Marxism; some were even card-carrying communists; but this was a disease to which these groups have been prone in all countries, fortunately not infecting the rest of society.

And yet, at a certain point in American history, things began to change. Whether this was the result of the '68 revolution and its sexual turmoil, or America's awakened sense of guilt about the plight of the black population in its history, or some other reason, or all of them together, the fact is that a form of neo-Marxism appeared in the States and soon was spreading by leaps and bounds. The concept of class was rehabilitated, but what is more important, two other concepts grew into such prominence that they colonized the modern American mind: race and gender. The class struggle was extended to the struggle between races and between genders, which meant that virtually every nook and cranny of human existence, whether physical or mental, emotional or intellectual, fell under this mechanism.

At the beginning, the concept of race referred to white Americans and black Americans, the former enslaving the latter, or, if not enslaving in the literal sense of the word, then degrading them to the status of inferior human beings. Later, however, the concept of race was reinterpreted to cover a lot more, for instance, the domination of European culture, an alleged race-based bias of the artistic canon, etc. In fact, any "Eurocentrist" statement, or any act of the positive singling out of the Western civilization, was condemned as racist.

The concept of gender turned out to be even more fecund. At first, the political narrative was about men discriminating against women, a narrative that had a long history both in the Western world and in the communist countries. But then the concept of gender appeared. Taken from the standard terminology of descriptive grammar, and given a rather absurdly opaque meaning, it soon denoted anything that anyone could claim to be his sexual preference. In fact, the pronoun "his" is inappropriate, and so is "her," because gender in its new meaning invalidates all pronouns, all of them being insufficiently opaque and dangerously binary. The genders were said to be many—no one knew how many—and any limitation of the number was considered discriminatory.

The concept of false consciousness also re-emerged, and quite triumphantly, though not necessarily under this name. The following argument has acquired the status of the unassailable truth. The people—and this view was in perfect accordance with what the Marxists had been teaching all along—are generally unaware of how deeply the discriminatory inclinations pervade their thoughts and emotions, how profoundly the education is infected by the supremacist prejudices, how imbued their language is with exclusionary phrases and categories. This dramatic situation requires a systemic and energetic action—through education, public pressure, but also through legal measures—so that the human minds be cleansed of the internalized stereotyping.

American liberals, who believed in the moral and political primacy of the rights-bearing individual, should have rejected all this as dangerous nonsense, that soon would lead to meticulous regulations on human behavior, both in public and in private, as a harbinger of censorship, indoctrination and ideological zealotry; in short, it was obvious that such a view had to lead to everything that the concept of rights was meant to prevent. But they did not, and it is not difficult to see why not.

The neo-Marxist view that America has been torn by the enduring, albeit often hidden conflicts between infinitely many groups (ethnic, racial, sexual, etc.), and that American minds have been overpowered by the false ideas that downplayed these conflicts, found a fertile ground. The neo-Marxists disclosed to Americans what seemed like an ocean of injustice, a massive, horrendous violation of the principle of equality by means of the perfidious, hitherto unseen instruments of oppression, the more perfidious that they allegedly blurred our cognitive, emotional and imaginative faculties which would have enabled us to detect them. The neo-Marxists also disclosed to them a shockingly large number of victims, of whose existence Americans apparently had not been aware before. Not only were classes subdued, not only was racism now exposed in its enormous hydra-like monstrosity, whose hateful touch polluted every aspect of life; the ideology of gender and its myriad forms were now the greatest providers of victims and of crimes perpetrated against them.

American liberals, with their standard notion of despotism as inequality, were not conceptually prepared to comprehend, and then to confront, the new situation, being overwhelmed by the alleged scale of newly-discovered inequalities, as well as by the number of individuals and groups whose rights—as it now became clear—were not respected, nor even recognized. The liberals did what seemed to them obvious and morally imperative, unaware that this was a self-destructive move. Once again, they invoked the rights—this universal solution for every oppression—and granted them to every new group that, according to the neo-Marxist ideology, existed, or was brought into being, or constituted itself, or simply claimed privileges. But they went further than that: after having accepted the neo-Marxist list of new victims, they had to accept the list of new oppressors.

What is significant is that this list was extremely long, much longer than that routinely presumed in the liberal doctrine of individual rights, but also longer than the list of enemies under communist regimes. In today's America, and, to a great extent, in the entire Western world, the sources of oppression and inequality are innumerable: misogyny, sexism, racism, homophobia, transphobia, islamophobia, eurocentrism, phallocentrism, logocentrism, ageism, binarism, populism, antisemitism, nationalism, xenophobia, hate speech, Euroscepticism, and many others. Every group that acquired the status of victimhood has its own list of oppressors; every self-proclaimed guardian of a new, oppression-free, egalitarian society feels obliged to identify his own candidates.

The fact that the liberals acquiesced to this new strategy of emancipation had far-reaching consequences. First, the individualism that, for better or worse, was at the heart of the American creed in proud contrast to the European identity, was now receding, being gradually replaced by collectivism. America was no longer a frontier nation of courageous pioneers practicing a virtue of self-reliance, but a battlefield of groups fighting for their collective rights. This new concept of America and her history naturally presupposed that the solution to the problem of inequality had to be collectivistic, and that it should consist in empowering certain groups, while taking power away from others. Second, the enemies were no longer the descendants of political hierarchies born in feudal Europe, which the American Constitution, Bill of Rights, and rights-based legal culture have managed to keep at bay—monarchy, aristocracy, established religion, the centralized state—but were home-grown and permeated the entire society with all its constituents.

Marriage, family, schools, universities, sex, matters relating to life and death, morality, language and its grammatical categories, literature, historical identity, memory, religion, even toilets—all these were the carriers of unbearable inequalities and, as such, had to be reordered according to the new rules to eliminate oppression. In a new strategy, like in every totalitarian strategy, no place was to remain intact. In communist society, even during the darkest times, there were some places of refuge, such as the family, where one could try to hide from the bulldozer of the communist state and its ideology. In the neo-Marxist, liberal society, the family was—right at the outset—pinpointed as a major stronghold of oppression; its destruction was, therefore, a top priority.

The strategy of emancipation, launched by the unholy alliance of the neo-Marxists and the liberals, had—as often happens—the reverse effects: freedom was dwindling, and rights turned out a convenient weapon to impose conformity. One of the paradoxes is that with more rights lavishly bestowed on the new victim groups, one can nowadays say less and less in America (and in Europe, let me add), and it has become much easier than in the past to be accused of violating somebody's rights, or of uttering a disrespectful remark, having racist, homophobic, misogynist, or otherwise offensive undertones.

The society ridden by all these sins, some of them purportedly having their roots deep in our minds, religious beliefs, upbringing, and cultural tradition, is becoming an increasingly dangerous place, similar to a minefield where every move is risky. Just as it is strongly advised not to make risky moves on a minefield, it is equally prudent not to say things that are unorthodox, potentially objectionable, too much dissenting from what is acceptable and politically correct. To ensure that this line is followed, one should enforce some mental discipline on oneself, so that the mind does not indulge in reckless thoughts: reckless thoughts generate reckless words, and reckless words—according to the orthodoxy reigning in this society—instigate oppressive acts.

The political logic is irrefutable, no matter what the system, whether American or Soviet, communist or liberal-democratic: the more victims, the more sins; the more sins, the more perpetrators; the more sins and the more perpetrators, the more self-policing and other-policing.

With so many ideological transgressions around, with so many inequalities, and political as well as cultural structures of oppression, the natural reaction of a typical human being would be to police his neighbors. Those who have taken to heart the new vision of society, and those who simply want to be safe, or to make careers by casting suspicion on others, cannot resist the temptation to play the role of the thought police. The results are sadly predictable: only the virtuous few defy the thought police, many cowardly obey and cooperate, the majority pretend not to see the problem, but occasionally, to be on the safe side, kowtow to the ideological idols.

In communist countries, the indoctrinated students regularly accused the old professors of reactionary views, shouted them down, and demanded they confess their ideological crimes and promise to repent. The American campuses continue that shameful practice. Europe has unfortunately followed suit. The persistent atmosphere of collective indignation—spontaneous or sparked by the ideological gurus—has contaminated education, media, and public life. There are still enclaves of common sense and civility, but the bad trend continues.

To conclude, Janowski's book is not a chronicle of the grotesque fringes of American life—some comic, some embarrassing, and some frightening—of the type one can find in any country or continent. His objective is to describe an emerging despotism, similar in its democratic genesis to what Tocqueville had indicated almost two centuries before as an endemic American product, but in its manifestations, similar to what the author himself experienced when living in a communist country. Janowski's ultimate conclusion is pessimistic: the American creed based on the idea of equality is helpless, *vis-à-vis* the new despotism. Whether he is right or wrong, the next decades will show. All despotisms ultimately fall, so this one will collapse sooner or later. The question is, how soon, and at what price?

SUGGESTIONS FOR FURTHER READING

Aczel Thomas, (and) Merey, Tibor, *The Revolt of the Mind: A Case History of Intellectual Resistance Behind the Iron Curtain*

Amalrik, Andrei, *L'Union soviétique survivra-t-elle en 1984?*

Applebaum, Anne, *Red Famine: Stalin's War on Ukraine*

—*Iron Curtain: The Crushing of Eastern Europe, 1944–1956*

Arendt, Hannah, *The Origins of Totalitarianism*

—*Eichmann in Jerusalem: A Report on the Banality of Evil*

—*On Revolution*

Aron, Raymond, *The Opium of the Intellectuals*

—*Main Currents of Sociological Thought*

Benda, Julian, *The Great Betrayal*

Besançon, Alain, *The Falsification of the Good: Soloviev and Orwell*

—*The Rise of the Gulag: The Intellectual Origins of Leninism*

—*Présent soviétique et passé russe*

—*A Century of Horrors: Communism, Nazism, and the Uniqueness of the Shoah*

Bukovsky, Vladimir, *The Collapse of Communism: The Untold Story*

—*To Build a Castle: My Life as a Dissenter*

—*Judgment in Moscow: Soviet Crimes and Western Complicity*

—*A Conversation with Vladimir Bukovsky: Held on June 12, 1979 at the American Enterprise Institute for Public Policy Research, Washington, D.C*

Conquest, Robert, *The Great Terror*

—*The Harvest of Sorrow: Soviet Collectivization and the Terror-famine*

France, Anatole, *Gods Will Have Blood*

Furet, François, *The Passing of an Illusion: The Idea of Communism in the Twentieth Century*

Howe, Irving (ed.), *1984 Revisited*

Huxley, Aldous, *Brave New World*

—*Brave New World Revisited*

—*The Island*

Jisheng, Yang, *Tombstone: The Great Chinese Famine, 1958–1962*

Judt, Tony, *Past Imperfect: French Intellectuals, 1944–1956*

Kim, Suki, *Without You There Is No Us: Undercover among the Sons of North Korea's Elite*

Koestler, Arthur, *Darkness at Noon*

Kołakowski, Leszek, *Main Currents of Marxism*

—*Modernity on Endless Trial*

—*My Correct Views on Everything*

Michnik, Adam, *Letters from Prison*

Miłosz, Czesław, *The Captive Mind*

Orwell, George, *Animal Farm,*

—*1984*

Panin, Dimitri, *The Notebooks of Sologdin*

Panné, Jean-Louis; Paczkowski, Andrzej; Bartosek, Karel; Margolin, Jean-Louis; Werth, Nicolas; Courtois, Stéphane; Kramer, Mark, *The Black Book of Communism: Crimes, Terror, Repression,*

Sakharov, Andrei, *Memoirs*

—*My Country and the World*

Solzhenitzen, Alexander, *The Gulag Archipelago*

—*The First Circle*

—*Solzhenitsyn at Harvard: The Address, Twelve Early Responses, Six Later Reflections*

Talmon, Jacob, *The Origins of Totalitarian Democracy*

Urban, George, *Stalin and Stalinism: Its Impact on Russia and the World*

—"*Can the Soviet Union Be Reformed*": *An Interview with Vladimir Bu-kovsky*

Vonnegut, Kurt, *Harrison Bergeron*

Wat, Aleksander, *My Century*

Wilson, Edmund, *To the Finland Station*

Yakunin, Gleb, *Letters from Moscow: Religion and Human Rights in USSR*

ABOUT THE AUTHOR

Zbigniew Janowski received his M.A. from The Catholic University of America, Washington, DC, and his PhD from The Committee on Social Thought at The University of Chicago. He is the author of *Cartesian Theodicy, Augustinian-Cartesian Index, How to Read Descartes' Mediations*, and (with Catherine O'Neil) *Agamemnon's Tomb*. He is also the editor of Leszek Kołakowski's *The Two Eyes of Spinoza and Other Essays on Philosophers, My Correct Views on Everything* and John Stuart Mill's writings *On Democracy, Freedom and Government & Other Selected Writings*. He is a member of Centre d'Etudes Cartésienne, Université de Paris-IV-Sorbonne